A-Z OF SOUTH AFRICAN POLITICS

Contributors:

Julia Beffon, Farouk Chothia, Carole Cooper, Lesley Cowling, Gaye Davis, Shaun de Waal, Jacqui Golding, Ferial Haffajee, Stephen Heyns, Claire Keeton, Bafana Khumalo, Stephen Laufer, Chris Louw, Mondli waka Makhanya, Eric Naki, Phila Ngqumba, Cathy Powers, Carmel Rickard, Reg Rumney, Pat Sidley, Paul Stober, Jan Taljaard, Andrew Trench. The chapter on negotiating forums was compiled by Claire Gordon-Brown of the South African Institute of Race Relations, with assistance from Robin Hamilton, Stuart Murphy, Shaun Mackay and Elizabeth Sidiropoulos.

WEEKLY MAIL & GUARDIAN

A-Z of South African Politics

The Essential Handbook

1994

Edited by
Anton Harber and Barbara Ludman

PENGUIN BOOKS

Published by the Penguin Group

27 Wrights Lane, London W8 5TZ, England

Viking Penguin, a division of Penguin Books USA Inc, 375 Hudson Street, New York, New York 10014, USA

Penguin Books Australia Ltd, Ringwood, Victoria, Australia

Penguin Books Canada Ltd, 10 Alcorn Avenue, Toronto, Ontario, Canada M4V 3B2

Penguin Books (NZ) Ltd, 182–190 Wairau Road, Auckland 10, New Zealand

Penguin Books, Amethyst Street, Theta Ext 1, Johannesburg, South Africa

Penguin Books Ltd, Registered Offices: Harmondsworth, Middlesex, England

First published by Penguin Books 1994

ISBN 0 140 24100 0

Typeset by Creda Press
Printed and bound by Creda Press
Cover design by Hadaway Illustration and Design

Contents

Acknowledgements vii
Introduction ix
1 Personalities
An A-Z of who's who in South African politics 1
2 Organisations and Institutions
An A-Z of what's what in South African politics 159
3 Forums
An A-Z of who's talking to whom in South Africa's negotiating forums 236
4 Issues
An A-Z of what matters in South African politics 253
5 Statistics
Vital indicators of the country's geo- and socio-politics 281
6 History
A concise chronology of what happened when in South Africa 302
7 Office Bearers
The key office bearers of the key political offices 331
8 Acronyms
An A-Z of the alphabet soup of South African politics 350
List of contributors 355

Acknowledgements

Special thanks to Sophie Perryer, Drew Forrest, Irwin Manoim, Lyle Britton, Mduduzi ka Harvey, Vuyo Mvoko, Emily Wintle, Alison Lowry, John Allen, Pam Thornley for their hard and valuable work, and to the East Cape News Agency (Ecna) and the South African Institute of Race Relations.

The Institute for Multi-Party Democracy sponsored the original *Weekly Mail* supplement (South African Politicians A-Z, October 1993) from which the idea of this book grew. David Beresford and Phillip van Niekerk are owed gratitude for their contributions to the concept.

A wide range of people, too many to name, have given help, advice and sympathy, and we thank them. In particular, our colleagues at *The Weekly Mail & Guardian* and our spouses offered patience, support and assistance. There are others who didn't and they, of course, are responsible for any errors that may have crept into the book.

Introduction

South African politics used to be simple. There was right and wrong, black and white, the powerful and the disempowered, the oppressed and the oppressors, the voters and the disenfranchised. It was relatively easy to find your way around and work out who and what fitted into these categories.

That changed in 1990, fortunately. Now, after four years of relative political freedom, the country boasts a bewildering array of personalities, organisations, institutions, ideas, issues, debates, conflicts and events, many of them new and unknown.

This book is an easy-to-read guide through that maze. It is a handy reference that is intended to be of use to specialists and laypeople alike. It should be of value to anyone who wants to be well informed for the country's first free elections and South Africa's first year of new democratic institutions.

It is *not* a bland fact-sheet. It is not intended to supply the full range of basic statistics, or every detail you may ever need about the individuals and institutions that are listed in it. We have limited the dry detail. We have tried, however, to give you a real, under-the-skin feel for these personalities and organisations. We have written of their characters, their foibles, their weaknesses and strengths, their reputations and our assessment of why they are likely to be important in the coming months. Embedded in each entry is the honest and candid analysis of our expert writers.

These contributors include a formidable array of

Weekly Mail & Guardian staffers and others who have covered every corner of South African politics, from the antics of the far-right to the debates within the ultra-left. They know the individuals they write about personally; they have tracked the organisations for many years; they have followed the issues doggedly.

We have drawn on a wide range of expertise — 28 writers — but this also accounts for some differences in style from entry to entry. Hopefully you will agree with us that this inconsistency is justified by the readability of the book and the richness of the analysis.

We have purposefully tried to avoid what has been done in other books. If you need more comprehensive facts and figures, we recommend the Institute of Race Relations' annual survey. And if you want more straight facts on the personalities, there is Sheila Gastrow's *Who's Who of South African Politics* (Ravan Press). If it's more businessmen you want to know about, there is the *Who's Who of Southern Africa* (Argus Publications).

But if you want to get under the skin of South African politics, this book will help you.

Our choice of entries — 182 profiles, 57 organisations, 18 issues — represents our best assessment of who and what will be important during 1994. The volatility of South African politics makes this an extremely risky task. Undoubtedly, people we have not dealt with will emerge unpredictably, and some will submerge unexpectedly. We have also had to exclude certain characters who will be important, so we have, for example, dealt with only a handful of the most important businessmen. But our lists are not just made up of politicians: there are policemen, soldiers, lawyers, priests, unionists, civic activists and academics. You will notice among them some surprises — younger, lesser-known, up-and-coming figures that we tip to emerge and make their mark in the coming months. Spot them and watch them.

Perhaps the most exciting part is that the book displays the rich and diverse pool of talent and skill that makes up our political life. Beyond the handful of internationally known leaders are fertile layers of leadership. There is also a wide range of organisations involved in everything from voter education to electrification. This is a country with a wealth of resources and leadership. That must give us all hope.

Anton Harber
Johannesburg
February 1994

1

Personalities

An A-Z of who's who in South African politics

Alexander, Benny Regarded as a political street-fighter, the Pan Africanist Congress's flamboyant general secretary shot from complete obscurity into prominence during the late 1980s, but has seen his star wane since the PAC joined the negotiations process. He is, however, expected to play an important role in the PAC's election campaign, with his fiery, crowd-swaying rhetoric.

Alexander was schooled in pan-Africanism by PAC founder Robert Sobukwe, who was banished to Alexander's home town of Kimberley. He was the third of five children of a labourer and was employed, after matriculating in 1975, by the Department of Manpower for six years. He moved to Johannesburg where, while working for a pharmaceutical company, he helped form the Black Health and Allied Workers' Union of South Africa. In 1986, he left to work full time for the South African Black Municipal and Allied Workers' Union.

He had joined the PAC underground in 1983, and when PAC president Zeph Mothopeng was released from prison in 1988 Alexander was constantly at his side. With his colourful language and distinctive missing front teeth, he quickly became the PAC's most recognisable face.

He was instrumental in the formation of the Pan Africanist Movement in 1989, a legal front for the PAC, and was duly elected general secretary. He assumed the same position at the PAC's first post-unbanning congress in 1990.

The 38-year-old former Baptist deacon is highly articulate and eloquent. His militant swipes at the 'settler regime' and his Cinderella-pitched voice get the crowds going whenever he addresses rallies. But his inflexible defence of every iota of PAC activity — such as armed attacks on white civilians — has sometimes painted the PAC into difficult corners.

Tel: (011) 836–0442/0457

Alexander, Neville This socialist intellectual and educationist was born in Cradock in the Eastern Cape in 1936. His father was a carpenter, his mother a teacher. He followed an early convent schooling with a BA and MA from the University of Cape Town before earning his doctorate in German literature from the University of Tübingen, but was already active in politics, mainly through the Teachers' League of South Africa and the Society of Young South Africa, a Non-European Unity Movement (NEUM) affiliate.

In Germany he had contact with the Socialist Democratic Students' Union and Algerian student and labour movements in exile, as well as with Cubans who persuaded him of the necessity of embarking on guerrilla warfare — a conviction which led to his suspension from the NEUM soon after his return to South Africa in 1961, when he formed the Yu Chi Chan Club, founded the National Liberation Movement, and forged links with Swapo.

He was convicted in 1964 of conspiring to commit sabotage and jailed for 10 years on Robben Island; for five years after his release he was banned and placed under house arrest. In 1980 he was appointed Cape Town director of the South African Council for Higher Education, and went on to launch the National Language Project and other cultural reform initiatives such as the Project for the Study of Alternative Education in South Africa. He is currently chairman of the tiny Workers' Organisation for Socialist Action.

Tel: (021) 650–4013

Anafu, Moses As the Commonwealth secretary-general's special representative, Ghanaian-born Anafu (46) made his reputation by succeeding where local peace mediators failed: brokering peace pacts between Inkatha Freedom Party and African National Congress supporters in parts of strife-torn Natal/kwaZulu. He earned respect for taking a more active role in attempts to bring peace than some of his international counterparts, and not confining himself to a strict interpretation of observing and monitoring.

His success was also largely due to his ability, as the son of a chief, to relate to Inkatha-aligned chiefs.

When he moved to Johannesburg, many of his peace initiatives in Natal crumbled and the peace community clamoured for his return. However, he will remain in Johannesburg to keep an eye on the April 1994 elections.

With the Commonwealth secretariat since 1979, Anafu also kept a close watch on the Lancaster House negotiations leading to Zimbabwe's independence and the transition to multi-partyism in Lesotho.

Tel: (011) 331–1162

Asmal, Abdul Kadera ('Kader') A lifelong commitment to human rights began with his meeting Chief Albert Luthuli while still a schoolboy in Stanger, Natal, where he was born in October 1934. He qualified as a teacher and taught while studying further through Unisa, realising a childhood dream when he enrolled at the London School of Economics in 1959.

In England he got the British Anti-Apartheid Movement off the ground before moving with his wife, Louise Parkinson, to Ireland where he lectured in law at Trinity College, Dublin. He formed the Irish Anti-Apartheid Movement and served as vice-president of the International Defence and Aid Fund while qualifying as a barrister at both London and Dublin's Bars and earning his LLM (LSE) and MA (Dublin). His involvement in Irish civil liberty campaigns led him to serve on a number of international inquiries into human rights violations, and in 1983 he was awarded the Prix Unesco.

From the mid-1980s he served on the African National Congress's constitutional committee, and soon after returning to South Africa in 1990 was elected to the ANC's National Executive Committee. He is currently professor of human rights at the University of the Western Cape.

Tel: (021) 959–3086

Barnard, Neil The strategic advice of the previous chief of the National Intelligence Service (NIS) is believed to have led to the unbanning of the African National Congress and release of Nelson Mandela. As the current director of the Department of Constitutional Development, this former professor of political studies at the University of the Orange Free State still plays an important behind-the-scenes role in negotiations and was often seen at the World Trade Centre, though he maintains the low-key habits of the intelligence world.

Born in Namibia in 1949, Barnard was a surprise PW Botha appointment in 1980 to head what was then called the Department of National Security (Dons, later NIS) because he came from an academic, rather than intelligence, background. He had written a number of articles on terrorism, the 'total onslaught' and international relations, and had served on a commission recommending the tightening up of security legislation in the late 1970s.

As NIS head, he was a member of the State Security Council and fulfilled a key function in the National Security Management System that was at the heart of the 'total strategy' approach of the Botha era.

He also played a quiet, but important, role in Namibian and Angolan peace negotiations and was one of the first government members to be involved in talks with the imprisoned Nelson Mandela.

After Mandela's release, Barnard was active in behind-the-scenes talks that led to negotiations, and attended Codesa I and Codesa II as a government representative.

Tel: (012) 341–2400

Bartlett, George As minister of Mineral and Energy Affairs, Bartlett has a dubious distinction: he faced 17 calls for his resignation in six weeks in Parliament in 1993. Bartlett refused, riding the storm over his handling of a fuel price rise.

The MP for Amanzimtoti was embroiled in controversy throughout 1993, over the St Lucia mining issue, maladministration during his period in the Ministry of Transport and, most recently, the petrol price rise. President FW de Klerk has kept him on, probably for fear that he would lead a defection of Natal Party MPs to the Inkatha Freedom Party.

He was born in 1931 in Port Shepstone in Natal, and studied in Toronto, Canada, where he obtained two BSc degrees. He was elected to Parliament for the old United Party, later the New Republic Party, and moved to the NP in 1984. In 1986 he was rewarded with the post of deputy minister of Economic Affairs and Technology, the first English speaker in the Afrikaans cabinet. In 1989 he was elected Natal NP leader. When negotiations began, he was a member of the NP team.

His reputation damaged, probably beyond repair, by the fuel price issue, Bartlett has announced that he will bow out of national politics to focus on regional issues.

Tel: (012) 322–8695

Bester, Hennie The Democratic Party has pinned its hopes of winning the coloured vote in the Western Cape on this bright young Afrikaner, recently naming the 30-year-old as DP Western Cape leader.

Born in Paarl, he received a BComm Law (cum laude) and an LLB (cum laude) from Stellenbosch University. In 1987 he obtained his LLM from Cambridge University.

He was the leader of a delegation of Stellenbosch students who proposed to meet a delegation of the then banned African National Congress Youth League in Lusaka, Zambia, in 1986, until PW Botha withdrew their passports.

His political career started in 1989 when he was the unsuccessful DP parliamentary candidate for Stellenbosch. He has been the MP for Green Point since 1991.

Tel: (021) 45–1420

Boesak, Allan Re-elected to the position of chairman of the African National Congress in the Western Cape for his third consecutive term, Boesak has indicated his keenness to serve the ANC but much will depend on his ability to deliver the coloured vote in the region.

Born in 1946 in Kakamas in the Northern Cape, he was raised in Somerset West before entering the Dutch Reformed Mission Church theological seminary. He was catapulted into prominence when he led the charge to have apartheid declared a heresy and was named president of the World Alliance of Reformed Churches. He made the speech that led to the formation of the United Democratic Front in 1983 and his charisma and powerful oratorical abilities played an important role in subsequent campaigns.

Security police exposed his marital infidelity in the early 1980s. In 1990, fresh revelations of a liaison with television producer and niece of a cabinet minister, Elna Botha, now his wife, saw him resign as minister and moderator of the Dutch Reformed Mission Church and surrender his post as leader of the World Alliance, while continuing to head the Foundation for Peace and Justice in Cape Town. As ANC candidate for regional premier, Boesak is viewed by some as an asset because of his superb oratorical abilities, and by others as a liability because of his repeated marital controversy.

Tel: (021) 948–9150 or (021) 448–5651

Boshoff, Carel Willem Hendrik Although considered the father of the volkstaat ideal, the urbane professor has found his influence in right-wing circles ironically waning with the recent wider acceptance of the notion. Still clinging to the belief that such a homeland can only be possible in the relatively unpopulated Northern Cape and that it must result from negotiations, Boshoff and his supporters have been overtaken by those proposing a volkstaat in parts of the Transvaal and Free State.

Boshoff (66) is a former chairman of the Afrikaner Broederbond and has chosen politics instead of a solid academic career as a theologian. He was dean of the Faculty of Theology and professor of missionary science at the University of Pretoria and also served as chairman of the apartheid think-tank, the South African Bureau for Racial Affairs and the Federasie van Afrikaanse Kultuurvereenigings. However, he relinquished his Broederbond position in 1983 because of opposition to the tricameral constitution.

He is now chairman of the Afrikaner Volkswag, a right-wing cultural umbrella organisation, and his wife — the former Anna Verwoerd, a daughter of assassinated premier HF Verwoerd — is deputy chairlady. Once the closest thing to unity in right-wing circles, the organisation's current influence is far from that exerted during its heyday in 1984.

Boshoff is also chairman of the Afrikaner Vryheidstigting (Afrikaner Freedom Foundation), the organisation that has been instrumental in setting up what is proposed to become the nucleus of an Afrikaner homeland at Orania in the Northern Cape. In June 1988, he wrote a position paper that rejected Conservative

Party policy and argued for the secession of an Afrikaner homeland, and in 1991 Orania was purchased, the local coloured community forced to move, and a homeland started. He also leads the Afrikaanse Gereformeerde Bond, which aims to prevent reform within the Dutch Reformed Church.

Tel: (053202) Orania 861

Botha, Roelof ('Pik') The world's longest-serving minister of Foreign Affairs is also one of South Africa's greatest political survivors. Publicly humiliated on more than one occasion by ex-president PW Botha — once for suggesting that South Africa may one day have a black president — the gravel-voiced foreign minister showed the necessary staying power and came back for more.

Not surprisingly, he was one of FW de Klerk's strongest supporters in the power struggle that saw PW Botha ousted as state president in 1989.

Pik Botha became minister of Foreign Affairs in 1977, after serving as a high-profile South African ambassador to the United Nations in 1974, followed by a stint as ambassador to the United States. An advocate by training, he had previously been a member of South Africa's legal team in the 'South West Africa case' at the International Court of Justice in The Hague, Netherlands, from 1963 to 1966, and again in the early 1970s.

In spite of his public image as a 'verligte' even in the days when this was not a popular asset, Botha has always been a great crowd-drawer for his party. An excellent public performer with an actor's sense for the dramatic, he was always the most popular speaker on the campaign circuit in white elections, and could swing marginal constituencies the NP's way.

He has, however, never been the typical party hack jostling for position. This aloofness has meant that he has almost always been the first candidate to fall out in leadership elections. It is also one of the reasons why he was only voted the NP's Transvaal leader in 1992.

In the country's new non-racial politics this may count in his favour, however: there have already been suggestions that he should stay on as minister of Foreign Affairs under an African National Congress dominated government. Whatever happens on election day, there is no doubt that Botha will be celebrating: it also happens to be his birthday. He was born at Rustenburg in 1932, matriculated at the Hoër Volkskool Potchefstroom, and received his BA and LLB degrees from the University of Pretoria.

Tel: (021) 45–5848 or (012) 351–0012/0005

Botha, Thozamile After a swift rise to fame in Port Elizabeth civic and union structures in the mid-1970s, at the cutting edge of the struggle against apartheid, Botha suffered long detention and banning and fled into exile in 1980. His profile lowered during three years in Lusaka, although he was elected to the national executive of the South African Congress of Trade Unions. He then moved to Essex where he studied for a PhD and chaired the African National Congress in the UK. On his return in 1990, he rose rapidly to a top position in the ANC's national executive.

Within two months of his return from exile, Botha was elected head of the ANC's Department of Local and Regional Government and Housing. He went on to play a key role in the Local Government Negotiating Forum, was a founding member of the National Housing Forum, and was elected to the executive of the South African National Civic Organisation.

Very popular in the Eastern Cape, personable, hard working and respected, Botha has been widely tipped to secure the Local Government and Housing portfolio in the new government.

Tel: (011) 330–7388

Bruwer, Dries President of the militant Transvaal Agricultural Union (TAU), Conservative Party MP for Lydenburg and member of the Executive Council of the Afrikaner Volksfront, he was born in 1936 at Reitz in the Orange Free State and obtained an MSc (Agric) at the University of Pretoria in 1964. He also holds a teaching diploma from the University of South Africa.

After starting his career as a researcher at the Council for Scientific and Industrial Research (CSIR), Bruwer taught at an agricultural school until he was once again employed as a researcher at the National Institute for Citrus and Subtropical Fruits at Nelspruit.

In 1970 he became a farmer in the Letsitele district where in 1973 he was elected as chairman of the Letaba regional agricultural union. In 1981 he was elected regional representative of the TAU in Northern Transvaal and in 1987 became president of the TAU, a position he still holds.

In 1989 he was elected to Parliament; he is also chairman of the CP agricultural committee.

Although the TAU has become increasingly politicised, Bruwer still concerns himself very much with purely agricultural matters. In this capacity he has received wide acknowledgement from fellow farmers and the organised farming community.

Tel: (01523) 51859

Buthelezi, Mangosuthu President of the Inkatha Freedom Party, chief minister of the kwaZulu homeland government and minister of the notorious kwaZulu Police, 65-year-old Buthelezi must surely win the title of South Africa's King of Controversy.

The current controversy is whether he is the peace-loving liberal democrat and leader of seven million Zulus he claims to be. But such issues have always dogged him: is he the hereditary chief of the Buthelezi tribe, or would his brother Mceleli have taken the post if he had not been fed to the police? Is he the traditional prime minister to the Zulu king or is the post a recent creation? Is kwaZulu a product of the homeland system, or does it represent the historic home of the Zulu nation? Is he a leader of the liberation movement, or is his record one of collaboration as a homeland leader? Is his organisation a perpetrator of violence, or the victim of ANC attacks? Is he genuinely unhappy with the new draft constitution, or does he simply fear the poll results?

Buthelezi had a traditional upbringing, working as a herdboy in his youth. At the University of Fort Hare in the late 1940s, he joined the African National Congress Youth League and came into contact with ANC leader ZK Matthews, Robert Mugabe and Robert Sobukwe. He was expelled after student boycotts and completed his degree at Natal University.

In 1953, he took up his position as chief and in 1970 was appointed head of the kwaZulu Territorial Authority. He became chief minister in 1976. Buthelezi used the kwaZulu homeland to build up a formidable power base in the 1970s and 1980s, based on homeland patronage, the exploitation of ethnic symbolism, policies on sanctions and violence that were much appreciated by the white establishment, and a combination of political guile and ruthlessness. However, he refused to enter into political deals with the government or accept homeland independence until Nelson Mandela was released and the ANC unbanned.

He formed Inkatha in 1975 with the sanction of the ANC, but broke with the ANC in 1980. Since then relations have grown steadily worse.

In recent years, severely damaged by revelations of covert and extensive security police and Military Intelligence support during the 1980s, Buthelezi has backed off from his claim to national leadership and moved to secure a regional base with a combination of ethnic nationalism aimed at a traditional constituency and liberalism aimed at white supporters.

The threat to his homeland base posed by the negotiations led him into partnership with the white right wing, originally in the Concerned South Africans Group, and more recently the Freedom Alliance.

Once secure in his partnership and likely election alliance with the National Party, Buthelezi was deeply affronted by the 1992 Record of Understanding between Mandela and FW de Klerk, which doused his dreams of recognition as a third and equal partner in negotiations. He has been further damaged by his refusal to rejoin the negotiations process, losing white and business support because of his attempts to disrupt the process and delay elections. As minister of Police in kwaZulu, he also assumes responsibility for the highly controversial activities of his police force, frequently accused of partisanship in Natal violence and found by the Goldstone Commission in late 1993 to have had a hit-squad among its ranks.

He remains a major factor, however, largely because of his uncanny political guile and threats of violence.

He holds the Guinness Book of Records entry for the longest-ever speech, a 400-page, five-day performance in the kwaZulu Legislative Assembly. He also had a brief film career playing Cetswayo in the Michael Caine/Stanley Baker movie Zulu. These are significant aspects of his character because, despite his extensive political experience, he is one of the driest of South African leaders. He is also the one who is most sensitive to criticism.

Tel: (0358) 20–2012/2016

Camerer, Sheila The deputy minister of Justice has risen quickly through National Party ranks and provided a highly visible presence in the negotiations process. She is tipped for a post in a government of national unity.

Camerer was born in Cape Town in 1941, finished her schooling in Pretoria and completed her BA LLB at the University of Cape Town in 1964. While she is mostly known for her background in the field of law, Camerer also did a stint as a journalist at the *Financial Mail* between 1966 and 1975.

She was elected MP for Rosettenville, Johannesburg, in May 1987 and re-elected in 1989. One of only a handful of English speakers in the NP, she was appointed deputy minister of Justice on 1 April 1993.

Tel: (021) 461–0150/1 or (012) 315–1022 or (011) 726–7290

Carolus, Cheryl As a politically correct candidate (an extremely able black woman who will be able to attract some of the elusive coloured vote to the African National Congress), Carolus surprised everyone when she turned down the opportunity to stand for Parliament and claim an almost certain top-level position in a new government. She has carried a huge load in the ANC, responsible for the Health, Education, Human Resource Development, and Arts and Culture portfolios, and has earned widespread respect for it.

A teacher by profession, Carolus (36) has been a political activist since her school days, but she began her climb to national prominence when she served on the Western Cape regional and national executive committees of the United Democratic Front. She cut her now extremely sharp political teeth in the mass struggles of the early 1980s.

Despite banning orders, Carolus remained active in the Western Cape until May 1990 when she was called to be part of the ANC delegation which met with the government. Later that year, the South African Communist Party appointed her to its interim leadership group, which was tasked with re-establishing the party as a legal organisation. After her election to the ANC NEC in July 1991, Carolus moved to Johannesburg.

She is married to another well-known activist, Graham Bloch.

Tel: (011) 330–7000/7204

Cassim, Farouk By switching from Solidarity in the House of Delegates (HoD) to the Inkatha Freedom Party early this year, Cassim salvaged a dying political career. Eager for Indian votes, Mangosuthu Buthelezi immediately appointed Cassim to the IFP Central Committee, negotiating team and election committee.

Cassim is breaking new ground for the IFP, canvassing for Indian support and establishing contact with potential funders in the Arab world. If Buthelezi contests and wins elections, he is likely to reward the suave Cassim with a government post.

Cassim's detractors argue that he is a political nonentity, having been nominated as an MP to the HoD under Solidarity's banner a mere four years ago. A lover of poetry, Cassim (48) is a former lecturer at the Springfield Teachers' Training College and a former deputy president of the now-defunct Teachers' Association of South Africa.

Tel: (0324) 21347

Chaskalson, Arthur Chaskalson (62) recently retired as director of the Legal Resources Centre which he helped establish over 15 years ago. During that period he fought and won many of the most important legal challenges to oppressive apartheid laws, continuing the work he began at the Bar before joining the LRC. He graduated cum laude from the University of the Witwatersrand with a BCom LLB, was admitted to the Bar in 1956 and took silk in 1971. He stands out as an obvious choice for the Constitutional Court and is widely believed to be a frontrunner for president of that court.

Like a number of his colleagues, Chaskalson has been

systematically overlooked for top honours by the government, although these have been heaped on him by international and local human rights and legal organisations. Among the most important is his election in 1985 as an honorary member of the Bar Association of New York, an honour shared by very few. He has also served as a board member of the Wits University law faculty since 1979 and has been honorary professor of Law at Wits since 1981.

He is a member of the African National Congress constitutional committee. He also served on the technical committee at the World Trade Centre which drafted the interim constitution. The results clearly demonstrate his strong influence. This was not his first experience of national constitutions: Chaskalson was a consultant to the Namibian Constituent Assembly on the drafting of the Namibian Constitution.

Tel: (011) 836–8071

Chikane, Frank As general secretary of the South African Council of Churches (SACC), this influential leader has the difficult task of taking his organisation through this period of change, casting aside the ecumenical body's tradition of resistance and participation in political struggles, drawing the more conservative churches back into the SACC and leading the churches during the elections. He is still struggling to throw off the image of the SACC as 'the African National Congress at prayer' and recast it as a neutral peace-making and mediating body.

Chikane was schooled in the Black Consciousness Movement on the campuses during the 1970s, his education repeatedly interrupted by detention. From 1975 to 1979 he trained as a pastor in the Apostolic Faith Mission church, but was defrocked because of his political activities. He was only recently reinstated and now heads the black section of the still-segregated church.

He has long been involved with the Institute for Contextual Theology, which has pioneered the development of a liberation theology and the publication of the seminal Kairos Document.

His allegiances switched to the United Democratic Front in the 1980s and he was elected as successor to Archbishop Desmond Tutu as SACC general secretary in 1987. He is 43 years old.

Tel: (011) 492–1380/9

Chiole, Joseph A former member of the Herstigte Nasionale Party (HNP), Chiole is representative of the hard-core 'Verwoerdian' element in the Conservative Party. In 1993 he rose to prominence when he was appointed to the position of chief secretary of the executive of the Afrikaner Volksfront. He is also CP MP for Pretoria West.

Chiole was born in 1948 at Vryheid in Natal. He obtained a BSc in mechanical engineering at the University of Pretoria and is still active in this field, serving on the national professional advisory committee of the Engineering Council of South Africa.

He served on the HNP executive from 1982 until 1987 when he resigned to join the CP. In the same period he was also regional chairman of Carel Boshoff's Afrikaner Volkswag in Pretoria.

In 1984 he was elected to the Pretoria Municipal Council and served as chief whip of the CP caucus in the council from 1988 to 1989, when he was elected as MP.

As hobbies he lists tennis, angling and singing — the latter not only in the bath as he sang for Pact in the 1970s.

Tel: (012) 43–7793 or (012) 386–0962

Corbett, Michael McGregor He became chief justice in 1989, after waiting in the wings several years beyond the retirement date of his predecessor, Mr Justice Rabie. Judge Rabie was the architect of highly controversial security legislation and a chief justice who ensured that certain, more conservative, judges always dealt with the sensitive political cases. The extension of his term beyond retirement age caused an uproar in legal circles.

However, so successful has Chief Justice Corbett proved in the post that when he reached retirement age (he is now 70) and was asked to stay on as acting chief justice, not a whisper of criticism was heard — rather, the move was greeted with acclaim.

Since his appointment as chief justice, the character and standing of the Appellate Division has changed significantly. Judge Corbett's scrupulous fairness has provided an enabling environment for pro-human rights judgments from the courts. However, he is no radical and speaks strongly about the need to preserve standards on the bench, even if this means that in the immediate future the judiciary continues to be dominated by white males. He has drawn recent criticism for a series of judgments that some commentators described as restrictive of press freedom.

He is expected to stay on as chief justice during the

transition, from which position he will play an important role in helping select members of the new Constitutional Court and other members of the judiciary.

Judge Corbett has degrees from the Universities of Cape Town and Cambridge, and honorary doctorates from UCT, Rhodes and the University of the Orange Free State. He was appointed to the bench of the Cape Provisional Division in 1963 and to the AD in 1974.

Tel: (051) 47–2631

Cronin, Jeremy As a good public speaker who combines wit and sincerity with an air of realism, Cronin has become one of the most public faces of the South African Communist Party. He has an impressive academic background with a BA Honours degree from the University of Cape Town and a Masters in philosophy from the Sorbonne, Paris. He lectured in political studies at UCT from 1974 until 1976 when he was sentenced to seven years under the Terrorism Act for producing and distributing ANC and SACP pamphlets. Over the years he has written an award-winning poetry collection (*Inside*) and numerous political tracts, including some important SACP strategy documents.

With these qualifications, all that will prevent Cronin from rapidly rising through the ranks of the African National Congress, or a future government, is a steadfast belief in the tenets of Marxism and unswerving loyalty to the SACP, although he cannot be described as a dogmatist.

As head of the SACP's Publications Department, he is on the party's list of office bearers who will not be allowed to stand for election to the Constituent Assembly. Cronin, who will almost certainly prefer to be outside government, is likely to emerge as a key figure in attempts to revive and unite South Africa's political left which currently appears fragmented and directionless.

Cronin (44) serves on the Political Bureau (politburo) of the SACP, edits the party's publications *African Communist* and *Umsebenzi* (The Worker), and serves on the ANC's National Executive Committee.

Tel: (011) 339–3621

Cronje, Pierre A 'grassroots politician', Cronje is one of a handful of African National Congress-supporting independents in Parliament, having crossed the floor from the Democratic Party in April 1992.

After being elected as DP MP for the Greytown constituency in Natal in 1981, Cronje immediately made it known that he was not only the MP for his white constituents, but also for the disenfranchised members of his community. He took the initiative to meet communities in the Valley of a Thousand Hills and elsewhere in the Greytown constituency and successfully assisted in preventing removals. He promoted interaction and joint initiatives in education, development and other fields between the white community and adjacent black communities.

As DP spokesperson for Indian Affairs, he met with Indian community leaders and took an active part in preventing removals in Clairmont and Cato Manor. He became an acknowledged expert on the causes of violence and has been actively involved in monitoring, exposing the causes and mediating in conflicts all over the Natal region.

Throughout his campaigning he shared and provided platforms for, first, United Democratic Front and, later, ANC leaders to expose the white electorate to the UDF/ANC leadership and positions.

Cronje was a member of the controversial 'Dakar safari' of 1987, when a group of South Africans, most of them Afrikaners, met with exiled ANC leaders in the capital of Senegal, West Africa.

Tel: (0331) 94–6558

Cronje, Rowan His role as a minister in Ian Smith's UDI cabinet in Rhodesia and his subsequent involvement in South Africa's homelands have earned this former Nederduits Gereformeerde Kerk dominee a reputation as a determined fighter for lost causes. Ironically, as Bophuthatswana's chief negotiator, he became one of the stars at the World Trade Centre, excelling as chairman of the negotiating council and proving to be pragmatic in closed-doors discussion with both the National Party and the African National Congress.

All this has now been suspended with the decision of the Bophuthatswana government to withdraw from the talks and form a Freedom Alliance with the likes of the Afrikaner Volksfront and Inkatha. Rumours are, however, that Cronje — a brother-in-law of the Conservative Party's Thomas Langley — is not very happy with President Lucas Mangope's decision.

Cronje's relationship with Bophuthatswana goes back to 1982 when he was appointed director of Development Co-ordination in the presidency. At present he serves as minister of State Affairs. He is 55.

Tel: (0140) 29–2002

De Beer, Zach Now 65, De Beer has had a long and distinguished career in liberal politics which began with the Students' Liberal Association and the presidency of the University of Cape Town SRC. In 1953, at the age of 24, he became the youngest-ever MP, representing the United Party in Maitland.

He was a doctor who gave up his practice for politics, but turned to business when defeated in the 1961 elections. By then he had left the United Party to become a founder of the more liberal Progressive Party. He joined the Anglo American Corporation's public relations division in 1968 and rose rapidly through the ranks. He headed the company's Zambia operation for two years and served as chairman of LTA, Southern Life, Anglo Properties and the AAC group board for many years.

He returned to Parliament in 1977–80, this time as Progressive Federal Party MP for Parktown, and in 1988 was brought back to lead the party. He played a key role in the formation of the Democratic Party in 1989 and, with Denis Worrall and Wynand Malan, was one of its troika of leaders until the other two withdrew the following year.

He has been prominent as a mediator in negotiations, commanding widespread respect for his leadership, his ability to mediate conflicts and his firm commitment to liberal principles. He has also been unbending in his leadership of the DP as an independent liberal voice. His detractors, however, argue that he is too close to the Anglo American tradition and too corporate and old-style in his approach to win the black votes that will be necessary for the DP's survival.

Tel: (011) 788–4425

De Klerk, Frederik Willem It is an ironic twist of history that the role of overseeing the transformation to democracy fell on a member of one of the staunchest families of Nationalists in South Africa. De Klerk's father was a member of Verwoerd's cabinet and former prime minister JG Strijdom was his uncle.

The most outstanding characteristic of De Klerk's political career since he joined Parliament in 1972 was probably his elusiveness. Always thought to be closer to the verkrampte section of the National Party, nothing prepared South Africa for his dramatic announcements on 2 February 1990, releasing Nelson Mandela and unbanning, among others, the African National Congress and South African Communist Party.

The calm and determined way in which he ousted his redoubtable predecessor, PW Botha, earned him respect, as did the sophistication he brought to the party. He was the first television president in this country, developing a friendlier relationship with the media than any of his predecessors and turning it to his advantage. He has also shown a steely determination in keeping the country on the negotiations path and a remarkable calm and self-confidence in the difficult period of the last few years.

Although he is credited with the abolition of apartheid, his refusal to admit that apartheid was immoral still counts against him in many quarters. He has also been criticised for failing to take adequate steps when irregularities in his security forces were revealed in the early 1990s.

De Klerk was born in Johannesburg, grew up in Krugersdorp and completed his BA LLB at the University of Potchefstroom. In January 1973 he was offered the chair of administrative law at Potchefstroom, but instead decided on a political career.

Apart from National Education, he served mostly in low-profile portfolios, including Posts and Telecommunications, Sports and Recreation, Mineral and Energy Affairs, and Internal Affairs.

He was elected leader of the NP in the Transvaal in 1982 following the breakaway of the Conservative Party. On 2 February 1989 he became leader of the NP and in August the same year state president.

De Klerk is 57 years old. In 1993, he shared the Nobel Peace Prize with Nelson Mandela, indicating how far he had come from leading a pariah government to one that was being embraced by the international community.

Tel: (021) 45–7300 or (012) 319–1500

De Lille, Patricia The Pan Africanist Congress's secretary for Relief and Aid, soft-spoken but forthright and hard-nosed in arguing her position, is a woman worth watching. A behind-the-scenes operator, she was thrust into the limelight when she took over from Benny Alexander as PAC chief negotiator at the World Trade Centre and won respect for her firmness and clarity.

De Lille's organisational and negotiation skills were honed in the trade union movement. After a brief involvement in the Western Cape uprising in 1976, she worked for a paint company where she and other workers, frustrated with trying to represent workers on an internal liaison committee, joined the South African Chemical Workers' Union. She became Western Cape regional secretary in 1983 and a member of the national executive in 1985. In 1987, she was the first woman to sit on the executive of the union federation Nactu and was elected vice-president the following year.

De Lille was involved in Africanist organisations in the Western Cape in the late 1980s. She left her job to work for the PAC in 1989 and declined renomination to Nactu leadership to concentrate on this. After the 1990 unbannings, she was elected PAC Foreign Affairs secretary. In 1992, she moved to the post of Relief and Aid.

Although De Lille claims to have no political ambitions and says she would choose to work in community projects rather than go to Parliament, she is likely to be propelled into a prominent PAC position. She has given herself the task of selling the PAC to the 'coloured' population by telling them they 'are Africans and not coloureds'.

Tel: (011) 836–0442/0457

Delport, Tertius Although late in 1993 he announced his intention to resign from national politics after the elections, the minister of Local Government is expected to play an important role in regional politics. He was known during the 1980s as one of the foremost verligtes in the PW Botha caucus, but has since earned a reputation as a critic of National Party accommodation with the African National Congress.

Since the days of Codesa II, when he acted as government's chief negotiator, it has become increasingly clear that he was uncomfortable co-operating with the ANC. Delport is widely held responsible for the collapse of Codesa, an allegation he strongly denies.

Delport — a former dean and law professor at the University of Port Elizabeth and a former captain of the Eastern Province rugby team — has always combined a lawyer's and rugby player's approach to politics. Critics say he preferred trying to outsmart the ANC negotiators and showed scant interest in building relations of trust.

He was instrumental in negotiating a deal with the ANC on local government. Its provision for racial representation on local government level has led to sharp criticism from within the ANC and from the Democratic Party.

Delport (53) is well liked in the kwaZulu capital of Ulundi and among conservative Afrikaners, and is an outspoken proponent of federalism with strong autonomous powers for the regions.

Tel: (012) 44–1879

Derby-Lewis, Gabrielle Whether as a nun in Australia or a leading light in the South African Conservative Party, Gaye Derby-Lewis has always been driven, a woman of bulldog-like tenacity and passion. They are attributes which saw her through several months in Pretoria Central Prison and equipped her for a court performance following the murder of Chris Hani which was rewarded with a verdict of not guilty. A second-class acquittal it may have been, but hers are strong passions, and they may well drive her to the forefront of ultra-right politics yet again.

Her statements to the court — vilifying moves to democracy and equivocal on the use of violence for political ends — and her appearance on a Volksfront platform immediately after her acquittal indicate that she may be looking for a role as the Joan of Arc of the right. But first, she will have to spend much of her energy keeping her husband Clive's neck out of a sling following the death sentence passed on him for having instigated the Hani assassination.

Tel: (012) 342–3408

De Villiers, Dawie A qualified dominee in the Nederduits Gereformeerde Kerk, the mild-mannered former Springbok rugby captain has distinguished himself as the National Party's moral philosopher. De Villiers led the NP team at the last round of negotiations, where he made his mark as one of the more capable chairmen.

De Villiers is provincial leader of the NP in the Cape, potentially one of the most influential positions if his party does well in this, the one region where it is well placed to challenge the ANC.

The 53-year-old former philosophy lecturer and ambassador to the UK has been in Parliament as long as FW de Klerk. He was first elected in 1972, and was appointed to the cabinet in 1980.

In spite of his philosophy background (he holds a PhD from the University of Stellenbosch) his cabinet positions were mostly of a technical nature: minister of Industrial Affairs, Trade and Tourism, Mineral and Energy Affairs, minister of Economic Co-ordination, and currently minister of Public Enterprises.

A staunch supporter of the NP since his student days at Stellenbosch — where he served on the management committee of the NP — De Villiers is now an equally staunch defender of human rights and is one of the severest critics in government of the Conservative Party.

Tel: (012) 326–1110

Dexter, Philip Just three years after his return from exile, Dexter is destined for a parliamentary future as one of the candidates on Cosatu's election list. He will leave his position as general secretary of the National Education, Health and Allied Workers' Union (Nehawu) when it merges with other Cosatu public sector affiliates in 1994.

Dexter joined the union as an organiser in Cape Town soon after he returned from exile in 1990 and was elected general secretary in March 1992. The young and outspoken militant inherited a rudderless union which threatened to fall apart through a lack of coherent structures and finances. Dexter, who was part of the co-ordinating team of last year's hospital strikes, has placed the union on a stronger footing, and its Cosatu membership has been restored.

He also sits on the National Economic Forum where he has gained a reputation as a sharp thinker — he is a politics and philosophy graduate — unafraid of grabbing the bull by the horns. He is a member of both the South African Communist Party and the African National Congress. He is 33 years old.

Tel: (011) 337–8516 or (011) 330–7000

Dhlomo, Oscar On the fringes of politics since his resignation as general secretary of Inkatha in 1990, Dhlomo is expected to return to the political limelight, having won respect for his quiet adherence to principle and his non-partisanship. In January 1994 he was appointed to the Independent Electoral Commission.

He has done so largely through his work in the Institute for Multi-Party Democracy (IMPD) which he founded shortly after quitting Inkatha in order to promote multi-partyism and national reconciliation.

Dhlomo's decision to leave Inkatha was a shrewd move: with the African National Congress unbanned, he apparently realised that his political career would make no headway in the organisation, which would take an increasingly hardline stance. He, however, has chosen never to speak publicly about what lay behind his surprise departure.

The Inkatha Freedom Party has thus been robbed of its more human face and worse still, its general secretary of 13 years who was schooled in the art of negotiations. Dhlomo was its chief negotiator at the kwaZulu/Natal Indaba and was also involved in negotiations with the government before the ANC's unbanning.

Holding an MEd degree, Dhlomo was also kwaZulu's minister of Education and Culture, where he controversially introduced 'Ubuntu-Botho' (Good Citizenship) as a compulsory subject. It was little more than an attempt to promote the IFP in the volatile schools.

Dhlomo is 50.

Tel: (031) 304–3863

Diba, Vincent Vuyisile Jailed in the 1980s for murder and terrorism along with trade unionist Oscar Mpetha, Diba was released in 1990 and was soon up to his neck in conflict as a mediator for the African National Congress in the Western Cape. His intervention in squatter crises and taxi wars earned him a well-deserved profile as an indefatigable fighter for peace and a place on the ANC's regional executive in 1991, where he headed the peace desk.

Born in Nyanga in 1959, he matriculated from Langa

High in 1979 after making his mark as a student activist during the 1976 schools uprising and as a member of the Black People's Convention. Arrested in 1980 on the point of leaving the country for military training, he was sentenced to 15 years in 1983 and sent to Robben Island, where he completed his BA.

He declined a nomination for the position of vice-chairman of the ANC in the Western Cape during 1992 but served on the regional executive. In 1993 he accepted a fresh nomination for the position of vice-chair and was elected. He is responsible for co-ordinating the ANC's election monitoring in the region.

Tel: (021) 448–5651

Dlamini, Chris A veteran unionist, Dlamini was one of the people seconded to the African National Congress's election list.

Dlamini has risen through the ranks of the modern trade union movement, in which he has been involved since its inception in the early 1970s. He is now the first vice-president of Cosatu and one of its negotiators on farmworkers' rights. Until 1993, he also headed the Food and Allied Workers' Union as its president and is a former president of the Federation of South African Trade Unions.

He remains a Central Committee member of the South African Communist Party and was one of the delegates who visited the ANC in Lusaka in 1990, paving the way for the return of that organisation to South Africa.

Dlamini lives in kwaThema and is active in the community. He is 49 years old.

Tel: (011) 813–1802

Dugard, John This law professor has, over many decades, built up a solid reputation as an academic, advocate at the Bar and outspoken opponent of human rights abuses. He practised at the Durban Bar for three years in the 1960s and has occasionally accepted important cases since then. These include a 1969 challenge to the validity of South Africa's administration of the then South West Africa; a 1982 claim for the return of Archbishop Desmond Tutu's passport; and the 1988 challenge to the legality of Bophuthatswana as a state.

Dugard (56) has degrees from Stellenbosch and Cambridge and he has won wide international acclaim for his academic work. In 1965 he joined the staff of the University of the Witwatersrand to teach international law, one of the fields in which he continues to specialise. His other specialities include human rights law and jurisprudence. He has published extensively on all these subjects and founded the Centre for Applied Legal Studies at Wits University.

Dugard is a longtime critic of the government's human rights record. At the same time he has strongly maintained an independent, liberal position which, in these days of political correctness, could explain why he was relegated to a comparatively obscure technical committee during negotiations at the World Trade Centre, instead of being asked to serve on a committee where his skills could be put to their best use. He would be likely to head the list of academics considered for the Constitutional Court.

He has an honorary doctorate in law from Natal University and was president of the South African Institute of Race Relations from 1979 to 1980. He is also president of the South African branch of the International Law Association.

Tel: (011) 716–5544

Duncan, Sheena The new South Africa can expect Duncan to play much the same role as she did in the old: that of a tireless worker for social justice, an independent voice of reason and an experienced and skilled organiser. This is what Duncan has been doing for over 20 years in various capacities. For many years she was the national president of the Black Sash; now she is an honorary life vice-president of the South African Council of Churches. She is still actively engaged in the Black Sash, a member of the National Co-ordinating Committee for the Return of Exiles, a member of the Independent Board of Inquiry, a patron of the Society for the Abolition of the Death Penalty and a canon of St Mary's Cathedral in Johannesburg. She has won a number of human rights awards and honorary degrees for her lifelong work.

Duncan (61) was born to the task; her mother, Jean Sinclair, was one of the six women who founded the Black Sash and was president for many years.

Tel: (011) 442–9713

Dutton, Frank His features tend towards the cherubic, but when it comes to tracking down criminals — including those within the police — he is tough and uncompromising. Now a colonel, 44-year-old Dutton started as a beat constable, becoming a national figure when he broke the Trust Feeds case in 1992, which exposed police involvement in a Natal massacre and a widespread attempt at a cover-up. His reputation for integrity and even-handedness has taken him to the Goldstone Commission as an investigator, and the South African Police would be well advised to consider him a model for a new breed of detectives orientated towards serving the community upon his return to the force.

Dutton grew up in Pretoria in a long line of policemen and says he never wanted to do anything else.

Tel: (031) 902–6247

Eglin, Colin The leading theorist in the Democratic Party and its longest-serving parliamentarian, Eglin is MP for Sea Point in Cape Town. He is currently chairman of the DP's parliamentary caucus, spokesperson on foreign affairs, and acted as the DP's chief negotiator at the multi-party negotiating forum. He has won respect for many years for his dogged commitment to principle, detailed knowledge of foreign affairs and dedicated liberalism. His dry and pedantic manner has served him well in Parliament and the negotiating council, but not during his two short-lived and unsuccessful terms as party leader.

Born in Cape Town in 1925, Eglin graduated with a BSc degree in quantity surveying at the University of Cape Town in 1946, having interrupted his studies for war service with the South African forces in Egypt and Italy in 1944/45. He was elected to the South African Parliament from 1958 to 1961 and re-elected in 1974. In 1959 he was one of the founders of the Progressive Party, which he served as leader from 1971 to 1979 and again from 1986 to 1988, by that time leading the Progressive Federal Party.

He was a member of the 10-person planning committee of the negotiating forum.

Tel: (021) 45–1420 or (021) 403–3118

Erwin, Alec Academic economist Erwin (46) is one of those diehard, overworked and underpaid white unionists who battled state opposition through the 1970s and 1980s to build the union movement to its present strength.

Erwin was general secretary of Cosatu's forerunner, the Federation of South African Trade Unions, from 1979 to 1981, but has since been content to play a backroom role, working for some years now as national secretary for education in the National Union of Metalworkers of South Africa.

He remains an influential economic thinker, shaping the rapidly changing economic thinking of the union movement. He has been Cosatu's co-ordinator of the Economic Trends Group, and is now active in the ETG's answer to South Africa's economic problems, the Industrial Strategy Project, as well as playing a role in the African National Congress-constructed Macro-Economic Research Group.

Once a doctrinaire socialist, Erwin is at the forefront of the labour movement's attempts to adjust to the new world order by mitigating capitalism rather than rebuilding the economy from scratch.

Rejecting 'a war of slogans', he has opted for participation in the consensus politics of the National Economic Forum, appearing on public platforms with Dr Japie Jacobs and Anglo American's Bobby Godsell.

Erwin, an SACP member, was seconded by Cosatu to the ANC election list.

Tel: (031) 32–6251

Fanaroff, Bernie A grey eminence in the labour movement, Fanaroff (46) is a quiet but powerful behind-the-scenes shaker as a sophisticated thinker who belongs to the inner circle of the Congress of South African Trade Unions (Cosatu).

In 1993 he was nominated to the Electricity Council, along with two other unionists — the first time unions won representation on that council.

Fanaroff also sits on the Electrification Forum, a tripartite body consisting of representatives of government, employers and trade unions. In November 1993 he spearheaded the formation of the Telecommunications Forum. This forum followed a Cosatu campaign, led by Fanaroff, against the granting of licences for the marketing and manufacture of cellular telephones. Trade unions demanded that the government negotiate the granting of licences. He is currently involved in negotiations with Armscor as part of a campaign to demand transparency in the arms industry.

In 1991, Fanaroff was part of a campaign against the implementation of Value Added Tax. The campaign failed, but trade unions managed to secure the exemption of basic foodstuffs from the implementation of VAT.

He holds a PhD in astronomy from Cambridge but chose trade union work over a promising academic career. He has worked in the metal and engineering industries since the late 1970s, initially for the Metal and Allied Workers' Union and now in charge of the organising department of its successor, the National Union of Metalworkers of South Africa. In the modern, independent union movement for decades, he has played an important role in building the unions to their current strength.

Tel: (011) 832–2030/9

Felgate, Walter Undoubtedly the most controversial politician among white members of the Inkatha Freedom Party, Felgate is also a doughty survivor: despite numerous enemies even within the IFP, he has maintained position and influence largely because of his personal and long-standing relationship with Chief Mangosuthu Buthelezi. White liberals in the IFP do little to hide their dislike for Felgate, complaining that he holds too much sway over Buthelezi.

Felgate has become prominent because of his uncompromising style at the Kempton Park negotiations and is now known as the most fiery militant of the IFP. The bearded anthropologist is largely blamed for the IFP's decision to withdraw from the constitutional talks.

Felgate (62) is a former African affairs adviser for the Rio Tinto-Zinc Corporation in London. He is a member of the IFP's Central Committee and a board member of the Inkatha Institute.

Tel: (0351) 53–3122 or (0351) 31814

Fismer, Chris One of the rising young stars in the National Party, the 37-year-old Fismer was appointed parliamentary and political assistant to the state president in 1993. His job is to 'communicate the president's views to the public at large'.

As one of the post-1976 graduates in the NP caucus, shaped by the demands of black politics rather than the fierce nationalism of an earlier generation of Afrikaners, he has shown more sensitivity for the new politics than most of his older colleagues. This, combined with a growing awareness of the importance of public perceptions, was the reason why he was appointed De Klerk's assistant.

In spite of his verligte tendencies, Fismer followed the typical Afrikaner road to NP office. Born and schooled in Pretoria at the prestigious Afrikaans Seuns Hoërskool, he obtained his BCom (Econ Science), BLC and LLB degrees from the University of Pretoria. As a student he served as SRC chairman, Central Rag Committee chairman and president of the Afrikaans Studentebond.

Fismer was first elected to Parliament in 1987 when he unseated the Conservative Party's Daan van der Merwe in the Rissik constituency. In 1989 he was re-elected with a majority of 3 533 votes.

In Parliament he quickly made his mark as an outspoken — if not very dynamic — member of the reform-minded left wing of the NP.

Tel: (021) 45–7300 or (012) 319–1500

Gasa, Faith The chairman of the Inkatha Freedom Party Women's Brigade, Gasa has given no sign in public that she intends to lock horns with the male chauvinists in the IFP. Instead, she projects an image of an organisation which does not discriminate against women — much to the chagrin of feminists outside the IFP. Relaxed, calm and humorous, she has led the Women's

Brigade into peace talks with their counterparts in the African National Congress in a bid to spearhead initiatives aimed at ending the political violence sweeping the country. Gasa, who is fluent in six languages, was part of the IFP delegation at the World Trade Centre and is on the steering committee of the National Women's Coalition. She is also a member of the IFP's election commission. She is 48.

Tel: (031) 309–6803 or (011) 397–1475/8

George, Mluleki A sports administrator and communist, George is a graduate of Robben Island where he spent five years during the 1970s. A founder member of the United Democratic Front, he was elected UDF Border president but fell foul of Ciskei security laws and spent long periods in detention.

He emerged as a powerful and influential sports administrator when he led a breakaway group from the South African Council on Sport in the early 1990s. The sports movement was divided on political ideologies at the time and George spearheaded the Congress tradition that later formed the National Sports Congress of which he was first president. He led the NSC delegations to Lusaka and Botswana to discuss the future of sport in South Africa with the African National Congress. In 1992, as a vice-president of the National Olympic Sport Committee, George was part of the South African delegation to the Barcelona Olympics. He is currently in the leadership of the ANC in the Border region.

Tel: (0431) 43–9734

Gerwel, Gert Johannes 'Jakes' This widely respected left-wing intellectual assumed the post of rector and vice-chancellor of the University of the Western Cape (UWC) in 1987 and immediately announced his intention of turning it into an intellectual home of the left. While these words would later return to haunt him, he succeeded in creating significant space for opposition to apartheid during the years of the Emergency.

Born in the rural district of Somerset East in the Cape in 1946, Gerwel attended a local farm school before being sent to boarding school by parents who refused to allow their impecunity to interfere with their desire to have their child educated. In a brilliant academic career, Gerwel graduated cum laude from the institution he would later head and, in 1979, earned a doctorate in literature and philosophy magna cum laude from the Free University of Brussels. His politics forged in the furnace of black consciousness, Gerwel led protests at UWC during the 1970s while lecturing there. Established as a 'bush college' for coloured people and staffed largely by reactionary white academics, UWC was to experience much travail.

Gerwel played a prominent role in the days of the United Democratic Front and later served on the regional committee of the African National Congress in the Western Cape. He holds two honorary doctorates, chaired the Committee of University Principals until the end of 1993, and serves on the boards of a number of educational and social assistance organisations.

Tel: (021) 959–2911

Ginwala, Frene The women's movement's most eloquent and elegant speaker, Ginwala (61) is deputy head of the ANC Commission on the Emancipation of

Women and heads the Women's National Coalition. She has been extremely influential in getting the African National Congress and the negotiating council to put women's issues high up on the agenda. But she turns her talents to more than just gender issues. A lawyer by training, she also heads the ANC's Research Department and is an executive member of the PWV region.

Of stern gait and even sterner countenance, she does not suffer fools gladly. The usually sari-clad Ginwala is an articulate and popular keynote speaker at any number of conferences and her early training as a journalist in East Africa, where she edited a state-owned newspaper, makes her a prolific writer.

From the early 1970s, she served as an ANC official in Tanzania, Zambia, Mozambique and the United Kingdom where she was the organisation's spokesman on various issues including military and nuclear technology, technology transfer, sanctions, the government's nuclear programme and the arms and oil embargo.

Tel: (011) 330–7054/7000

Godsell, Bobby Godsell has left his mark on South Africa's difficult interface between business and politics and will undoubtedly continue to play a role in this area.

Born in 1952, and holding an MA in liberal ethics from the University of Cape Town, Godsell was a rising star in the Progressive Party from the age of 15. He joined Anglo American's Industrial Relations Department in 1974 and rose through the ranks rapidly. He is now an executive director of the giant corporation.

He is a former president of the Chamber of Mines, a

member of the South African Employers' Consultative Committee on Labour Affairs, and is a member of the State President's Economic Advisory Council and an active member of the National Economic Forum.

More than merely the acceptable face of corporate capitalism that Anglo shows to the world, Godsell is a rare example of a business leader who has a sophisticated understanding of society as well as influence in business circles. His contribution to efforts like the National Economic Forum has strengthened these initiatives and enhanced the perception of business as a willing partner in change.

Tel: (011) 638–9111

Golding, Marcel A sharp and ambitious young unionist, Golding (33) left his second-in-command job at the National Union of Mineworkers (NUM) to stand for Parliament as one of Cosatu's nominees on the African National Congress's list.

Together with Cyril Ramaphosa, he built up the country's biggest union during the 1980s, steered it through the 1987 strike — the biggest in the country's history — and through the trauma of massive retrenchments in the past few years. But he is thought to be disillusioned by his failure to win the post of general secretary after Ramaphosa left to join the ANC.

Golding is the NUM's chief negotiator and is one of the architects of the union's ground-breaking profit-sharing agreements with various mining houses. He is also a key player in the mining industry summit which is considering proposals for the restructuring that industry will face in the future.

Tel: (011) 330–7000 or (011) 833–7012

Goldstone, Richard He heads the Standing Commission of Inquiry into Violence and Intimidation named after him, while continuing to work as an Appellate Division judge and involving himself in a number of legal issues, including business law reform.

Judge Goldstone joined the bench in 1980 as a top commercial lawyer, with no significant interest or experience in public interest or human rights law. He rapidly gained a reputation in the latter with precedent-setting decisions, while retaining his authority in the commercial field. Perhaps his most famous precedent was the case in which he prevented Group Areas Act evictions unless alternative accommodation was provided, thereby making unworkable a key apartheid race law. He is responsible for most of the precedent-setting AD labour law judgments.

Judge Goldstone headed an important inquiry in 1990 into the Sebokeng shootings. In his report, he criticised all parties, as he has continued to do in his current commission.

During the State of Emergency, he also developed a reputation as one of the very few judges who used his powers to visit and assist detainees, and became colloquially known among Transvaal detainees as 'the comrade judge'. However, he also adjudicated in a controversial case, where he declined to order the release of a 12-year-old Emergency prisoner.

It was a measure of the widespread respect he commanded that he was the candidate agreed among the parties to head the crucial inquiry into violence. His work has not been without controversy: some have argued that it is inappropriate for a judge to be involved in such political work; others feel the commission has become ineffectual as a whole range of violence-related problems are dumped at its doorstep, so far with little result. He has added to this controversy by showing a nose for political opportunity — particularly in the timing and wording of his pronouncements — as strong as his nose for the evidence before him.

Despite these issues, however, the ambitious judge is frequently tipped for a seat on the Constitutional Court or as a candidate to replace the acting chief justice.

Judge Goldstone now leads a peripatetic existence, travelling between his home in Cape Town, the Appellate Division in Bloemfontein and the commission headquarters in Johannesburg. He is also president of the National Institute for Crime Prevention and Rehabilitation of Offenders.

Tel: (011) 884–0440

Gomomo, John Twenty-seven years ago Gomomo was making silencers on Volkswagen's Uitenhage production line. Today he is president of Cosatu.

Gomomo's rise to power started slowly, from his humble beginnings as a peasant boy on an Eastern Cape farm. In 1963 he started work at Volkswagen where, he confesses, he was 'a cheeky lad'. It was 10 years later that he became involved in union activity through the United Automobile Workers, which became part of the National Automobile and Allied Workers' Union (Naawu) in 1980. A full-time shop steward since 1984, Gomomo was made vice-president of Naawu in 1987 and was elected Cosatu second vice-president in 1989. After the February 1990 unbannings, Gomomo became part of the

internal leadership corps of both the African National Congress in the Eastern Cape and of the South African Communist Party.

Gomomo (48), a big man, is a devout Roman Catholic who fasts on Fridays. He is a hard worker with a strong reputation for his organisational and procedural skills. He is also known as a tough disciplinarian, totally committed to both the struggle for democracy and to his family. It has been said Gomomo removed his name from the list of Cosatu officials selected to stand for elections under the ANC flag because he was concerned about the drain on Cosatu leadership.

Tel: (011) 339–4911/4

Gordhan, Ketan ('Ketso') The third member of the youthful triumvirate of former mass democratic movement activists now running the African National Congress election campaign, Gordhan has made a quick name for himself as an organiser and strategist.

Gordhan (32) comes from a politicised family (Pravin Gordhan is his uncle) and was involved in resistance politics from school, cutting his teeth on civic youth work in Phoenix and Newlands, Durban. In 1984, he was appointed full-time organiser for the United Democratic Front in Natal, joined the Natal Indian Congress executive and co-ordinated the Million Signature Campaign.

He was detained in 1987 and left to study in England, where he did an MPhil in development economics at the University of Sussex. He returned in 1990 to work for the Labour Economic Research Project in Durban and joined the ANC Department of Economic Policy in July

1990 for two years. In September 1992, he became assistant co-ordinator of the ANC elections commission.
Tel: (011) 330–7109/7000

Gordhan, Pravin Long an influential Natal 'struggle' figure, Gordhan was thrown on to the national stage with a vengeance when he was elected co-chairman of the multi-party negotiations forum at the World Trade Centre. He won widespread respect for his skilful and firm handling of the talks, and was in the chair at two crucial points: when 27 April 1994 was adopted as the election date, and when delegates met for a tense, last-minute agreement in November 1993.

Sidelined after the African National Congress's unbanning because of allegations that he was manipulative, undemocratic and part of a Natal 'cabal', Gordhan overcame this with his sharp thinking and good organisational skills and he is now tipped for a top government post. He is one of four joint chairpersons of the Transitional Executive Council.

He has been elected to the ANC southern Natal regional executive committee as well as its election committee, though he has little time to spare for this work. He is also a leading member of the South African Communist Party. Gordhan built his political career through the ranks of the Natal Indian Congress and the Durban Housing Action Committee but was also in the ANC underground network and played a role in Operation Vula. He is 44 years old.
Tel: (031) 301–4333

Gous, Pieter A one-time assistant professor in agriculture at the University of Wisconsin in the United States,

Gous is one of the more influential volkstaat proponents in the Conservative Party caucus. As president of the very much politicised Free State Agricultural Union, he holds sway over one of the strongest right-wing pressure groups in the country. He is also Conservative Party MP for Parys, a post that he has held since his election in September 1989. In contrast to his friendly and outgoing personal style, Gous is an articulate firebrand on public platforms, at times given to threatening rhetoric. He has been associated with the volkstaat think-tank, Vekom, since the early stages, and it is thought that he is aligned more closely to the generals of the Afrikaner Volksfront than to his parliamentary CP colleagues.

He was born in 1941 at Keimoes in the north-western Cape province. He obtained an MSc in agricultural chemistry at the University of Pretoria. A PhD at the University of Virginia followed and at the moment he is busy with his final year of an LLB degree at Unisa.

Apart from his academic qualifications, Gous is no stranger to management. He was assistant director of technical services of the Department of Agriculture as well as senior manager of national agricultural interest groups.

He is a prolific author and his articles on chemistry and agriculture have been published widely in specialised as well as popular publications. He has also travelled extensively in the Americas and Europe.

He serves on the CP study groups for trade and tourism, agriculture, foreign affairs, finance, and environment and water affairs.

Tel: (051) 47–7671

Govender, Pregaluxmi (Preggs) Becoming the overall project manager of the Women's National Coalition seemed a natural step for this feisty Durban unionist. Govender graduated from the University of Durban-Westville with a BA degree, an HDipEd and an Honours degree and spent the next three years teaching in House of Delegates schools. She left quite a reputation behind her after heading the first Labour Committee at the University of Durban-Westville and was elected national education officer of the new Garment and Allied Workers' Union in 1987.

Govender co-ordinated research for the clothing negotiations nationally and developed, directed and managed the Western Cape Workers' College launched in February 1991. With a history of organisational involvement, she was a founder and media co-ordinator of the Natal Organisation of Women and is also a member of Cosatu's National Women's Committee. An excellent speaker, panellist and evaluator, she is currently responsible for conceptualising, planning and implementing the coalition's campaign for equality. As an ANC parliamentary candidate, she can be expected to play an important role in the new government.

She is 33.

Tel: (011) 331–5958/9

Gqozo, Oupa Joshua Once feted as Ciskei's liberator, the homeland military ruler swiftly achieved national notoriety. Gqozo, Ciskei's former military attaché in Pretoria, took over from homeland president Lennox Sebe in a bloodless coup on 3 March 1990. He initially embraced the African National Congress and other mass-based organisations. But, by the end of 1991, following decisions influenced by a South Africa-linked covert intelligence unit operating in the homeland, that relationship was permanently soured.

His rule has been marked by bloody incidents. He was widely blamed for the 7 September 1992 massacre of 29 people by Ciskei troops during an ANC march on Bisho. He was charged for the 1991 killing of homeland rebel — and former security chief — Charles Sebe during an abortive coup, but in December 1993 was found innocent.

With his conservative politics, Gqozo has found a place in the newly formed Freedom Alliance along with the Inkatha Freedom Party, the Conservative Party, Bophuthatswana and others. He has attempted to find a constituency for his policies in the African Democratic Movement, which he founded and leads. Gqozo (42) was born and grew up in Kroonstad. His background lies largely in the military, serving with the South African Defence Force's 21 Battalion from 1977. He joined the Ciskei Defence Force in 1981.

Tel: (0401) 95–1407 or (0401) 91415

Groenewald, Tienie Arguably wielding more back-room influence than any other single person in the far-right sphere, it was this former head of Military Intelligence who, more than anyone else, engineered the formation of the Afrikaner Volksfront, played an instrumental role in the formation of the Concerned South Africans Group — a forerunner of the Freedom Alliance — and whose fervent volkstaat ideals eventually became part of broad right-wing policy.

Although articulate and an ambitious power-player during his tenure as a career officer, Groenewald managed to avoid the common right-wing failing of trying to be king of his own heap. By electing to work largely behind the scenes, he continues to exert considerable influence on right-wing strategy without having to play the role of public flak-catcher.

A former fighter pilot and military attaché, Groenewald was born in July 1937 on a farm outside Koster in the Western Transvaal. He joined the Air Force in 1955 and obtained an Honours degree in military science. After rising to the rank of major general, he was appointed security adviser to the State Security Council by PW Botha in 1982.

In 1985/86 he held the post of chief director of Military Intelligence. After a four-year spell as deputy head and chief director of planning of the Bureau of Information, he requested early retirement in June 1990. Since then he has involved himself full time in right-wing activities.

Tel: (012) 342–2872/3

Gwala, Harry 'How can you negotiate with a man who has a sword when you have no sword yourself?' This statement by Gwala in 1990 encapsulates the African National Congress stalwart and current Midlands, Natal, leader: a hardliner who places little faith in negotiations as a vehicle for liberation and is prepared to take up weapons when he feels it is necessary, even in defiance of ANC head office.

Gwala is immensely popular in his region, but his militancy and war talk have become a thorn in the flesh of the ANC's national leadership. Nelson Mandela personally tried in 1993 to force Gwala to resign as regional chairman because this conflicted with his national executive position. Instead, Gwala resigned the latter post, and remained on the national executive as a regional leader.

To offset the criticisms fired at him, Gwala points out that he is in tune with the ANC's grassroots — many believe he is the most popular ANC leader in Natal/kwaZulu — and still lives in Pietermaritzburg's Edendale township rather than a leafy white suburb.

A political animal since 1942 when he first joined the Communist Party and later the ANC, Gwala never opted for exile. After being released from an eight-year jail term in 1972, he continued his Umkhonto weSizwe activities, resulting in his re-arrest in 1975. He was given a life sentence.

The old-style communist at first indicated that he did not want to serve in a future government and would prefer to hold classes in political education, play with his grandchildren and raise vegetables on a small farm.

But under pressure from supporters, Gwala put his name forward for the regional premier slot, only to be defeated by the moderate Jacob Zuma. Nevertheless his voice is likely to be heard in any internal radical revolt in the ANC.

Tel: (0331) 94–6558

Hanekom, Derek The choice of a former farmer as head of the African National Congress's land commission was either inspired or a political blunder.

While Hanekom, as the ANC spokesperson on agricultural matters, may be marginally more palatable to the conservative farmers who own South Africa's prime agricultural land, he is an unusual choice to represent blacks demanding land reform.

He has a firm grasp of the political and economic complexities of land redistribution in South Africa; as co-ordinator, he is responsible for developing land policy.

Hanekom served three years in prison for leaking information about South African Defence Force support for Renamo to the ANC. After his release he worked for development projects before joining the ANC in his present position.

Tel: (011) 330–7000

Hartzenberg, Ferdinand The author of a highly acclaimed doctoral thesis on cattle breeding, Hartzenberg is the leader of the Conservative Party as well as chairman of the Afrikaner Volksfront's Executive Council.

His election to the leadership of the CP, following the death of Andries Treurnicht in early 1993, was widely seen as a sign of the ascendancy of the militant element of the party. But while following a more hardline tack, the leadership's change to a more affirmative style has served to consolidate the CP's support base. Unabashed about contact with previously shunned organisations such as the far right-wing AWB, Hartzenberg has emerged relatively unscathed.

Active in National Party politics from his days as a student, Hartzenberg was elected MP for Lichtenburg in 1970. Six years later he was appointed deputy minister of Development Aid and in 1979 he was promoted to minister of Education and Training.

In 1982 he left the NP to become one of the founding members of the CP. He is 58.

Tel: (012) 342–3408 or (01441) 26218

Haysom, Nicholas ('Fink') From ex-detainee to member of the Police Board, Haysom (42) has come some way since his days as a student leader. However, this affable and energetic lawyer has always exerted a strong influence both as an attorney and a politician and is likely to continue to do so.

Haysom cut his teeth in student politics, serving on the SRC of the University of Cape Town and as president of the National Union of South African Students. He went on to law, and is now a partner in the leading civil rights firm, Cheadle Thompson and Haysom and deputy director of the Centre for Applied Legal Studies at the University of the Witwatersrand. He is an associate professor of law and a member of the African National Congress constitutional committee.

He has written extensively on human rights and policing issues, and this may account for his appointment to the Police Board in 1992 where he has played a leading role in helping reshape the South African Police.

Tel: (011) 403–2765

Heyns, Johan As moderator of the Nederduits Gereformeerde Kerk, known as the 'National Party at prayer' since it played a critical role in providing the moral and theological justification for apartheid, Heyns is now overseeing the transformation of the church into a non-racial body.

Heyns, born in 1928 on a farm near Tweeling in the

Orange Free State, was educated at Potchefstroom and Amsterdam with a speciality in ethics and dogmatics. He was ordained in 1954, and held various positions in the church before becoming moderator at a crucial synod in 1986. The government, followed by the NGK, was trying to become more non-racial and in 1986, led by Heyns and others, the church moved significantly away from its past and admitted, albeit in equivocating terms, that apartheid was not entirely a good thing.

Heyns is a gregarious person who has had surprising success in improving relations with other churches and the ecumenical movement.

He retired at the end of 1993 from his professorship at Pretoria University, but will continue with his church work and his other great love, 'cultural organisations'. Those admitted to are the Federasie van Afrikaanse Kultuurverenigings and the Akademie vir Wetenskap en Kuns. Not admitted to is his continuing senior membership of the Afrikaner Broederbond.

Despite the baggage of the past, Heyns will remain influential as he is able to bridge some of the gap between the conservative nature of his church and his ecumenical contacts.

Tel: (012) 420–9111

Holomisa, Bantubonke Released from detention in April 1987 at the demand of Transkei troops, Major General Bantu Holomisa seized power in a bloodless coup eight months later. The crafty and popular 38-year-old military ruler has since established himself as a key critic of the South African government and a voice for its opponents, in the process often drawing the wrath of Pretoria. Seen as an ally of the liberation movements, Holomisa has, however, refused to align himself directly to either the African National Congress or the Pan Africanist Congress. He was the first South African leader to free political prisoners and to allow banned organisations to operate freely.

How sharply Holomisa's path diverged from that of his predecessor, George Matanzima, became clear when he advocated the reincorporation of Transkei. Early on, he purged ex-Selous Scouts from the Transkei Defence Force and he easily survived a coup attempt, allegedly orchestrated by Pretoria, in November 1990.

The 'comrade general', Holomisa has long been a thorn in South Africa's side. His well-timed exposure of a Military Intelligence signal that appeared to authorise the 1985 murder of activist Matthew Goniwe led to the reopening of the inquest and seriously embarrassed the military.

Holomisa, a friend of the late Chris Hani and of Nelson Mandela, has widespread support among the youth. His rising popularity, particularly in the Cape, is seen in frequent invitations to address conferences, rallies and universities and his prominent showing in the ANC elections for parliamentary candidates. Holomisa is known for his 'open-door' policy and practice of wide consultation.

A strategist, Holomisa has an impressive background in the military, rising swiftly from lieutenant (1978) to commander of the Transkei Defence Force (1987 to present). He is in charge of the Department of Defence, the Audit — having vowed to root out corruption — and the Military Council. He has been tipped for a senior position in the new South African Defence Force.

Tel: (0471) 31–0436 or (0471) 22510

Jiyane, Ziba In a major coup for the Inkatha Freedom Party, Dr Jiyane rejoined the organisation early this year after leaving it in 1978 to join the Pan Africanist Congress and to carve out an academic career in the United States.

Jiyane's decision to return to his political roots is ironic: at the time the chairman of the Inkatha Youth Brigade, he left the organisation because of its failure to embark on militant protest action against the government. He returns to the IFP at a time when it is showing signs of militancy, but of a very different sort from what he wanted to see in the 1970s.

Today, Jiyane is the IFP's leading media spokesman at its Durban headquarters — an appointment that moderates pushed for in the hope that it would keep hardliner Walter Felgate out of newspaper headlines.

Jiyane brings with him the experience he gained as the PAC's director of Publicity and Information from 1979 to 1984, though he often gives the impression that he would be more comfortable behind a computer than in front of a television camera.

He is, perhaps, more comfortable in his other roles: serving on the IFP's election committee and acting as its constitutional adviser. An academic at heart, Jiyane earned his BA in political science at the University of California, Los Angeles, before going on to a demanding joint PhD/JD degree programme at Yale Law School, which he completed in 1992.

Jiyane is 35.

Tel: (031) 309–6803

Jordan, Pallo Jordan is the foremost left-wing thinker inside the African National Congress and outside of the South African Communist Party. He has impeccable left-wing credentials, but has always been strongly critical of the SACP. His fiercely independent thinking has not always been well received, and he was detained for six weeks by the ANC's security department in the early 1980s. However, his intellectual leadership and strategic input ensure that his voice carries weight within the ANC.

Jordan comes from an intensely political Free State family, with both parents prominent in the Non-European Unity Movement. Since receiving history degrees from the University of Wisconsin and the London School of Economics, he has worked for the ANC in various capacities: head of Radio Freedom and head of Research before moving to Information and Publicity.

As the current head of the Department of Information and Publicity, Jordan (51) will play a key role in projecting the image of the ANC during elections. He led the argument against Joe Slovo's proposal for 'sunset clauses' in the new constitution but, as a loyal ANC member, fell back into line when his position was defeated. His popularity was evident, however, in his strong showing in the ANC national election list.

Tel: (011) 330–7000/7096

Kalako, Mziwamadoda 'Lerumo' Elected in late 1993 to the key post of general secretary of the African National Congress in the Western Cape after a leadership tussle with his predecessor, Tony Yengeni, Kalako has been involved politically since his school days in the Eastern Cape, where he was born in New Brighton township, Port Elizabeth, in 1955.

A student leader of note, he was detained in 1976 and on his release formed the first SRC in Port Elizabeth, and was also active in the South African Students' Movement. He joined the ANC's underground in 1977, forming cells, distributing literature and recruiting for MK. Arrested in 1978, he was convicted of furthering the aims of a banned organisation and sentenced to nine years on Robben Island, where he completed matric.

Released in 1986, he remained in the Western Cape, operating underground, helping relaunch the Cape Youth Congress which spurred the revival of a beleaguered United Democratic Front. In 1987, while registered at the University of Cape Town, he was arrested while distributing Communist Party pamphlets. He jumped bail and left the country, undergoing training in Angola.

He saw active service against Unita, opened an ANC camp in Tanzania and spent time in Moscow at the Marxist Leninist Institute of Social Science and in the ANC's headquarters at Lusaka before returning to South Africa in 1991. He was elected to the ANC's regional executive in the Western Cape, serving as vice-chair the following year. He has meanwhile completed his BSocSci degree.

Tel: (021) 448–5651

Kasrils, Ronnie Having spent his early years in the advertising industry, Kasrils has a natural flair for self-presentation which, to the casual observer, can obscure the political savvy he couples with a tenacious and essentially romantic commitment to a set of increasingly unfashionable communist ideas.

Not that he ever really needed PR skills of his own, given the consistent effort by the government to boost his image among black people over the years by demonising him as a revolutionary and messenger of the devil. His popularity reached a peak during Operation Vula, when he became known as the 'scarlet pimpernel' for his ability to evade the security forces.

At 55, the 'Yeoville boykie', as he likes to refer to himself, is a member of the politburo of the South African Communist Party (which he joined in 1961, two years before he went into exile) and the national executive of the African National Congress. He seems to have largely overcome the criticism he took for his leadership of the Bisho march, which ended in a massacre by Ciskei troops.

Currently working in the ANC electoral commission, he has been a member of Umkhonto weSizwe's negotiating team with the South African Defence Force which has led him to a significant career choice: the pressure is on from within the ANC for Kasrils to don an SADF general's uniform, possibly specialising in the Military Intelligence field in which he gained experience during years building and running MK's information gathering operation. But, despite the high esteem in which he is held by cadres for his willingness — unusual for a white

— during years as a commissar to spend extended periods in the camps, Kasrils is reluctant. As a street-fighter and populist with a taste for adventure, he is unlikely to feel happy tied into a bureaucracy.

Tel: (011) 330–7380/7000

Kerzner, Sol The son of poor Russian immigrants, Kerzner has had a career which resembles most closely that of Bugsy Siegel — except for the strong Mafia connection and homicidal tendencies.

Born on the wrong side of the tracks in Troyeville, Johannesburg, in 1935, he went on via chartered accountancy to become a business megastar. En route, he also gained a few university welterweight boxing titles, a reputation for irascibility and business vision, and the hand of former Miss World Anneline Kriel, the last of his three marriages.

He formed the Southern Sun hotel chain in 1969 and later Sun International, and most recently unveiled the grandiose Lost City hotel complex in Bophuthatswana. But it was the Transkei homeland operation which got Kerzner into hot water in 1989 when he admitted Sun International had paid a R2-million bribe to then Transkei leader George Matanzima for permission to establish one of his casinos there. He has never been far from controversy, with his long-standing close relationship to the homelands, and more recently his public courting of African National Congress leaders.

Tel: (011) 780–7444

Keys, Derek When he was brought into the Cabinet in 1992 as minister of Economic Co-ordination and of

Trade and Industry, Keys was warmly welcomed by the business community. He came with an impressive CV, including a spell as executive chairman of Gencor when he changed the image of the conglomerate from that of a dour Afrikaner mining house to that of a world class company.

His appointment in mid-1992 as minister of Finance also met with approval all round. At last here was a Finance minister who understood the subtleties of business — he has been a member of a number of boards, including Price Forbes, National Discount House, Malbak and Sandvik — and could be expected to represent its interests.

He was also seen by labour and others in opposition to the government as a reasonable bargaining partner. Keys — advocating a 'golden triangle' partnership between business, labour and government — has shown himself willing to be part of the negotiating process led by the National Economic Forum.

Now 62, he has proved not only flexible, but independent-minded as well, venturing to criticise both business and labour. And he has turned out to be more of a politician than his private sector background would suggest, acting as a consummate deal-maker in a difficult transition period.

Tel: (012) 323–8911 or (012) 21–8675

Kgositsile, Baleka Feisty, forthright, fearless — this executive member and former general secretary of the ANC Women's League couldn't be better equipped to give women a stronger voice in South African politics. A leader in the battle for permanent places for women on all delegations to the multi-party talks at the World Trade Centre, she has also worked to increase her organisation's influence within the African National Congress, preventing attempts to get involved in beauty pageants and modelling schools, and instead pushing for substantive policies towards women.

Born in Durban 44 years ago, Kgositsile was strongly influenced by the heady political atmosphere at Fort Hare University during the late 1950s, where her father was librarian before losing his job because of his Communist Party membership. A trained teacher, she fled South Africa in 1976 after hearing that the police were looking for her in connection with illegal political activities. She worked as a journalist on the ANC's Radio Freedom and was active in both cultural and women's politics before returning to South Africa in 1990 as a member of the interim leadership corps.

Tel: (011) 330 7390/7000

Khanyile, Vusi From treason trialist and community activist to managing director of Thebe Investment Corporation has been no easy walk for Khanyile. As the head of the African National Congress's hived-off investment arm, he and his company have been subject to close scrutiny by business (and the press) locally and abroad because they travel the narrow path between black empowerment and privileged political access.

Khanyile, who served as the ANC's national treasurer after the organisation was unbanned, left to start Thebe in 1991. Initially intended as a conduit for ANC funds (political organisations cannot receive international funds), Thebe has branched into various subsidiary companies and uses black empowerment as its catchphrase. It was started by funds from the Batho-Batho trust, of which Nelson Mandela and Walter Sisulu are the major trustees, as well as from loan capital.

Thebe has interests in property, car rental, travel, computer, ANC memorabilia and hawking companies and is also said to be interested in the cellular telephone industry. A Thebe-owned company, Dakawa Properties, owns Shell House, the ANC's headquarters. In September 1993, together with publishing giant Macmillan Boleswa and black publishing house Skotaville, Thebe established a textbook publishing company, Nolwazi publishers. The draft business plan from Macmillan Boleswa to Thebe set alarm bells ringing when it was suggested that in return for a percentage shareholding, Thebe would provide privileged access to a new government for the new company. Among Thebe's board members are former kaNgwane minister Enos Mabuza and Tokyo Sexwale, chairman of the ANC PWV region.

Khanyile (43), who has BComm Hons, is also on the board of SA Express, a joint Thebe and Canadian-owned domestic airline due to be launched in 1994. He does not hold office in the ANC, though he remains a member.

Tel: (011) 29–2741

Khoza, Themba Reputed to be the most powerful Inkatha Freedom Party leader in the Transvaal, Khoza traces his interest in politics to the Zulu wars against British imperialism and says his great-grandfather fought in the Battle of Isandhlwana in 1879, when Zulu warriors defeated the British army.

Khoza's own involvement in politics came only in 1975 when he joined the Inkatha Youth Brigade, but he was not in the public eye until January 1990, when he opened the IFP's first organisational office in the Transvaal. He played a key role in that post in projecting a national profile for the IFP which had been seen only as a regional party, based in Natal/kwaZulu. In 1991 he was appointed to the IFP's top decision-making body, the Central Committee.

As violence flared on the Reef, Khoza was accused of supplying weapons to hostel-dwellers; an arms cache, including AK47 rifles, was found in his car in September 1990 but, in January 1992, he was acquitted on charges of illegal possession of firearms, ammunition and explosives.

He has recently played the role of peace-maker, serving on the National Peace Committee and the local dispute resolution committee in Soweto.

He was born in Eshowe in Northern Natal in 1959.

Tel: (011) 838–4127 or (011) 339–3647

King, Angela As chief of mission of the United Nations Observer Mission in South Africa, King is responsible for the organisation's activities in the country. She has been cautious about exceeding her mandate by going beyond watching developments in South Africa. This, and the failure of the United Nations to act decisively in Angola and Bosnia, has resulted in debate about what purpose a UN presence would serve if some parties decided not to recognise a negotiated settlement and revived the armed struggle.

Despite these reservations, UN involvement is still seen as a key aspect of the monitoring of violence and the election and joint control of the security forces, especially by the liberation movements.

King (55) is a Jamaican who joined the UN in 1966 after serving in her country's foreign service. At the UN she worked chiefly in human development, resource process and resource planning.

Tel: (011) 331–2311

Kriegler, Johann Christiaan Judge Kriegler, who heads the Independent Electoral Commission, was confirmed as a member of the Appellate Division in December 1993 after an acting appointment of several years.

Born in 1932, he matriculated at King Edward VII High School in Johannesburg before going on to the University of Pretoria and Unisa. He was a member of the Johannesburg Bar, at one time serving as its chairman. Apparently because of political differences with the authorities, he was appointed to the bench later than he might otherwise have been, which in turn meant he had a rather longer career at the Bar than is usual for a judge.

That career was studded with a number of important cases, whose variety indicates quite clearly his belief that advocates should be prepared to defend any client. He was a member of the legal team which acted for the Rev Beyers Naudé and Professor Albert Geyser when they brought a defamation claim against the church publication *Die Hervormer*. During the case it soon became clear they were taking on the international right-wing establishment, but they succeeded in winning the highest defamation order ever made up to that time — R13 000 each.

He also acted for Eschel Rhoodie when he was prosecuted for allegedly having stolen public funds, and successfully defended Breyten Breytenbach when he was charged with terrorism after an alleged attempt to break out of prison. Another famous trial involved defending members of the AWB charged with terrorism. His reputation as a liberal from whom all sides may expect scrupulous fairness will help him in the difficult task of chairing the IEC, which has responsibility for overseeing the elections and ensuring they are free and fair.

Tel: IEC (011) 397–2222

Kriel, Hernus As minister of Law and Order, Kriel has the task of steering the South African Police through the difficult waters of transition and is choosing to do this with a combination of bluster, threats and kragdadige posturing.

His most infamous moment came during 1993 when Pan Africanist Congress members, including PAC chief negotiator Benny Alexander, were arrested in a night-time raid later termed a 'fishing expedition'; nearly everyone arrested was later released. He was summoned by the multi-party negotiating council to explain the actions of his police, the first time a South African cabinet minister had ever been forced to account for himself in public.

In spite of his image as the National Party's 'Mister Tough', he is not averse to having a drink with political opponents in the parliamentary bar. A lawyer, he became an MP in 1984, representing Parow. He recently announced he would not be standing for national elections in 1994, preferring to represent the Western Cape on a regional level.

He is 52.

Tel: (012) 323–8880

Kuzwayo, Ellen When Kuzwayo was nominated in 1993 to the governing body of electricity supplier Eskom, she became the first black woman on the Electricity Council — just one more in her list of 'first black woman' accolades. She was also the first black woman to receive an honorary degree from the University of the Witwatersrand (in 1987) and to bag the CNA Literary Prize — for her autobiography *Call Me Woman*, published in 1986.

Kuzwayo serves on the Electricity Council as a consumer representative and because she is the national president of the Black Consumer Union. She is a teacher and social worker and was trained early in her career by Chief Albert Luthuli.

Regarded as one of the true Mothers of the Nation, alongside women like Albertina Sisulu, Kuzwayo became active in the 1970s when she was detained for five months as one of the Soweto Committee of Ten.

After her detention, she turned her attention to social welfare work — especially for black women and children — and served as the leader of various organisations including the Young Women's Christian Association, the self-help group called the Zamani Soweto Sisters' Council, and as a member of the Urban Foundation.

Kuzwayo remains the president of the Black Consumer Union. She is 78 years old.

Tel: (011) 337–6210

Langa, Pius Nkonzo This respected advocate has an unusual breadth of working experience. He started out as a factory worker in 1957. Three years later the Department of Justice employed him as an interpreter and messenger. He continued studying and in 1971 was transferred to Ndwendwe as prosecutor and later magistrate. As soon as he completed his LLB he resigned from the department. Langa has practised at the Durban Bar since 1977.

He was a founder member of the Release Mandela Committee in Natal and an early member of the Democratic Lawyers' Association, a forerunner of the National Association of Democratic Lawyers (Nadel). Langa is well thought of as a member of the Bar, and can expect appointment to higher office at some stage. However, it is as president of Nadel that he is currently most prominent. Nadel has been the prime mover behind the National Legal Forum and Langa has been deeply involved in getting this project off the ground.

Langa, who comes from a deeply religious family, is the second of seven children. One brother was killed in political conflict in 1984. Two others have been in exile since the late 1970s.

Tel: (031) 301–5402

Lekota, Mosiuoa Patrick ('Terror') One of the triumvirate of former United Democratic Front activists running the African National Congress elections department (with Popo Molefe and Ketso Gordhan), Lekota will have a major role to play in the build-up to the April 1994 ballot. And, as a popular figure and extremely competent organiser, his influence is likely to be felt well beyond that. As the ANC's number one candidate in the OFS, he is a certainty for the premiership of this historical bastion of the National Party.

Lekota, born in the Free State 45 years ago, rose to prominence in the Black Consciousness Movement while a student at Turfloop. He served six years on Robben Island for his part in organising pro-Frelimo rallies, and joined the ANC while in prison.

In 1983, not long after his release, he was appointed publicity secretary of the UDF and played a key role in the campaign against the tricameral Parliament. He was imprisoned during the marathon Delmas Treason Trial, and only released after four years when his appeal against conviction was upheld.

Since the ANC's unbanning, he has served the organisation in Natal, the Free State and at head office, first as deputy head of the Intelligence Department and latterly as deputy head of the elections commission.

He is known for his courage, his campaigning experience and his dedication to the 'struggle'. The nickname 'Terror' was earned on the soccer field.

Tel: (011) 330–7291/7000

Leon, Tony The tenacity and audacity of this ambitious 37-year-old MP for Houghton have won him almost as many supporters as critics in his short parliamentary career.

A lawyer, he first made his name in politics as a skilful

and eloquent Johannesburg city councillor but chose to leave local politics when Helen Suzman retired from her safe Houghton seat in 1989. Amid controversy, he took on Suzman's hand-picked successor — and won, demonstrating his ruthless determination and campaigning skills.

He has been clearly identified with the old-style liberals of the Democratic Party, having no time for those who have flirted with the African National Congress and aiming some of his most potent eloquence at the left.

At the multi-party negotiations, Leon has made his mark as an uncompromising defender of free market guarantees in the Charter of Fundamental Human Rights, taking the technical committee to task for emphasising equality in its draft documents and not, as he would prefer, freedom. He also led the attack, eventually successful, on a proposal to allow the cabinet to appoint Constitutional Court judges.

He was tipped to make a bid for the party leadership at the 1993 congress, but held off for tactical reasons.

Tel: (011) 337–2100 or (011) 483–2743

Louw, Michael As head of the National Intelligence Service, Louw has a natural tendency towards the shadows. But he will play a central role in reforming and re-aligning the intelligence services in the coming years — not least because he knows more than most about how the military and civilian intelligence agencies work, whom they employ, and what they did in the past. As a civilian Louw is likely to support models currently under discussion which would place the spy agencies under some sort of centralised control, with a national director of intelligence responsible to the president and Parliament. He is 54.

Tel: (012) 317–5911

Maharaj, Satjandranath Ragunanan ('Mac') He is a wily and influential military leader and strategic thinker for the African National Congress. Maharaj's law studies at the University of Natal were repeatedly interrupted by politics, although he completed a BAdmin, an MBA and part of a BSc degree while serving 12 years in prison for sabotage. On his release, he left the country and worked for the ANC in Lusaka.

He was sent back into the country in 1987 as a leading member of Operation Vula and was underground when the ANC and SACP were unbanned. He left the country in order to return with indemnity. He was detained in 1990 in connection with Operation Vula and after his release resigned his ANC and SACP posts and quit politics. However, in 1991 he was re-elected to the ANC leadership and joined the negotiations team. Although he had acted as an SACP spokesperson after its unbanning, he never rejoined the organisation on his return to politics. Maharaj (59) is the ANC's alternate member of the Transitional Executive Council and is headed for Parliament and, it is likely, an important place in government.

Tel: (011) 330–7301/7236

Mahomed, Ismail Appointed acting judge of appeal in November 1993, Mahomed was the first judge to break the all-white mould. He is known for his brilliant legal mind, his flamboyant eloquence, his workaholic habits and his commitment to civil liberties. Despite being only recently appointed to the Witwatersrand bench, he is the judge with the widest experience in other jurisdictions, such as Namibia, Botswana, Swaziland and Lesotho.

He has had personal experience of the humiliation of apartheid, even as it has been practised at the Bar — having been prevented from practising in his home city of Pretoria and passed over for the bench for decades.

Mahomed led, with dogged determination, a number of legal challenges to apartheid and the State of Emergency, scoring some notable human rights victories, such as the dismissal of all charges at the massive Pietermaritzburg treason trial in the mid-1980s.

As acting chief justice of Namibia, he has made a number of precedent-setting human rights decisions in terms of that country's Bill of Rights.

Soon after his appointment to the supreme court, he was appointed co-chair of the constitutional negotiations. This high-profile role was followed by an appointment to chair the committee that appointed the new SABC board. He was subsequently criticised for not standing up firmly enough against the interference in the selection by President FW de Klerk.

With his experience and reputation, Mahomed (63) is an obvious candidate for one of the two top judicial jobs — chief justice or head of the new Constitutional Court.

Tel: (011) 333–8707

Makwetu, Clarence Although leading a party that thrives on militant rhetoric and symbolism, the Pan

Africanist Congress president is one of the most colourless and dour of South Africa's leaders. Attempts to bestow on him the mantle of his fiery predecessor, Zeph Mothopeng, 'Ibhubesi' (the lion), have not been successful. Makwetu (63) has failed to electrify the PAC's militant constituency, least of all the youth.

A Transkei farmer, he was a founder member of the PAC and was subjected to long periods of banishment and imprisonment. He was the president of the Pan Africanist Movement, a PAC internal front, and elected PAC president in 1991 as a compromise candidate when the PAC was wracked by bitter internal conflict over whether to negotiate. He succeeded in holding the movement together and took it back into the negotiations process.

He lives in Cofimvamba, Transkei.

Tel: (011) 836–0442 (PAC)

Mandela, Nelson Rolihlala Mandela is the man who, with FW de Klerk, can take the credit for breaking South Africa's political deadlock and leading the country down the road of negotiations. He is the one South African political leader who commands universal respect and has played a pragmatic role in moderating the policies of the African National Congress since his 1990 release.

Mandela was groomed to lead from his birth in Transkei in 1918. He attended Fort Hare, whence he was expelled, and later the University of the Witwatersrand, where he received an LLB and, with Oliver Tambo, opened the first black law practice.

He was a leading figure in the young guard that took

control of — and radicalised — the ANC Youth League in the late 1940s and the ANC itself in the 1950s. He was 'volunteer-in-chief' in the Defiance Campaign of the early 1950s and the M-plan, drawn up to deal with the possibility of going underground, was named after him. He was one of 156 accused in the 1956 Treason Trial and, although acquitted, was detained during the 1960 Emergency.

As chairman of the All-In National Action Council, he was central to the underground organisation of a three-day stayaway in 1961, and its failure in the face of severe repression led him down the path of armed struggle.

When the formation of Umkhonto weSizwe was officially proclaimed on 16 December 1961, Mandela was named commander-in-chief and sent to Algeria for military training. He was captured near Howick in 1962 and was serving a sentence for incitement and leaving the country illegally when his colleagues were arrested in Rivonia and he was put on trial with them. His speech from the dock ('I am prepared to die for what I believe') received international attention and he was sentenced to life imprisonment.

During his 27 years in prison, he was recognised as the leader of the political prisoners and a massive international campaign for his release made him by far the best-known prisoner in the world. In the early years, he and his colleagues were subjected to extremely harsh conditions and punishing hard labour, but this eventually eased off. He began contacts with the government in 1986, leading to his release in 1990 and the beginning of negotiations.

Despite personal trauma — he separated from his wife Winnie in 1992 — he is a fit, healthy and extremely hard-working 75. He brings to bear an old-worldly dignity and courtesy, combined with a firm and sometimes imperious leadership. He remains the unchallenged leader of the liberation movement.

Tel: (011) 330–7000/7273

Mandela, Winnie Mandela captured the presidency of the African National Congress Women's League in December 1993, 15 months after she had been suspended from office in the League's PWV region and resigned from all her positions in the ANC, including membership of the National Executive Committee. Her 1992 withdrawal followed accusations of abuse of ANC funds and staging demonstrations against the leadership — but her 1993 League triumph indicated still another comeback for this fiery, determined woman.

Mandela (59) is likely to remain an influential and divisive figure in the organisation because she has shown a talent for mobilising grassroots support, an unequalled commitment — and a high level of ruthlessness.

Mandela has won significant support in the poverty-stricken, strife-torn townships of the East Rand where her militant rhetoric goes down well. The Civic Association of the Southern Transvaal has also been a steadfast support base and pushed Mandela on to the national leadership of the South African National Civic Association.

A social worker, she married Nelson Mandela in 1958 after his divorce from his first wife. During his imprisonment, she won local and international admiration for her defiance of the government in the face of severe harassment: she was repeatedly banned and in the late 1970s banished to Brandfort in the Orange Free State. Her bravery, as the only person within the country who would publicly mouth ANC positions, drew international acclaim.

Her problems with the ANC began before her husband's release from prison. Her controversial bodyguard, the Mandela United football team, was wreaking havoc in the township when young activist Stompie Seipei and four colleagues were kidnapped. In February 1989, representatives of Cosatu and the former United Democratic Front accused her of involvement in Seipei's kidnapping and murder. She was later convicted of kidnapping and accessory to assault; in an appeal, the conviction was upheld but the jail sentence was set aside. In April 1992, Nelson Mandela announced his separation from his wife for 'personal reasons'.

Mandela has shown her resilience and can be expected to maintain a strong influence on the left wing of the ANC with her close allies Harry Gwala and Peter Mokaba.

Tel: (011) 330–7000/7288

Mangope, Manyane Lucas Mangope's attitude to elections will be crucial to whether they can be conducted in a free and fair manner in his homeland. President of Bophuthatswana since 1977, he has so far held out firmly against reincorporation into South Africa, although he participated in negotiations before deciding to join the Freedom Alliance.

Mangope takes credit for building the most economically successful of the homelands, but he also takes criticism for ruling it with an iron, intolerant fist. For the first, he has relied a great deal on Sun International, which has used his homeland as a casino base. And for the second, he has been aided by Pretoria, which sent troops to reverse a coup in 1988.

Born in north-west Zeerust 69 years ago into a family of ruling chiefs, he was sent to an Anglican mission school. He trained as a teacher, specialising in Afrikaans, but his interest in politics led him eventually to the post of chief councillor of the Tswana Territorial Authority, then first chief minister of Bophuthatswana and the homeland's first and only president.

Tel: (0140) 29–2041

Manie, Salie Born in District Six in February 1949, Manie, a radio and television technician, ran his own business before joining the Cape Town City Council as an electronics technician — a move that would change the course of his life. Elected a shop steward, six months later, in 1985, he became vice-president of what was then the Cape Town Municipal Workers' Association. His leadership and negotiating skills came to the fore during the unification of bodies representing municipal workers which followed.

Elected president of the Cape Town branch of the South African Municipal Workers' Union, a post he still holds, he was also recruited into the underground of the African National Congress, became a member of Cosatu's central executive and was part of a delegation to Lusaka (before the ANC's unbanning) to discuss winding down the South African Council of Trade Unions.

His major focus now is local government: he is a member of the Western Cape ANC regional executive, he has served as deputy chair of Cape Town's Local Government Negotiating Forum, where he represents Cosatu, and also serves on the National Economic Forum. At Cosatu's September 1993 congress, he was selected as one of 20 candidates to represent the trade union federation in general elections.

Tel: (021) 448–5651

Manuel, Trevor Despite initial reservations about the appropriateness of this Cape Town activist's appointment to head the African National Congress Department of Economic Policy, he has rapidly made himself a vital element of the organisation's economic strategy. He faced a tough task when appointed in 1992, given his lack of formal economics background and experience: to develop a pragmatic and realistic economic policy in the face of tough criticism and competing demands from the business community and the ANC's Cosatu and South African Communist Party alliance partners.

However, he quickly familiarised himself with the debates, and by virtue of his position and his extensive networking, he is central to attempts to win over local business and bring international investment into South Africa.

Manuel (37) is on the ANC committee dealing with socio-economic reconstruction and development and will have to continue to play an important role balancing Cosatu's demands in the Reconstruction Accord — to which the ANC committed itself in exchange for its support in the April 1994 election — with a workable economic policy acceptable to the broader electorate.

Manuel is well placed on the ANC's election list, given president Nelson Mandela's determination to show 'coloureds' they have a home in the ANC. If he does not get a ministerial position, he is a definite for a senior civil service post.

He has a history of involvement in civic associations active on the Cape Flats. In 1983 he was elected to the national executive of the now-defunct United Democratic Front which resulted in extensive harassment, including a two-year stretch in detention. After the unbanning of the ANC in 1990, Manuel was one of those appointed to establish the organisation in the Western Cape. In 1991, he was elected to the ANC's National Executive Committee and later to the national working committee.

Tel: (011) 330–7267/7000

Marais, Jaap The grand, obstinate old man of far-right politics clings desperately to the Verwoerdian concept of white supremacy in a white South Africa. As the leader of the marginalised Herstigte Nasionale Party, he is still tilting at windmills after more than 25 years in the political desert.

Marais is regarded as the voice of the civilised ultra-conservatives, but may be speaking on behalf of more people than just those inside the HNP. However, a certain quaintness, bad timing, the formation of the Conservative Party, a pedantic political style and, of course, his obstinacy have prevented Marais and the HNP from capitalising on that potential support.

Marais is a lover of poetry, with TS Eliot and John Keats among his favourites. A prolific author, he has translated Shakespeare's *Julius Caesar* into Afrikaans. He is a connoisseur of fine wines and cuisine, and a breeder of budgies.

Tel: (012) 329–3119

Marcus, Gill Her years in exile were spent clipping South African newspapers for the African National Congress, discussing radical politics and making sandwiches in Knightsbridge's best lunchtime hangout, activities which all seem to have left their mark. The clippings service became Shell House's Department of Information and Publicity, the radical politics have been honed to fit the election campaign, and from the sandwich shop comes a passion for hard work and long hours which has made Marcus an important figure in the ANC.

Given the choice, she'd get out of politics once Nelson Mandela is president, says the 44-year-old Marcus — but those around her cannot imagine a passion capable of competing for her attention. In any case, she has accepted nomination to Parliament. She criss-crosses the country tirelessly, training ANC media workers and voter educators, accompanying Madiba on his forays into the provinces. And although she is less visible than Pallo Jordan, Carl Niehaus or Ronnie Mamoepa these days, she continues to play an important role in shaping the public face of the ANC.

Tel: (011) 330–7277/7096/3000

Marks, Joe Currently deputy leader of the Democratic Party in the Western Cape, Marks was born in Mossel

Bay in April 1936 and raised in Pacaltsdorp. He left school after Standard Five and, after he was fired from his job for staying away during the 1976 Soweto uprising, he became a fruit and vegetable seller.

A former member of the Coloured People's Congress, he founded the Cape Areas Housing Action Committee, in which he is still active, and helped form the United Democratic Front in 1983, which he twice served as vice-president.

Detained under the State of Emergency three times and then banned for two years until 1990, Marks clashed with the African National Congress in the region which led to his resignation from the movement and its ally, the South African Communist Party. He joined the DP and was recently elected its deputy leader in the Western Cape. He was involved in the launch in 1993 of the Western Cape Community Organisation (Wecco), a civic organisation set up in opposition to the ANC-aligned South African National Civic Organisation.

Tel: (021) 45–1420

Masekela, Barbara This highly respected woman has been, as head of staff in the office of the president of the African National Congress, a behind-the-scenes power-broker, but she can be expected to play a more public role after the elections. She is known for her forthrightness, independence of thought and sharp political skills.

Masekela, born in 1941, came from a political and socially involved family and grew up in the cauldron of Alexandra township. She left the country in 1963 and began a long period of study and teaching in the United States. She received her BA and studied for an MA at

Ohio University and taught English at Rutgers University while publishing poetry. While in the US, she chaired the ANC's regional political committee and worked hard organising support for the movement.

In 1982, she moved to Lusaka to work for the ANC administration, but was appointed head of the Department of Arts and Culture (DAC) at its formation the following year. It was an important time for arts and culture, because of the increasing mobilisation of artists against apartheid and the long debate over the cultural boycott of South Africa. It was in this job that Masekela made her mark, becoming known for her diplomatic and political skills in dealing with a tough area.

Masekela played a major role in the 1988 speech by Oliver Tambo that changed the blanket cultural boycott into a more selective one.

After the ANC unbanning, she returned to head the DAC in Johannesburg, later moving to head the ANC fundraising drive. However, Mandela asked her to move to his office where she plays an important role advising him and controlling his schedule. She is a national executive member and served on the ANC's negotiations commission, but declined nomination to Parliament.

Her brother is the world-famous musician Hugh Masekela.

Tel: (011) 330–7350/7000

Matsepe-Casaburri, Ivy The head of the SABC board was chosen as a compromise candidate in mid-1993 after President FW de Klerk's choice, Frederik Van Zyl Slabbert, stepped down in favour of Njabulo Ndebele, vetoed by De Klerk. It is arguably one of the most powerful and important positions in the country. It is also a highly visible position, and Matsepe-Casaburri has been criticised by SABC staff for her membership of the African National Congress and by the press for her reticence in talking about herself or her job.

With a BA from Fort Hare, an MA and PhD from Rutgers University in the United States and fluency in five South African languages, she has, however, silenced those who criticised her inadequate communication skills.

Born in Kroonstad and widely travelled, she formalised links with the ANC Women's League after a spell in Lusaka and participated in defining the ANC's position on gender issues. She has a list of publications behind her name ranging from the country's economy and labour issues to the development of women in East Africa. She was also a founder member of Women's World Banking in South Africa and is seen to be dedicated and conscientious.

Tel: (011) 714–3900

Matthews, Joe The son of the famous ZK Matthews, Cape leader of the African National Congress in the 1950s, Joe Matthews (64) has come a long way since his days as national secretary of the ANC Youth League. As chief executive officer of the Inkatha Freedom Party, Matthews has earned a reputation for his argumentative debating style and almost complete lack of diplomacy.

His background as a communist, sentenced twice under the Suppression of Communism Act, makes his joining of the IFP something of a surprise. But his friendship with Mangosuthu Buthelezi dates back to 1948 and their years at Fort Hare University.

Both ZK and Joe Matthews were charged in the 1956 Treason Trial. In 1960 Joe Matthews went into exile and after stints in England, Holland, Botswana (where he was assistant attorney-general) and Canada as a member of the ANC's external mission, he returned to South Africa in 1991.

Tel: (031) 307–4962

Mayekiso, Moses An enigmatic figure, Mayekiso is credited with being a driving force behind the powerful National Union of Metalworkers of South Africa (Numsa) and the country's civic movement, while courting controversy with a militant line on bond boycotts and nationalisation.

He was elected general secretary of Numsa at its formation in 1987, while still in detention facing a treason charge. He remains general secretary of the largest trade union in the country, but is leaving to stand for Parliament as one of the unionists seconded by Cosatu.

He joined the then Metal and Allied Workers' Union while employed by Toyota and, when dismissed by the company for organising a strike there, joined the union full time. He became its general secretary in 1986.

Late in 1993 he stepped down as president of the South African National Civic Organisation, where he had concentrated on the provision of low-cost housing, but remains a national executive member. He is likely to continue focusing on the housing field in Parliament.

He spearheaded the formation of the Alexandra

Action Committee in 1985, which organised the community into yard, block and street committees to oppose local councils; the AAC laid the foundation of civics around the country. Mayekiso (44) is also a Central Committee member of the South African Communist Party.

Tel: (011) 832–2030 or (011) 330–7000 or (011) 403–6009

Mbeki, Thabo After a brief spell on the edges of the leadership of the African National Congress, Mbeki (51) recently shot to the fore again when he was elected national chairman. His diplomatic experience, personal acumen, eloquence and personal charm — and his surprise endorsement by the ANC Youth League in his bid for the national chairmanship — are likely to offset the most frequent criticism of him: as a jet-setter, he represents an ANC leadership losing touch with the grassroots.

Mbeki's background is an unusual mixture of strong family influence (as son of ANC stalwart Govan Mbeki), academia (MA in economics from Sussex University), and military training (in the Soviet Union in 1970). He left the country in 1961 after a short spell in the underground and, after his studies, represented the ANC in London, Botswana, Swaziland, Nigeria and Zambia. He became best known as president Oliver Tambo's right-hand man and was frequently the ANC's most visible diplomatic face.

As head of the ANC Information Department and later International Department, he played a key role in the international campaigns of the 1980s. He returned in 1990 to be part of the ANC's Groote Schuur talks team.

Tel: (011) 330–7286/7238/7000

Mboweni, Tito While Trevor Manuel has largely soothed white business fears, Mboweni — the other most active member of the African National Congress Department of Economic Policy — has gone from conciliation to the creation of anxiety with suggestions of a wealth tax along the lines of the German levy after World War II to rebuild the country, and by his backing for anti-trust legislation.

Nevertheless, as a trained economist, he has tried to rein in the more irresponsible tendencies in the movement and is careful to make economic sense.

Born in 1959, he went into exile at the age of 21 and earned a BA from the University of Lesotho and an MA from the University of East Anglia.

Tel: (011) 330–7271/7000

McBride, Robert The journey from the bloody destruction of the Why Not Bar on Durban's beachfront, which became known as the Magoo's Bar bombing, via Death Row to the peace desk of the African National Congress PWV region would be sufficient to boggle the minds of most people, but McBride has managed the transition with a gentle charm. It belies the tough commitment of the soldier who, in 1986, freed his wounded Umkhonto weSizwe commander in a shootout with police guards at Edendale hospital and went on to command the unit which bombed the seaside bar. Like many from all sides involved in ongoing efforts at peace, McBride has taken on a dual role since receiving amnesty — he is also the eyes and ears of his party on the Witwatersrand's peace structures, one of the few places where representatives of the ANC, Inkatha and the police meet on a regular basis. He was married while on Death Row to the former Paula Leydon.

Tel: (011) 29–6066

McCauley, Ray He has risen from a bodybuilder who left school in Standard Eight and came third in the 1974 Mr Universe competition to the status of Pentecostal clergyman with political clout. His one-congregation church, Rhema, has one of the largest single congregations in the country and was once noted for its belief that all the ills of the world, including apartheid and poverty, would be healed by fervent prayer.

The leadership of the 44-year-old McCauley is charismatic, his congregation is non-racial and his theology is conservative. His easy communication with whomever he talks to has made him well liked, despite some official disdain for his church and his perceived lack of sophistication. He has pulled the politics of his church across the political spectrum, accepting criticism that his church supported the status quo of apartheid, and has since played a mediating role on the political playing field.

Tel: (011) 792–3800

Mdlalose, Frank One of the few true gentlemen of South African politics, the urbane Inkatha Freedom Party national chairman won the respect of some of the IFP's harshest critics for the calm and conciliatory tone of his contributions to negotiations. In bilaterals with other parties, Mdlalose has consistently taken a moderate line, often to be overruled by his principals in Ulundi. With Inkatha's withdrawal from negotiations and entry into the Freedom Alliance, Mdlalose appears to have been sidelined by more militant voices. It was reported, and denied by Mdlalose, that he attempted to resign in 1993, but was blocked by Mangosuthu Buthelezi.

A medical doctor, Mdlalose has served in the kwaZulu government since 1978 and is a close confidant of Buthelezi. His modesty belies a sharp sense of humour and an acute intellect. He obtained BSc and BEd degrees from the University of Fort Hare, and an MB ChB from the University of Natal. Mdlalose (61) is one of many senior IFP leaders who received their early political training from the African National Congress: he was a member of the ANC Youth League from 1950 to 1960 and joined the IFP at its launch in 1975.

Tel: (0358) 79–1031 or (0358) 20–2432

Meiring, Georg It is not without irony that the new chief of the South African Defence Force will oversee some of the most momentous changes in the history of the South African military. With a reputation as a no-holds-barred opponent of the African National Congress and its military wing, General Meiring will be responsible for the integration of thousands of Umkhonto weSizwe cadres into the SADF.

Like his predecessors, Meiring (54) has signed a three-year contract, and although some observers believe an ANC-led government is likely to ease him out after the transition in favour of a general with stronger democratic credentials, others believe the ANC is happy to see him in the job because he commands the loyalty of the Army, the largest and most politically engaged section of the military. Internal political unrest and the threat of secession by kwaZulu and an Afrikaner homeland could feature in South African politics for some time to come, circumstances under which an ANC government will be pleased to have the Army within the fold, loyal and ready for action if called.

With a background in signals and logistics, Meiring saw action as commander of South African forces in Namibia and the far northern command, which was responsible for counter-insurgency on the Zimbabwe border. He holds an MSc in physics from the University of the Orange Free State.

Tel: (012) 428–3839

Meyer, Roelf Unassuming and quiet, Meyer came into the public limelight in 1993 as the government's chief negotiator, taking over from his cabinet colleague Tertius Delport after the failure of Codesa II. Both are lawyers, but while Delport preferred drawing a line in the sand, Meyer is a proponent of the behind-closed-doors, coming-to-terms approach.

Accepting that there were only two major parties and that most of the other participants would follow in their slipstreams allowed Meyer and his African National Congress counterpart, Cyril Ramaphosa, to get on with their work.

It also led to accusations by Meyer's more conservative cabinet colleagues that his relationship with Ramaphosa was 'too cosy'.

Meyer has not always been known as a leading verligte. He openly supported the detention of youths during the State of Emergency, when he was deputy minister of Law and Order. At the University of the Orange Free State, where he completed his BCom and LLB degrees, he was national president of the conservative Afrikaanse Studentebond. Later he became national chairman of the Junior Rapportryers which is closely linked to the secretive Broederbond.

Meyer (47) was elected to Parliament in 1979. His nine-month stint as minister of Defence ended in May 1992 amid allegations that he was not accepted by the Defence Force's tough guys. He is now Minister of Constitutional Affairs and Communication and the government's chief representative on the TEC.

Tel: (012) 341–1380 or (021) 462–1441

Mlaba, Zibuse As the only Zulu chief who is a regional African National Congress leader in Natal/kwaZulu, Mlaba (38) holds the key to the organisation's success in winning rural voters in the province.

The boyish-faced Mlaba earned the ire of the Inkatha Freedom Party in 1993 when he organised a mass rally to demonstrate Zulu support for the Transitional Executive Council and the April 1994 elections.

A shy person, he prefers working behind the scenes, travelling through rural areas to woo chiefs who wield enormous influence over their subjects. In attempts to allay the chiefs' fears, he points out that he has survived — indeed, succeeded — without Ulundi's help. For example, he has successfully negotiated the launch of a R10-million water project in his area of kwaXimba.

His support has paid handsome dividends for the ANC: its kwaXimba branch is the second largest in the Midlands.

Officially installed as a chief in 1989 after his elder brother, Msinga, was assassinated, he is also the Natal secretary of the ANC-aligned Contralesa.

Tel: (0331) 94–6558/9

Mlambo, Johnson The Pan Africanist Congress's first deputy president used to be the single most powerful man in the organisation. But his popularity and power have declined as his views have become more moderate than those of the militant faction he used to lead, which pushed for the coupling of negotiations and armed struggle. He is a former chairman of the organisation's Central Committee and a former commander of the Azanian People's Liberation Army.

Mlambo was born in the Eastern Transvaal in 1940 and did most of his schooling at mission schools there. Joining the PAC in 1959, he worked underground in Daveyton after the movement was banned two years later. In 1963 he was sentenced to 20 years on Robben Island for his political activities, and he used this time to complete a BSc in economics.

On his release Mlambo was restricted to the Eastern Transvaal, but soon fled to Tanzania. He immediately took over the foreign affairs post and in 1985 was elected chairman after the death of incumbent John Phokela. Mlambo lost the presidential race to Clarence Makwetu at the PAC's first conference inside the country in 1991. He is, however, a front runner to succeed Makwetu.

Tel: (011) 836–0442/0457

Modise, Joe Umkhonto weSizwe's commander since 1965, Modise has been praised for his professionalism by all sides negotiating the integration of the armed wing of the African National Congress into the South African Defence Force, including top SADF generals. Despite never having commanded regular forces, nor being universally popular as a leader, he is likely to be a major player in the future military.

Born in Doornfontein, Johannesburg, 64 years ago, Modise has led a life of militancy which took him from resistance to the Sophiatown removals via the 1956–60 treason trial to participation in MK's first acts of sabotage. He received military training in Czechoslovakia and the USSR, and was involved in the planning and execution of MK operations, including the Wankie campaign in then Rhodesia and the strategy of 'armed propaganda' in South Africa after 1976. The mild criticism he received recently from the Motsuenyane commission into torture at ANC camps looks unlikely to affect his future role. The portly Modise was part of the ANC team at the May 1990 talks with the government at Groote Schuur.

Tel: (011) 330–7167/7000

Mogoba, Mmutlanyane Stanley The 60-year-old head of the Methodist Church was converted to Christianity while in solitary confinement during a three-year sentence on Robben Island for Pan Africanist Congress activities. His is an influential voice for peace despite his own more radical background.

He is also vice-chairman of the National Peace Committee and president of the Boy Scouts of South

Africa. Both positions have made it possible for the bishop to argue eloquently for the cause of peace and negotiations, despite calls within the church and other groupings for a more radical approach. At the same time, he is more able than most church leaders to communicate with left-wing lobbies. He is chancellor of the Medical University of South Africa and in 1990 was the recipient of the human rights award of the Swiss Foundation for Freedom and Human Rights.

Tel: (031) 21–6424/5

Mokaba, Peter A strategist, the flamboyant president of the African National Congress Youth League relishes the cut and thrust of internal politicking and will play a key role in the manoeuvring for position which is sure to take place in the ANC as it prepares for government.

He is credited with having brokered the key position of ANC chairman for Thabo Mbeki, setting Mbeki up as a possible successor to Mandela.

At 35, he controls the ANC Youth League, is one of the few ANC leaders who has the unreserved respect of township militants and is influential among elements of Umkhonto weSizwe and the ANC Women's League.

He also has a strong political base in his home territory in the Northern Transvaal, where he owns hairdressing salons. He was a founder of the South African Youth Congress, launched in March 1987 with Mokaba as national president. After the unbanning of the ANC, Sayco decided to dissolve and re-establish ANCYL. In December 1991, Mokaba was elected ANCYL president at its first conference, a position he held until January 1994.

His tough talk has made him a controversial figure —

his refusal to stop leading crowds in chants of 'Kill the Boer, kill the farmer' last year set him on a collision course with the ANC leadership, which repudiated the slogan. But he has modified his rhetoric substantially since assuming the tourism portfolio for the ANC. In November 1993, he was nominated by the Youth League as a candidate in the April 1994 elections and is likely to play an important role in helping the ANC keep the support of young militants.

Tel: (011) 333–6750 ext 202

Mokae, Gomolemo His is going to be one of the loudest dissenting voices in the post-election period. As the Azanian People's Organisation's publicity secretary, he will be voicing the movement's rejection of the power-sharing deal which Azapo regards as a betrayal of the black liberation struggle. He is also a prolific writer, making regular contributions to publications.

Mokae was born near Potgietersrus, son of a Methodist minister. His political awareness began as a teenager when Warmbaths municipal police used to hound township residents in search of people without permits to stay there. He dabbled in journalism during his matric year in Garankuwa.

Mokae's political activism intensified while at the University of Natal Medical School in the 1980s, during which time he served as publicity secretary for the Azanian Students' Movement.

Tel: (011) 333–0132/3

Molefe, Popo A graduate of the 1976 uprising, Molefe moved from a black consciousness background to the non-racial movement in 1981. He learnt his politics on the Soweto SRC, in Azapo, the Soweto Committee of Ten and the Anti-Republic Day Celebration Committee, and in 1983 became national secretary of the United Democratic Front. Detained two years later, he was one of the Delmas treason trialists, sentenced to 10 years in 1988 and released on appeal at the end of 1989. His organisational experience was key to his appointment to head the ANC's election department, where he is certain — in his quiet but determined manner — to play a central role in the campaign. He is 41.

Tel: (011) 330–7000/7189

Molobi, Eric A founder of the National Education Crisis Committee, Molobi was appointed chief executive officer of the Kagiso Trust at a crucial time in the organisation's history. As the 1990 unbanning of political organisations was changing the face of South African politics, former 'struggle industries' that had been supported through the late 1980s by the KT — a conduit for, among others, European Community funds — appeared to have been made irrelevant by events. At the same time, the direction in which the funds had been channelled during the struggle years, and the way those funds had been accounted for, were being questioned.

Molobi's direction of the trust, which handles an estimated R240-million annually, has been considered successful by funders and recipients alike.

Born in Alexandra, educated in Lesotho, Molobi was trained as a technician but earned a BA from Unisa, where he also studied towards an Honours degree. A friend of black consciousness student leader Abram

Tiro, he moved into the African National Congress camp while serving five years on Robben Island for political offences. He subsequently served on the United Democratic Front national executive committee and helped to establish the Joint Enrichment Project, a programme dealing with marginalised youth. He was detained for 18 months from December 1987 under Emergency regulations.

Molobi (46) heads the National Housing Forum, is a member of the Wits University Council and a member of the boards of the Urban Foundation's housing company, Newco, and the Independent Development Trust.

Tel: (011) 403–6319

Momberg, Jannie A former right-winger in the National Party, and once a target of an ANC bomb on his farm, Momberg is now a prominent member of the African National Congress and sits on a regional committee with the person who planted the bomb. Back in his student days at Stellenbosch University he was responsible for the expulsion from the National Party of Hernus Kriel, who would later become Law and Order minister, because of Kriel's alleged 'liberal views'.

In one of those ironic twists of politics, Kriel has since built a reputation as a hardliner, while Momberg has shifted his preference for populist politics to the mass-based and non-racial ANC.

Momberg (55) is well known in the wine farming industry in the Western Cape, and is an athletics and cricket administrator.

Momberg joined the NP in 1957, and twice fought a nomination contest for the provincial council. In 1985 he resigned from the NP and two years later managed Denis Worrall's independent campaign in Helderberg; Worrall lost by 39 votes to then Constitutional Development minister Chris Heunis. In March 1988 Momberg helped to form the Independent Party which merged a year later with the Progressive Federal Party and the National Democratic Movement to form the present Democratic Party. He was elected to Parliament in 1989 for the DP.

In 1992 he resigned from the DP to join the ANC and was elected to its Western Cape executive. He is now an ANC parliamentary candidate.

Tel: (021) 728–3494

Moosa, Mohammed Valli His role in negotiations belies his youthful 36 years. He studied for a BSc at the University of Durban-Westville where he became active in black consciousness politics. He turned to the politics of local civic associations thereafter and played an important role in the revival of the Congress tradition in the Indian community.

He rose to prominence through the Anti-South African Indian Council Committee and later the United Democratic Front, where he was Transvaal general secretary, taking over as national general secretary after the arrest of Popo Molefe. In 1993 he served as the co-ordinator and secretary of the African National Congress's negotiations commission, in which role he was an important ANC talks strategist.

He is married to journalist Elsabe Wessels.

Tel: (011) 330–7000/7236

Mosala, Itumeleng The president of the Azanian People's Organisation is faced with one of the toughest tasks of all political leaders: ensuring his party and its ideology are not marginalised by the politics of transition. Having opted not to take part in the negotiations process and constituent assembly elections, Azapo has been pushed further and further to the periphery.

Born in 1950 in Bloemfontein, Mosala adopted black consciousness at the Federal Theological Seminary in Alice where he had come into contact with South African Students' Organisation activists, including Steve Biko.

A theologian and deeply religious man, Mosala has written extensively on theology, particularly black theology, and has lectured widely, in Africa, North America and Europe. He is presently a professor in theology and African religion at the University of Cape Town.

Tel: (021) 650–9111

Moseneke, Dikgang The deputy chair of the Independent Electoral Commission and one of the two practising African silks in the country, Moseneke has experience on both sides of the courtroom. When just 15, he was sentenced to 10 years for sabotage on behalf of the Pan Africanist Congress.

He was also the first black member of the Pretoria Bar, excelling in that bastion of conservatism with his eloquence, dignity and quiet reasoning.

He was elected deputy president of the PAC in 1990, but quit in 1992. Although a key player in taking the PAC into talks, he was rumoured to be uncomfortable with the organisation's increasing militancy. It has also been apparent that he will be more likely to get the judicial appointment for which he has been tipped if he has no political ties.

He is 46.

Tel: (012) 322–1511 or (011) 928–1000

Motlana, Nthato The grandfather of Soweto politics has, with the unbanning of the African National Congress, turned his hand more to his medical practice and to the business deals that go with black empowerment.

Motlana earned his MBBCh degree at the University of the Witwatersrand in 1956.

He was active in the ANC Youth League in the 1950s, but shot to national prominence during the 1976 uprising when he was instrumental in the formation of the Black Parents' Association and the Soweto Committee of Ten, for which he served a long period in detention. He has also served a number of banning orders.

He has remained active and outspoken, often taking liberal and pro-capitalist lines that were unfashionable, but always commanding respect for his dedication and firmness. He served for many years as president of the Soweto Civic Association.

He continues to run his Soweto clinic while serving as chairman of the Get Ahead Foundation and a director of Southern Life, and has been pioneering major black financial interventions in the economy. He is chairman of Prosper Africa, whose subsidiary, New Africa Publishers, agreed in January 1994 to buy a controlling interest in the *Sowetan* newspaper.

Tel: (011) 933–1682 or (011) 938–3318

Mthintso, Thenjiwe Courage and a powerful intellect are the two attributes most readily mentioned when talk turns to Mthintso, social work student and member of the South African Communist Party politburo. A close associate of Steve Biko, she was horribly tortured by the security police on several occasions in the 1970s, and still suffers painful after-effects.

She joined the party and Umkhonto weSizwe in exile, rising rapidly to command the African National Congress's military structures in Botswana.

Currently an alternate member of the Transitional Executive Council, she is coming under increasing pressure from the party to play a more visible role than she has been able to recently, when she juggled a full-time course at Wits University with the painful and time-consuming job of nursing her companion, Skenjana Roji. Dressed in her MK uniform, she surprised and delighted many at his funeral in 1993 when she criticised the hypocrisy and outdated attitudes of the ANC and the SACP to permanent relationships not formalised in marriage.

In her early 40s, Mthintso can be expected to play a significant role in government and politics for many years to come.

Tel: (011) 339–3621

Naidoo, Jay The man who has personified the trade union movement in any number of cartoons and dinner conversations, bade an official farewell in 1993 to Cosatu, which he has led since its formation in 1985.

He heads the group of trade unionists on the African

National Congress election list and is likely to take up a ministerial post in a new government. Though early pundits suggested this was likely to be in the Labour ministry, Naidoo is said to be keen on the Trade portfolio.

The articulate and outspoken trade unionist left the federation with over a million members and as a major negotiating partner in the National Economic Forum, whose establishment he called for after anti-VAT protests in 1991.

After acquiring a BSc at the University of Durban-Westville, where he was an adherent of black consciousness, he became general secretary of the Sweet, Food and Allied Workers' Union in 1983.

Naidoo (39) has forged a clearly political role for the federation: he met the ANC in 1985 and again in 1986 when he led a Cosatu delegation on a safari to Lusaka. And the trade union movement has made representations to the constitutional technical committees on worker rights.

Naidoo is married to French Canadian journalist Lucie Page.

Tel: (011) 339–4911 or (011) 403–6009

Naidoo, Jayendra Despite being trounced in the running for assistant general secretary of Cosatu early in 1993, Naidoo has already made his mark in important sectors at the federation. He is the negotiations co-ordinator of Cosatu, a key participant in the National Economic Forum and an architect of the National Peace Accord, where he continues to play an active role.

An appointed official, Naidoo began his labour career

in the catering union Saccawu, where he was involved in major strikes including those at the Spar Group, Pick 'n Pay and OK Bazaars.

He served as chair of the Durban Western Areas branch of the African National Congress, but stepped down to concentrate on his education work in the labour movement.

Naidoo (33) set tempers aflare in 1993 when he suggested, at an NEF meeting, that all those who have swimming pools should pay a pool tax. He later said it had been a joke.

Tel: (011) 339–4911

Napier, Wilfred The immediate past-president of the Southern African Catholic Bishops' Conference is less overtly political than his predecessor, Archbishop Dennis Hurley. But insiders say the 53-year-old Franciscan, who is the Catholic archbishop of Durban, is a fiery crusader for justice and intensely political outside the glare of publicity. He is highly considered internationally and serves as information officer in the African synod of his church.

With 3,5-million Catholics in South Africa, his attitudes in the election will be an important influence.

Tel: (011) 402–6400 or (031) 303–1417/2991

Ndebele, Njabulo The new vice-chancellor and principal of the University of the North seems divided between a successful academic career and appointments such as his vice-chairmanship of the SABC board that make demands on his time. A subtle and flexible thinker, known for his firm independence, he has had a great influence on South African cultural politics through his critical writings, pronouncements and his leadership of the writers' group Cosaw since its foundation in 1987. The imperatives of education in a new South Africa are also close to his heart.

He is the author of the much acclaimed *Fools and Other Stories*, which won the Noma Award for Publishing in Africa in 1984 and remains a seminal work of black South African fiction.

In his critical work (collected in *Rediscovery of the Ordinary*), Ndebele takes the cultural debate into a new realm, away from the broadly instrumentalist views of the era of cultural struggle. He insists that 'society is the content of politics' and argues against the reduction of complex social realities to a few political shibboleths.

With his impeccable academic qualifications and commitment to the broadest notions of cultural liberation and intellectual freedom, Ndebele is perfectly placed to influence, possibly to oversee, the development of a truly multi-cultural South Africa. The president of the National Arts Initiative, founded by a range of groups seeking independence for the arts, he accepted the presidency late in 1993 of the National Arts Coalition, which grew out of the NAI.

Ndebele was born in Charterston township near Nigel and involved in the black consciousness-inspired students' movement. He received a Masters degree from Cambridge and a doctorate from the University of Denver in the United States, returning to his first alma mater, the National University of Lesotho, to become pro-vice-chancellor. Since then he has been head of the Department of African Literature at the University of the Witwatersrand, vice-rector (academic) of the University of the Western Cape, and is now vice-chancellor at Turfloop.

Tel: (01521) 68–2100/9111

Ndlovu, Louis The new president of the highly influential Southern African Catholic Bishops' Conference grew up in Swaziland, where he is now bishop of Manzini. Born in March 1945, he was ordained 33 years later and consecrated as a bishop in 1985. He is a member of the Servite Order (Order of the Servants of Mary) and studied in Rome, giving him a fluency in Italian.

Tel: (09268) 52348

Ndude, Hilda Sharing her father's cramped single-men's quarters in Langa while a schoolgirl awoke Ndude to apartheid's injustice, but her husband Alpheus's harassment by security police — he was an organiser for the General Workers' Union in Cape Town — drew her firmly into politics. Born in Jagersvlei near Cape Town in June 1955, she was raised in Transkei before returning to Cape Town and marrying in 1974. She was drawn to the non-racial stance of the African National Congress by the support she got from white as well as black activists during her husband's detention in 1976.

Ndude was a founder member of the United Women's Organisation, one of the driving forces behind the formation of the United Democratic Front in 1983. She was UDF publicity secretary in 1987 but the following two years saw both her and her husband detained. On her release she was banned and, unable to work for the

UDF, joined the Theology Exchange Programme as administrator.

After the ANC's unbanning she was elected vice-chair of the first Western Cape regional executive and in 1991 was re-elected as a member of its working group. She was already serving as a member of the ANC Women's League national executive. In 1993 she was elected co-chair of Cape Town's local government negotiating forum and re-elected to the Western Cape regional executive of the ANC.

Tel: (021) 448–5651

Nemadzivhenani, Maxwell Unless something goes drastically wrong, Nemadzivhenani (37) is bound to be one of the most prominent figures on the post-election scene. The national organiser of the Pan Africanist Congress has all the makings of a rising star: a sharp mind, charisma and the mobility of youth.

A former organiser for the South African Students' Movement in the Northern Transvaal, Nemadzivhenani left the country in 1977. He studied economics in Australia but left his degree uncompleted to take up the post of chief PAC representative for Australia and the South Pacific. While there, however, he was charged with sabotaging the vehicles of the United States military attaché and a South African diplomat. The charges were dropped after a three-year trial, but it was too late for Nemadzivhenani to take up a post as PAC ambassador to the United Nations. However, he served as PAC chief representative in Nigeria for nearly two years, until December 1991.

Tel: (011) 836–0442/0457

Ngqungwana, Lizo ('Bright') Expelled from school after taking part in protests against Bantu Education, Ngqungwana left Alice, where his father was a Presbyterian minister and his mother a nursing sister, for Port Elizabeth, where he joined the South African Students' Movement and continued his protests until the banning of the organisation forced him into exile in 1978, at the age of 18.

His parents only saw him eight years later when he was on trial as the commander of Umkhonto weSizwe in the Western Cape — a position he assumed after receiving military training in African National Congress camps in Angola and Lesotho and in the Soviet Union, and after training ANC cadres himself in Lesotho. Sentenced to life imprisonment on Robben Island in 1987, Ngqungwana served two and a half years before being indemnified. He returned to Cape Town and was co-opted on to the interim executive of the South African Communist Party in the Western Cape, having joined the party in 1982. He currently serves on the regional executive of the ANC in the Western Cape.

Tel: (021) 448–5651

Ngubane, Ben The kwaZulu government's chief negotiator at Kempton Park, Ngubane was given the task of breaking the deadlock in bilateral discussions with the government's negotiating team. In spite of the breakdown in efforts to find a meeting of the minds, government representatives described Ngubane's contributions as 'constructive'. Earlier, at open sessions of the negotiating council, Ngubane's contributions were mostly of an intellectual nature.

The 52-year-old medical doctor is minister of Health in the kwaZulu government. He has no history of political activism, but serves as a moderating influence in the Inkatha Freedom Party leadership.

Tel: (0358) 20–2471/69

Nhlanhla, Joseph The African National Congress security and intelligence department has often been compared to Swiss cheese, with Nhlanhla time and again the dairyman tasked with plugging the holes—or at least explaining how they got there.

Appointed to head Mbokodo, or NAT as the department is also known, in a 1987 revamp made necessary by the abuse of dissidents in Umkhonto weSizwe's Angolan camps, Nhlanhla has won the respect of the department as a clear strategic thinker, despite his lack of formal intelligence training. His was a political appointment, a signal to the trained intelligence and security officers following the abuses that their first allegiance must be to the democratic principles of the ANC and not to the closed corps spirit of an elite.

Since returning to South Africa in 1990, Nhlanhla (57) has been involved in negotiations on several fronts, most recently on the future of the intelligence services. As a member of the ANC's National Executive Committee, he can be expected to play a prominent role in the future, although not necessarily in an intelligence capacity.

Nhlanhla was born in Sophiatown and grew up in Alexandra, the son of a priest. He was active in the 1957 bus and potato boycotts and left the country in 1964 to join MK. Between 1973 and 1978 he was ANC representative in Egypt and the Middle East.

Tel: (011) 330–7000

Niehaus, Carl An Afrikaner from a conservative working-class family, Niehaus joined the then banned African National Congress in the early 1980s after an exhausting process of political introspection. His autobiography released late in 1993, *Om Te Veg Vir Hoop* (To Fight For Hope), tracks this political conversion which started during the 1976 uprisings, when he was in Standard Nine, and peaked in 1980 when he was expelled from Rand Afrikaans University after putting up Release Mandela posters on campus.

He continued his studies at the University of the Witwatersrand and at the same time became involved in Umkhonto weSizwe activities, including assisting young blacks to cross the borders to receive military training and scouting the Johannesburg Gas Works for the ANC military.

Niehaus, then 23, and his student friend Jansie Lourens were jailed on convictions of treason. They married in prison. Niehaus was released after seven and a half years of his 15-year sentence in terms of an amnesty contained in the Record of Understanding reached between the government and the ANC. He has since served as ANC information officer.

Niehaus is known for his uncompromising views, but is also respected for his honesty. He has made it his main task to lead Afrikaans speakers to the ANC.

Tel: (011) 29–0151 or (011) 330–7000

Nkuhlu, Wiseman The former principal and vice-chancellor of the University of Transkei was appointed chief executive of the Independent Development Trust in March 1993, two months after being named chairman of the board of the Development Bank of Southern Africa. He was the first black chartered accountant in the country, founded the University of Transkei's Department of Accounting a year after he qualified in 1976, and has concentrated throughout his career on black empowerment through the accounting profession, management and commerce.

Nkuhlu (49) holds an MBA from New York University and is national president of the Black Management Forum. He serves on a number of boards, including Standard Merchant Bank and Old Mutual. He is also chairman of the National Electrification Forum.

Tel: (021) 23–8030

Nqakula, Charles Elected general secretary of the South African Communist Party following Chris Hani's assassination, Nqakula decided not to move into his predecessor's office, a sign of his self-effacing modesty. Yet this quality may give the party a headache as it works to reclaim the public ground so convincingly occupied by Hani.

Nqakula's biography parallels Hani's in many ways. Both were born into devastatingly poor backgrounds in the Eastern Cape, and both attended mission schools. Later, Nqakula took over the ANC underground built by Hani in Lesotho. But to see him as a carbon copy is to underestimate him.

Of intense, quiet passion, he has come a long way from a rural background as one of 10 children of an illiterate labourer and a washerwoman. His simple, forceful advocacy of economic and political justice for ordinary South Africans has the ring of authenticity.

Challenged on socialism's realities, Nqakula, who spent time in the USSR and East Germany, says he believes it was bureaucracy which killed socialism, 'which is why we feel that democracy must be the focus of our party. We are drawing on the experiences of the trade unions, which are steeped in democracy.'

He says SACP membership must continue to come primarily from within the labour movement, strengthening its watchdog role when the African National Congress is in government. But first comes party building and that is why he declined nomination to Parliament. His true passion lies in grassroots organising. He is 51.

Tel: (011) 339–3644/4244/3621

Nyanda, Siphiwe Like all of Umkhonto weSizwe's senior cadres, politics came before soldiering for the chief of staff. But unlike most of MK's top brass, he has adopted a decidedly military bearing, the product perhaps of several training spells in East Germany and the USSR. At 43, Nyanda has the confidence and at least some of the conventional military background he will need for a senior staff career within an integrated South African Defence Force, and with time and some fast-track adaptation training he could be the first black chief of the Defence Force. Through his close involvement in the integration talks with representatives of the SADF and the armies of the TBVC states, Nyanda has gained insights into the workings of all of the standing armies in South Africa.

Born in Soweto, the son of a traffic inspector, Nyanda

grew up in an African National Congress household, making early attempts to join the underground. He was commanding guerrilla activities in the PWV region within a few years, rising to become MK's Transvaal chief of staff at the age of 33. Together with Mac Maharaj, Nyanda was infiltrated back into South Africa in mid-1988 as one of the commanders of Operation Vula, surviving underground until July 1990. He is a member of the ANC National Executive Committee.

Tel: (011) 330–7000

Nyati, Eugene Nyati is one of South Africa's few black economists and is a successful political analyst. A former financial journalist and investment researcher, he knows the value of explaining the facts in clear English. He is the director of the Centre for African Studies, an independent consultancy based in Johannesburg. Its main work is scenario-planning and economic and political policy analysis for companies in South Africa and overseas.

Born in Natal, Nyati (36) grew up in the then Rhodesia, returning to South Africa in 1983. He holds an MA in economics from the University of Pittsburgh.

Tel: (011) 642–9856

Ogilvie Thompson, Julian The quintessential English colonial, Anglo American chairman Julian Ogilvie Thompson (60) strikes the British as having a manner and accent more English than the English.

He is a Rhodes scholar who went into Anglo soon after graduating from Oxford and easily slid into the top seat of the giant conglomerate's 44 Main Street headquarters in 1990 as his predecessor Gavin Relly retired, though he is seen to represent the more conservative face of liberal Anglo.

Both Ogilvie Thompson and Relly were professional managers, in contrast to previous chairman Harry Oppenheimer and his father Sir Ernest Oppenheimer. But JOT, as Ogilvie Thompson is jocularly known, fits into the Anglo corporate mould as well as Relly did. He is articulate, intelligent, impervious to criticism from the hoi polloi and comfortable with the Anglo family business set-up.

He has vigorously defended the group's size against those who think it is the epitome of the over-concentration of economic power in South Africa.

Tel: (011) 638–9111

Olivier, Pierre A supreme court judge in the Orange Free State, in 1986 he was seconded to the South African Law Commission and has held the position of vice-chairman ever since. In December 1993 he was appointed an acting judge of the Appellate Division.

With Appeal Court Judge JJ van Heerden, who chairs the commission, Judge Olivier can take significant credit for moving the government towards accepting the need for a Bill of Rights. Mandated to study the question, he became convinced the Bill of Rights route was the only way for the country to go — a radical shift from the idea, current at the time, that apartheid and separate development could be justified through the application of group rights.

Much of the groundwork in preparing the government

psychologically and ideologically for negotiations was done by the commission through its reports, which shook up established thinking in Pretoria.

Judge Olivier stresses the independence of the commission, and guided by him its thinking has clearly been far ahead of the government on many issues.

He was born in Namibia 57 years ago. He graduated with a BA Law and an LLB from the University of Pretoria and a doctorate in law from Leiden in the Netherlands. He was a member of the Bloemfontein Bar from 1973 to 1985 until his supreme court appointment, and he still sits regularly to hear cases.

His wide-ranging work on the commission as well as his experience on the bench must make him a likely candidate for the Constitutional Court.

Tel: (012) 322–6440

Oppenheimer, Harry Now 84, Oppenheimer took over the reins of Anglo American from his father, Sir Ernest Oppenheimer, in 1957 and brought the family company to even greater heights. The involvement of the Oppenheimer family continues with his son Nicholas, deputy chairman of associate De Beers, and a member of a number of Anglo boards; he may well be destined for the top seat at Anglo itself.

Though professional managers like Julian Ogilvie Thompson play a big part in the company, the family still controls the giant empire with its eight per cent shareholding, a stake enhanced by a web of cross-holdings.

Harry Oppenheimer, who bowed out of direct management around 13 years ago, still commands admiration and respect for having continued the stewardship of Anglo with at least as much skill as his father. With his cultured mien he came to personify the Anglo aristocratic style, somewhat aloof from the hurly-burly of the Johannesburg business world.

He has been a longtime supporter of the Democratic Party and its predecessors, and brokered the meeting that led to Zach de Beer taking over the party leadership.

Tel: (011) 638–9111

Patel, Ebrahim The only thing the 50-year-old former head of the South African Rugby Football Union (Sarfu) has in common with the stereotype of the South African rugby player is his home language: Afrikaans.

This devout Muslim — he is principal of Lenasia's Muslim School — did not play rugby during his active sporting days, preferring soccer and cricket. He represented Transvaal at both sports at provincial level, playing alongside Kaizer Chiefs boss Kaizer Motaung in the Transvaal soccer team.

Born in Vrededorp, Johannesburg, of Cape Malay parentage, he was late in developing a love of rugby. He served for 15 years under Abdul Abbas in the South African Council on Sport-affiliated South African Rugby Union, before becoming Saru president after Abbas's death. His Saru delegation met the white South African Rugby Board in Harare in 1988 for preliminary unity talks which culminated in the formation of Sarfu in 1992.

Patel took over the Sarfu reins after the death of Danie Craven in January 1993. His tenure at the top had been in jeopardy since his ousting from the Transvaal Rugby Union executive, his support base, in November 1993 on a technicality and he resigned in February 1994.

Tel: (011) 857–1062

Patel, Ebrahim The youthful general secretary of the Southern African Clothing and Textile Workers' Union (Sactwu) and one of the architects of the National Economic Forum cut his labour teeth while in high school where he ran a students' support committee for striking pasta workers. Though an academic, he has stayed close to the labour movement ever since.

He started a trade union for university workers while at the University of Cape Town and was elected its first general secretary in 1985; he moved to the then National Union of Textile Workers in 1986 and became the general secretary of that union (now Sactwu) in 1993.

But it is his work in the National Economic Forum that will be most worth watching in the next few years. Patel (31) has been instrumental in shaping a co-determinist relationship between labour, business and government.

He convened one of the first industry summits in 1991, where he presented well-received plans for the restructuring of the clothing and textile industries. He is the chair of the NEF's short-term working group.

Tel: (021) 47–4570

Pienaar, Schalk Widely regarded as the militant voice of the Young Turks inside the Conservative Party, Pienaar was one of the main contenders for the role of deputy leader in 1993.

A combination of circumstances eventually led to the

more conciliatory choice of Dr Willie Snyman, but Pienaar is expected to play an increasingly important role inside the CP, especially by virtue of his close links with extra-parliamentary right-wing structures in the Northern Transvaal.

A lawyer, Pienaar (40) was involved in National Party politics during student days at Rand Afrikaans University in the 1970s. He has served on several committees and regional structures of the CP and in 1987 was elected to Parliament.

Tel: (0154) 3619

Pieterse, Herman The deputy commander of the South African Police Internal Stability Unit in Thokoza/Katlehong, Captain Pieterse is the kind of policeman South Africa will need in future. In the conflicts which have raged through the East Rand townships, he has often been the voice of reason and moderation, his readiness to talk rather than shoot bringing a peaceful solution to many tense situations. Trusted by the African National Congress and the Inkatha Freedom Party, he is often sought out when tensions begin to rise.

At 37, he is in many ways typical of increasing numbers of his mid-ranking compatriots. Thoughtful and flexible, his revised approach to questions of law and order reflect an increasing realisation by young SAP officers that they must change in order to survive in the force.

Like many, Pieterse believed his country and its values were in mortal danger in 1976, and donned the blue uniform, convinced he had to defend the world as it was. His was the SAP of the sjambok and the pass raid. Now he attends training sessions on negotiating strategies and seminars on conflict resolution. In Thokoza/Katlehong he avoids confrontation if he can, seeking consensus as the best route to public order. And he says sincerely, without a hint of glibness, it is because he feels a responsibility to the community he has been sent to serve.

Tel: (011) 909–7781

Pruis, Andre To the sceptics, the general is just another song-and-dance man, pulling public relations rabbits out of the hat while the vast body of the police force continues to act like thugs in uniform. To others, he represents the future of the South African Police — community policing, a service to the population which will, with time, change the image of the force. A former academic, journalist, and adviser to the SAP on the suspension of the armed struggle, Pruis is said to have accepted a generalship on condition that he be given a free hand to develop a new type of police force.

Since then he has implemented several visible changes, but he has also faced an uphill battle against the old guard, which is resisting moves away from its paramilitary style. For Pruis, the final showdown is likely when a successor is chosen to SAP commissioner Johan van der Merwe. If the job goes to a traditionalist, he might return to the ivory tower of the University of the Orange Free State. He is 40.

Tel: (012) 310–1911

Radebe, Jeff Chairman of the African National Congress Southern Natal region, Radebe has found his points on the organisation's national leadership's scoreboard increasing as he pushes for peace in the region.

Unlike the hawks in the Natal Midlands and Northern Natal, Radebe has made peace a central theme in Southern Natal in the run-up to elections, hoping that it will lead to free political activity and votes for the ANC.

But Radebe's image as a man of peace has been questioned — as was the case early in 1993 when he resolutely defended Umkhonto weSizwe cadres arrested while trying to smuggle a huge arms cache into the region.

Radebe earned a Masters degree in law at Leipzig University in East Germany in 1981. While on a mission to South Africa in 1986, he was arrested and sentenced to 10 years' imprisonment on terrorism and other charges, reduced to six years on appeal. In 1990 he was among prisoners who embarked on a hunger strike, forcing the government to release them.

Tel: (0358) 20–2422 or (031) 307–5460

Ramaphosa, Cyril Ramaphosa rose fast to the number two position in the ANC/Cosatu/SACP alliance, playing a key role in relations with the government and the steering of negotiations towards success. African National Congress general secretary since 1991, he has also been important in reorganising the movement and preparing it for elections. His main strengths are an ability to negotiate without damaging a grassroots reputation for firmness and a good capacity for using the media. His personal relationship with government negotiator Roelf Meyer has been important in breaking negotiation deadlocks.

Ramaphosa comes from a black consciousness background. Born to modest beginnings in Soweto, Ramaphosa (41) studied law at the University of the North and later Unisa and held positions in the South African Students' Organisation, the Black People's Convention and the Students' Christian Movement. He spent long periods in detention in 1974 and 1976.

The Council of Unions of South Africa appointed him to form the National Union of Mineworkers, where he quickly proved his organisational and strategic abilities. He broke with black consciousness when he led the NUM into Cosatu and played an important role in union-liberation movement relations thereafter. In 1987, he led mineworkers in one of the largest strikes in the country's history.

Tel: (011) 330–7067/7000

Ramphele, Mamphela Social anthropologist, medical doctor, author, administrator, activist, community worker . . . Ramphele has turned her hand to many disciplines and succeeded at all of them. In 1991 she was named a deputy vice-chancellor at the University of Cape Town, but has continued, despite heavy administrative and teaching duties, to write both for academic journals and for local publishers — roughly a book every year. She was recently appointed to the board of Anglo American.

As a powerful and prodigious intellectual, with a long record of community service, her voice and influence carry far. In the mid-1970s, as a newly qualified doctor, she was banished to the Northern Transvaal for her close association with the Black Consciousness Movement and her work in its programmes. During her banishment she founded the Ithuseng Community Health Programme. When it was lifted, she joined UCT, taking diplomas in public health and tropical health and a BComm in administration before registering for a PhD in social anthropology. She has edited a book on land issues — *Restoring the Land* — and co-edited a book on the Black Consciousness Movement, *Bounds of Possibility*. She co-authored *Uprooting Poverty* with Professor Francis Wilson; the result of their work for the second Carnegie Inquiry into Poverty and Development in South Africa, it won several honours, including the Noma Award for Publishing in Africa. Her current research area is hostel life, the subject of her most recent book, *A Bed Called Home: Life in the Migrant Labour Hostels of Cape Town*.

Her elder son was born some weeks after the death of his father, Black Consciousness leader Steve Biko.

Tel: (021) 650–9111

Ramsamy, Sam This 54-year-old former beach lifeguard has never been far from water — often hot water. He was branded Public Enemy Number One by white South African sports administrators during the apartheid era and is now the driving force behind the country's bid to host the 2004 Olympic Games.

A former teacher and swimming coach, Ramsamy left South Africa in 1972 and soon rose to prominence as spokesman, later chairman (1986), for the London-based South African Non-Racial Olympic Committee (Sanroc), the overseas arm of the South African Council on Sport (Sacos). He campaigned avidly for the isolation of South African sport: victories included the disruption of the 1986 Commonwealth Games (after a rebel rugby tour), and the rejection of South Africa from most international sporting bodies.

In 1989, after a squabble with Sanroc founder Denis Brutus, he returned to South Africa and was soon back in business uniting sporting bodies in the Interim National Olympic Committee of South Africa (Inocsa), which has since dropped its interim status. Abandoning the hardline Sacos for the more pragmatic National Sports Congress in forming Nocsa, of which he is now president, he was instrumental in getting South Africa back into the Olympic movement.

He has been criticised for the influence he wielded over the selection of the team for Barcelona (particularly the exclusion of javelin thrower Tom Petranoff), and for receiving a 'present' of a R30 000 watch in 1991 from former soccer PRO Abdul Bhamjee, who has been jailed.

He is married to a former East German basketball star.

Tel: (011) 483–3788/3883

Rockman, Gregory Searing public criticism of the 'brutal, unprofessional conduct' of the riot police catapulted this former police lieutenant into the spotlight in 1989, turning him into something of a folk hero. Born in Port Elizabeth in 1959 to working-class parents, he left school in 1976 without completing Standard Nine and joined the South African Police in 1977. He completed his matric and earned his national diploma in police administration and law in 1984 and was posted to Mitchell's Plain, a coloured dormitory suburb outside Cape Town, as a crime prevention officer in 1987.

Detailed to liaise with the community and smooth out points of friction, Rockman was driven publicly to criticise the riot police after watching them break up a peaceful demonstration by schoolchildren, one sjambok charge breaking down months of painstaking liaison work. He described them as behaving 'like animals'.

Rockman went on to form the Police and Prisons Civil Rights Union (Popcru), to provide a home for the 'hundreds' of policemen and women and prison warders he said shared his opposition to apartheid. After Popcru's first national strike in March 1990 he was dismissed from the force but continued organising for the union, which now claims a membership of 20 000.

He works as a minibus taxi-driver in Port Elizabeth when not fulfilling his duties as Popcru's national president.

Tel: (041) 988–2834

Rupert, Anton Ageing and legendary Afrikaans entrepreneur Anton Rupert (87) has more or less handed over the reins of the secretive Afrikaner conglomerate Rembrandt to son Johann. Rembrandt has diversified from its base in tobacco and alcohol products into every nook and cranny of the economy and established profitable links overseas, notably through Richemont, which owns luxury brands like Dunhill.

Though Stellenbosch-based Rembrandt is identified with the rise of Afrikaner capital, Rupert is famous for the phrase about blacks, uttered during the dark years of apartheid, 'If they don't eat, we don't sleep', and his son has supported President FW de Klerk's reform initiatives.

Nevertheless, the company's regime of secrecy, the boost it is supposed to have got from Afrikaner nationalism, and its sinful birth from liquor will not endear it to the politically correct.

Tel: (0218) 83–2331

Samuel, John The former national director of the Sached Trust, now head of the African National Congress Education Department, Samuel (54) is tipped as a possible minister of Education in the first post-election cabinet.

As an educator and administrator in Zambia, Ghana, England and South Africa in the 1960s and 1970s, he dealt with curriculum development and educational policy before his Sached appointment in 1979.

The Sached Trust, concerned first with distance education and, later, with curriculum development and publishing, became a major educational player during his tenure, beginning in 1979. In August 1990 the ANC appointed him head of its department involved in formulating a post-apartheid education policy; he managed both jobs for a year before stepping down at Sached.

Samuel's first degree is from the University of Natal and his Masters, in applied linguistics, from the University of Essex. Among his publications are a play entitled *Strike a Blow and Die*; *I Remember*, an anthology of poetry; and *An Introduction to African Poetry*.

Tel: (011) 330–7000/7326

Schutte, Danie The minister of Home Affairs is known to have strong sympathies with the Inkatha Freedom

Party, and is also popular in white right-wing circles. During the negotiations he distinguished himself as a stickler for detail, sometimes to the exasperation of his own colleagues.

He was elected to Parliament in 1977 for the first time as the member for Pietermaritzburg North, although in recent years he served as a nominated MP for Natal.

He served as deputy minister in a range of departments after his first appointment as deputy Justice minister in September 1989. In 1991 and 1992 these included the departments of Correctional Services, Education, and Training and Manpower. In January 1992 he was appointed deputy minister for the National Intelligence Service as well. In April 1993 he was named minister of Home Affairs.

Schutte was born in 1947 in Pretoria. He obtained his BComm Honours degree (economics) and LLB at the University of Stellenbosch, where he was a member of the Afrikaanse Studentebond executive.

Tel: (012) 326–8081 or (021) 461–5818

September, Connie When Cosatu's only woman national office bearer assumed her post as second deputy vice-president in September 1993, she was determined not to become 'Cosatu's women's desk'. She brought with her a new focus on gender issues, but made it clear she considered the federation's negotiations in the National Manpower Commission and the National Economic Forum as important.

Her immediate focus has been on increasing Cosatu's membership to 1,3-million by 1994. She has also supported the movement on the labour front, pushing for a body of worker rights to be enshrined in the constitution.

September (34), who remains a factory worker, is also the national treasurer of the South African Clothing and Textile Workers' Union. With this experience, many hope she will bring a strong administrative hand to the federation. She is more a doer than a fiery union speaker; when she commits herself to a campaign she sees it through. September was, for example, instrumental in the SITE tax campaign, which saw the federation secure the refund late in 1993 of about R700-million for workers who had overpaid the tax in the three years it had been in operation.

Tel: (021) 474–570 and (011) 339–4911

Seroke, Jaki The secretary for political affairs of the Pan Africanist Congress, Seroke describes his task as 'making sure the party has a clear ideology and that it is not submerged under other parties during the transition period'.

He faces a difficult task attempting to create ideological cohesion in a party very prone to factionalism. He has himself often fallen victim to this factionalism. The pro-negotiations faction of the PAC has often kept Seroke, who is on the far-left of the organisation, in the dark about developments.

Born in Alexandra in 1960, he became active in the South African Students' Movement in high school. During the 1976 uprising he was at the forefront of protests in Alexandra. This and his continued activism after the uprising earned him several spells in police detention. He was eventually convicted for membership of the then banned PAC and in 1987 sent to Robben Island, where he served four years, beginning a BA degree through Unisa. He was elected to his present post in 1992.

A founding member and former book editor of Skotaville Press, Seroke is also a writer and poet. His works have been published in journals and magazines; his poem Era, about the 1976 uprising, has been reproduced widely in literary journals. He is the current chairman of the African Writers' Association. At the time of his imprisonment Seroke was working on a novel, which is still incomplete.

Tel: (011) 836–0442/0457

Serote, Mongane Wally Serote may be wishing he had never become involved in anything besides poetry, an area where his reputation is secure. In the last year, he has taken much flak for his involvement in deals between the African National Congress's Department of Arts and Culture, of which he is head, and interests such as Sun International and Elmo de Witt Films.

This is a long way from the darkest years of repression and struggle, when Serote was a leading formulator of the 'culture is a weapon of the struggle' approach and one of the key figures in the development of the cultural boycott. His progress from such positions to his current attempts to reconstruct a new South African cultural milieu has not been unfaltering. In 1993 he came into conflict with a range of discipline-based organisations (film-makers, dancers, actors and others) whose formation the ANC had encouraged but which now sought independence for the arts; although ANC policy holds that culture should be dealt with by civil society, Serote has been accused of turning the DAC into a policy-making body. Despite the controversy which surrounds him, he remains a hugely influential figure and could well be one of the chief policy-makers of a new government's treatment, including funding, of the arts.

The roots of Serote's place as a major cultural arbiter lie in his attachment to black consciousness politics in the late 1960s and early 1970s, and his prominent position in the parallel emergence of a renaissance of black poetry. Born in Sophiatown in 1944, Serote focuses on life in the townships, especially Alexandra, in his early poems. A deep concern with conscientisation and black self-awareness runs through his oeuvre, including his recent book-length epic poem Third World Express, which won the 1993 Noma Award for Publishing in Africa. *To Every Birth Its Blood* (1981), his novel about the 1976 uprising, is a key text of South African political literature.

Serote studied fine art at Columbia University, founding the Medu Arts Ensemble in Botswana in 1979. From 1986 to 1989 he was the ANC's cultural attaché in London.

Tel: (011) 330–7229/7000

Sexwale, Gabriel ('Tokyo') A leader in touch with the grassroots, Sexwale (40) rose to national prominence following the death of his close friend Chris Hani in April 1993. He has since displayed astuteness and an ability to control tens of thousands of ANC supporters at mass rallies — qualities he had used in calming jobless Umkhonto weSizwe cadres returning from exile.

An ANC member since student days and a specialist in conventional warfare — he was trained in the Soviet Union, specialising in army engineering — he has gained a reputation as a cross between a calm negotiator and a fiery militant.

He went underground in the 1970s after matriculating in Soweto and completing a short spell in the Black Consciousness Movement, and in 1975 he went into exile.

On his return, he was convicted of terrorism and conspiracy and jailed on Robben Island where he spent 13 years. Four months after his release under the amnesty provided for in the Groote Schuur agreement, he was elected to the ANC's executive committee in the PWV region. His popularity was confirmed when once again in 1992 he was re-elected (unopposed) as chair of the ANC PWV area. He is currently a member of the ANC's National Executive Committee. He is also a board member of the ANC-linked Thebe Investment Corporation. He is married to Judy van Vuuren, a lawyer he met while in prison.

Tel: (011) 29–6066/7

Shabalala, Thomas Mandla Shabalala's charismatic, friendly personality belies his reputation as the most feared Inkatha warlord in Natal/kwaZulu. A street-fighter all his life, he should play a crucial role in consolidating IFP support at grassroots level in the run-up to elections.

Pessimists fear he will do so violently but optimists believe he has now assumed the role of a peacelord, leading the IFP's Southern Natal delegation to the regional dispute resolution committee.

In charge of his own fiefdom — the Lindelani squatter settlement near Durban — he has been instrumental in its development, ensuring that purified water is available and roads are tarred.

But he still strikes fear among African National Congress supporters: there were claims recently that he had threatened teachers with death for embarking on a chalk-down. It was reminiscent of the mid-1980s when he expelled two medical doctors, suspected to be United Democratic Front supporters, from his fiefdom. Although Shabalala has been accused of murder, he has never been found guilty, but in 1989 two of his bodyguards were convicted of killing UDF-supporting youth.

Now 50, Shabalala had to change residences a number of times as the government implemented the Group Areas Act. When his father fell ill in 1962, Shabalala, then in Standard Nine, was forced to leave school in order to become a breadwinner.

Tel: (031) 509–3551/5445

Shaik, Mo As the strategic thinker and de facto number two of ANC intelligence and security, Shaik looks back on years as an underground cadre and a leading Vula operative in Natal, but he claims that optometry remains his abiding interest. Now, at 34, Shaik is among those in the African National Congress who are feeling increasing pressure to give up their civilian careers for a future in the bureaucracy or security forces. There is a greater need for his clarity of vision within the National Intelligence Service, argue his compatriots, than in the optometry department at the University of Durban-Westville.

Involved in negotiations over the integration of the armed forces and intelligence services, he is destined to remain intimately connected with the country's security matters for decades to come, whether as a policy-maker or a senior operative. As someone who believes in transparent government and the need for clear direction of the intelligence and security services by a democratically elected Parliament, he says he will work to prevent the creation of a new, secretive and all-powerful securocracy.

Tel: (031) 820–2293

Shill, Louis In 1993, at the age of 62, Shill metamorphosed from distinguished businessman to Nationalist politician by accepting the Housing portfolio in President FW de Klerk's outgoing cabinet.

Shill established the Sage Group, founded the pioneering unit trust Sage Fund and helped introduce the unit trust concept to South Africa.

It was thought that Shill, though a long-standing National Party supporter, would copy Finance minister Derek Keys — the other outstanding businessman who moved into government — in bringing some statesmanship to the troubled area of housing. But Shill has proved to be disappointingly expedient, introducing an unexpected extension of the state subsidy scheme which has been seen as a cynical move to buy votes. It has also been seen as a show of power by the government, which bypassed the National Housing Forum, in which Shill took part even before he was made minister.

Tel: (012) 324–1510 or (021) 462–4184

Shilowa, Sam Shilowa's rise to the hottest seat in the trade union movement — he was elected in 1993 as Cosatu general secretary — has been meteoric. Largely self-taught, he is energetic, articulate and ambitious, a trade unionist who has moved up through the ranks.

He began organising security guards for the Transport and General Workers' Union in the early 1980s. He quickly made his mark at the transport union, becoming vice-chair of the Transvaal branch, second vice-president and president within two years. At Cosatu's 1991 congress, he was elected assistant general secretary.

Some suggest that Shilowa had his eye on Parliament, but stayed on at Cosatu when his predecessor, Jay Naidoo, topped the list of trade unionists who will run for office. He also served on the South African Communist Party negotiating team at the World Trade Centre and was information officer in the ANC's Dobsonville branch.

In the short term, Shilowa (35) is likely to turn his attention to Cosatu's voter education programmes, but in the long term it will be his duty to see that the federation makes its target membership of 1,5-million by the 1994 congress, to organise white collar workers and to establish a strong presence among domestic and farm workers.

Tel: (011) 339–4911

Sigcau, Stella Nomzamo A daughter of the late paramount chief Botha Sigcau, Transkei's first state president, Stella Sigcau was the first woman prime minister in Africa, even if she held the office only in a homeland, Transkei. Nor did her tenure last long. In 1987, after only 86 days in office, she was toppled in a bloodless coup by the homeland military led by Major General Bantu Holomisa, who accused her government of corruption and has run Transkei ever since. The coup was the culmination of a turbulent year in Transkei politics, which ended the rule of its long-standing rulers, the Matanzima brothers.

Sigcau entered the political scene in 1968 as MP for Lusikisiki in Eastern Pondoland and held various portfolios in the Matanzima cabinets, including Works and Energy, Education, Interior, Commerce, Tourism and Industry, and Posts and Telecommunications.

After her overthrow, Sigcau dropped from public view, but has recently begun to make her mark as an African National Congress supporter: she heads the ANC's Women's League in the Transkei. She was also a delegate to the negotiations, representing Transkei traditional chiefs.

Before entering politics, Sigcau (56), a Fort Hare graduate, taught in Natal high schools.

Tel: (0471) 31–2341

Sisulu, Max For the direction of macro-economic planning in South Africa, Sisulu will be the man to watch in the years to come. As director of the National Institute of Economic Policy (the successor to the Macro Economic Research Group or Merg), he will have a strong influence on the development paths the South African economy will take.

Born into the Sisulu dynasty, he had most of his education abroad, beginning with a pre-university preparatory course in Moscow. He earned a Masters degree in economics at the Plekhanov Economic Institute in the former Soviet Union. That was followed by a research fellowship at the University of Amsterdam to look into transnational corporations and South Africa's electronics industry, and a course in industrial restructuring at the University of Sussex's Institute of Development Studies.

Sisulu had a meteoric rise in exile through the ranks of the African National Congress, as deputy head of the Youth League, unofficial ANC representative in Hungary and, in 1986, head of the ANC's Economic Planning Department, co-ordinating the movement's economic policy research and representing the movement on bodies such as the Preferential Trade Area and Southern African Development Co-ordinating Council.

Upon his return from exile in 1990, he became involved in setting up Merg. He spent part of 1992 and 1993 as a fellow at Harvard University doing an MA in public administration and is currently working on a research project on the transformation of apartheid institutions, in consultation with Harvard University.

Tel: (011) 403–3009

Sisulu, Sheila *Femina* magazine chose Sisulu as its Nedbank woman of the year in 1993 because 'she's a woman you could trust with the future of a country'.

One has to: in a way, she holds a major segment of the country's future in her hands. She is director of the Joint Enrichment Project, an organisation founded by the South African Council of Churches and Southern African Catholic Bishops' Conference to find a way back for South Africa's marginalised youth — its 'lost generation'. She recently organised a three-day national youth and development conference which ended in the establishment of a National Youth Forum to 'address the challenges confronting marginalised youth'.

Sisulu, born Sheila Mashile 45 years ago, has been an educationist all her professional life, holding a degree from Roma University in Lesotho. In the 1980s she was national co-ordinator of student services for Sached's Turret correspondence college and editor of a range of Sached publications, including *Upbeat* and *Learning Post*. In 1988 she moved to the Council of Churches as Education Desk co-ordinator — in 1993 she became a vice-president — and in 1991 was appointed to the JEP.

She is a member of the council of the University of the Witwatersrand, the board of the Education Development Trust and the Equal Opportunity Trust, and in 1993 was appointed to the SABC board. She is also active in organisations designed to empower women.

Walter and Albertina Sisulu are her parents-in-law; she is married to their second son, Lungi.

Tel: (011) 834–6865/9

Sisulu, Walter Deputy president Sisulu is one of the most powerful men in the African National Congress, second only to Nelson Mandela. He has earned the universal respect of ANC members because of his position, his unquestionable commitment to the organisation, and an almost religious determination to stay above internal politicking.

He is known to want to withdraw from active politics, and his age — he is 81 — may prevent him from taking part in a new government. He may, however, stay active in the ANC as a stabilising factor while the organisation struggles to convert into a formal political party with a presence inside and outside government. He is also a prime candidate for an ambassadorship after a new government is installed.

Sisulu first joined the ANC in 1940 and rose into the leadership of the Youth League before becoming secretary-general of the ANC in 1949. In 1963 he went underground to join the newly formed Umkhonto weSizwe. In July 1963 he was captured at Rivonia, and the following year sentenced to life imprisonment.

He was released in October 1989, and after the unbanning of the ANC he was asked by the movement to re-establish its structures inside South Africa. At the July 1991 conference he was elected deputy president.

He is married to Albertina Sisulu, a well-known activist in her own right. They live in Soweto.

Tel: (011) 330–7000/7057

Sisulu, Zwelakhe Appointed at the end of 1993 to the second most powerful position in broadcasting — executive assistant to the group chief executive of the SABC — Sisulu (44) is the son of African National Congress deputy president Walter Sisulu and his wife Albertina. He was educated in Swaziland and in 1975 started working, as a reporter, for the Johannesburg-based liberal daily, the *Rand Daily Mail*. In 1980, after stints at a number of publications, he was appointed news editor of the *Sunday Post*, a weekly which replaced the banned *Weekend World*. The *Sunday Post* soon followed in the footsteps of its predecessor.

He was instrumental in the founding of the Media Workers' Association of South Africa; his activities within and without this organisation soon invited the attention of state organs and he spent numerous spells in detention. These were accompanied by a banning order.

In 1984 he was awarded a Nieman Fellowship at Harvard University. On his return he was appointed editor of *New Nation*, an alternative newspaper launched by the Southern African Catholic Bishops' Conference. His appointment to second Wynand Harmse — who is on shorter-term contract at the SABC — came as a surprise to most observers, who had believed Sisulu was in line to edit a new ANC daily newspaper.

Tel: (011) 714–9111

Slabbert, Frederik Van Zyl Slabbert has earned his spurs as academic, rugby player, TV presenter, political facilitator — and extremely unconventional politician. In February 1986, at the height of the State of Emergency, this hugely popular figure resigned both as MP and leader of the Progressive Federal Party, stating that the tricameral Parliament had become irrelevant. He co-founded the Institute for a Democratic Alternative for South Africa (Idasa), aimed at facilitating the transformation towards democracy, and developed a powerful reputation for political analysis and commentary.

In 1987 he led a delegation of white South Africans to Dakar, Senegal, for a meeting with the then banned African National Congress. Although the 'safari' was condemned by the PW Botha government and participants threatened with treason charges, the venture is today widely regarded as the beginning of the negotiations process.

Slabbert, who comes from a conservative Afrikaner background, started at the University of the Witwatersrand and moved to Stellenbosch, gathering on the way a BA (Hons), BDiv, MA and PhD, most of it cum laude. He switched to sociology when he became disillusioned with Afrikaner nationalism.

FW de Klerk's choice for chairman of the SABC board in 1993, he stepped down in favour of Njabulo Ndebele, who did not assume the post. Late in the year, he resigned from the SABC board, saying he needed more time to concentrate on the work of the Metropolitan Chamber, where a range of players, including the Johannesburg City Council, township councils and civic associations, are developing a new form of 'one-city' local government. His frequent and indecisive changes of direction have often been cited as his greatest weaknesses.

He is 54.

Tel: (011) 402–4603

Slovo, Joe Tenacity and loyalty to the battle against apartheid and for justice have been central traits through 40 years of bannings, a treason trial, over two and a half decades of exile, the assassination by the South Africans of his first wife Ruth First, and attempts on his life — which may be why he seems to have a perpetual air of satisfaction at having lasted the course through 67 years.

But victory has only been partial. The death of the apartheid system in South Africa has been paralleled by the demise of socialism, Slovo's abiding passion and the cause of many a semantic slalom-trip since his days in the Young Communist League in Yeoville in the early 1940s. Slovo, for many years a hardline Stalinist, later led the move to Gorbachevism in the party and most recently wrote the key paper arguing for the African National Congress to accept pragmatic compromise and coexistence with the National Party.

While sticking to his vision of a future free of exploitation, he has emerged as a pragmatist, accepting and arguing for a multi-party democracy, and on more than one occasion giving fresh impetus to the negotiations process, where he represented the South African Communist Party, whose chairman he is. His central role as mentor and motor during the talks is likely to continue into the period of multi-party government, despite his fight against cancer, currently in remission. A lawyer by training, Slovo served during his years in exile as chief of staff of the ANC's military wing, Umkhonto weSizwe, and general secretary of the SACP.

Tel: (011) 330–7063/7000

Smuts, Dene The Democratic Party spokesperson on women's rights first assumed the political limelight in 1987 when she was dismissed as editor of *Fair Lady* by Nasionale Pers for writing approvingly about Denis Worrall, who had resigned as ambassador to the UK to stand for election against Constitutional Development minister Chris Heunis.

Smuts (44) has consistently taken up the cudgels for women, both at Codesa and the multi-party negotiating forum that followed, both of them male-dominated.

She is a founder member of the Western Cape Women's Alliance and the National Coalition of Women.

Tel: (021) 45–1431

Sonn, Franklin Abraham A former school principal, Sonn (54) rose to prominence as president of the traditionally conservative Cape Teachers' Professional Association and its umbrella body, the Union of Teachers' Associations, under which coloured teachers were organised. An outspoken campaigner for political and educational reform, he provoked the ire of the Labour Party-dominated House of Representatives in frequent clashes while campaigning for equity in teachers' salaries and working conditions, but also came under fire from progressive quarters for maintaining a neutral political stance and leading teachers along a path of disciplined, rather than radical, protest.

Sonn adopted a more high-profile political stance during the 1980s, marching against police brutality alongside Archbishop Desmond Tutu and University of the Western Cape rector Professor Jakes Gerwel, around the same time that a compilation of his speeches appeared under the title *A Decade of Struggle*. He was born in the Vosburg district of Victoria West and raised in Queenstown and Cape Town by parents who were both educators with a track record of involvement in public affairs. He studied at the Hewat College of Education, Unisa and UWC. He was appointed rector of the Peninsula Technikon in 1978, a position he still holds. He serves on the boards of a number of education and service organisations, chaired the Committee of

Technikon Principals for two consecutive terms and was recently appointed a member of the SABC board. He is currently chairman of the National Education and Training Forum.

Tel: (021) 959–6201

Steenkamp, Johan A one-time National Party right-winger in Natal, Steenkamp has now emerged as the strongest ally of chief government negotiator Roelf Meyer in the province. As Meyer pushed the NP towards power-sharing with the African National Congress, he faced stiff opposition from Natal Nats who preferred an alliance with the Inkatha Freedom Party. But Steenkamp acted as a counter-balance, supporting Meyer as he staved off the pressure.

The MP for Umhlatuzana since 1987, Steenkamp has made a dramatic about-turn: he was one of the last NP parliamentarians to accept the demise of the Group Areas Act and campaigned vigorously against 'infiltrators' in white areas. In 1988, he expressed his opposition to 'a unitary one-man, one-vote South Africa, in other words black majority government'.

But he emerged as a strong supporter of negotiations with the ANC and is the vice-chairman of the NP's study group on constitutional development. He is also the NP's director of information in Natal and a member of its head committee.

Having matriculated in 1961, Steenkamp enrolled at the University of Pretoria where he obtained his BSc and MSc degrees. He went on to write his thesis on the Theory of Nuclear Fission at the University of Heidelberg, West Germany, graduating three years later. He took up a lectureship in applied mathematics at the University of Port Elizabeth in 1972 and thereafter a senior lectureship in mathematics and applied mathematics at the University of Natal.

Tel: (031) 78–4330

Steyn, Pierre For some, General Steyn was the 'Jesuit' of the South African Defence Force — intellectual, uncorruptible, an upholder of the highest principles of service. For others, mainly military colleagues, his acceptance of President FW de Klerk's mandate to clean up Military Intelligence in late 1992 was tantamount to betrayal. Which is possibly why Steyn, an Air Force officer and the SADF's number two as chief of Defence Force Staff, was overlooked as successor to 'Kat' Liebenberg for the top military job. It is also why he may get the job next time round, when a new government is looking for an experienced officer with proven democratic credentials — even though he retired in October 1993 and the police seconded to him for the MI investigation failed to produce hard evidence.

Steyn has been a high flier since he joined the Air Force in 1960, progressing rapidly through the ranks after taking top honours at the Military Academy and a Masters degree in business leadership through Unisa. A former Mirage jet pilot, he is 50 — and young enough to be a serious contender for SADF chief when the incumbent, General Georg Meiring, retires.

Tel: (012) 428–4201

Strydom, Barend On 15 November 1988 Strydom, then 23 and a former policeman, shocked the world when he embarked on a racially motivated killing spree in central Pretoria.

Armed and dressed in camouflage uniform, he began firing indiscriminately at black people. Within the space of minutes he shot 22 people, killing eight. He was apprehended while reloading his pistol and sentenced to death on each count of the eight murders in May 1989. While on Death Row he married Karen Rautenbach, the daughter of well-known right-wingers from Brits. In September 1992 he was released as part of a general amnesty.

During his trial Strydom alleged that he was a member of a secret organisation, the Wit Wolwe (White Wolves). A police investigation, however, found no proof of the existence of such an organisation.

A few months after his release, in January 1993, the Wit Wolwe was officially formed with one Boerstaat Bosman acting as spokesman and Lodewyk Putter introducing himself as chief of staff. Within days the organisation had fallen apart because of internal strife.

Sunter, Clem Born in Suffolk, England, genial Anglo American director Clem Sunter shot to fame towards the end of the 1980s when he developed a seminal scenario exercise, sponsored by Anglo American, which depicted a high-road and a low-road future for South Africa. The scenario, persuasively presented by the boyishly eccentric Oxonian, sparked real debate about South Africa's future and probably nudged the democratic process along.

He has since published other books along scenario lines, and one that is not, entitled *Pretoria Will Provide, and Other Myths*.

Author Sunter is unique in being not only one of Anglo's intellectuals but also an active executive, chairman of Anglo American's gold and uranium division and of its property arm, Anglo American Property Services.

Tel: (011) 638–9111

Terre'Blanche, Eugene Despite court cases in London, unruly horses, purges and brushes with the law, Terre-'Blanche has by now proved himself the true survivor and arch opportunist of the far-right.

With the far-right Afrikaner Weerstandsbeweging (AWB) inextricably intertwined with the mixed fortunes of its leader and vice versa, the movement (and the leader) has gained a new lease of life with the advent of increasing right-wing militancy.

Both Terre'Blanche and the AWB experienced a serious setback after the Jani Allan débâcle, but the organisation has restructured itself to become a high-profile army, with membership rising from about 8 000 at the end of 1989 to an estimated 18 000, and acceptance in mainstream right-wing circles.

Formal co-operation between the AWB and white labour unions began this year, and Terre'Blanche has been appointed to the Afrikaner Volksfront executive council.

However, Terre'Blanche and the AWB are adamant that they will not take part in a general election. He is 50.

Tel: (01480) 2005/7

Till, Christopher The influence of Johannesburg's director of culture extends far beyond the limits of his office. Locally, he is a member of the city's Olympic bidding committee, project director of the Newtown Cultural Precinct and a trustee or member of the board of almost every major cultural group, from the Market Theatre Foundation to the Soweto Dance Theatre. At the same time, he was active in the National Arts Initiative in late 1993 that led to the establishment of a National Arts Coalition pledged to lobby for the independence of the arts and the founding of a British-style national arts council in place of the current provincial performing arts councils.

He is a member of the Standard Bank National Arts Festival committee; he is consulted on the participation of South African artists in overseas exhibitions, and serves on committees debating a range of cultural issues, including the establishment of a national gallery in Namibia and fine arts education at university level.

It was in fine arts that Till (43) made his mark. Schooled at Hilton College, he became curator of the National Gallery of Rhodesia a year after earning his Masters in fine arts at Rhodes University. He moved quickly up the ranks and by 1980, three years after his arrival, was director of what was by then the National Gallery of Zimbabwe. In 1983 he came home as director of the Johannesburg Art Gallery and presided over its renovation, creating an exciting venue out of a dank and dusty museum.

He is seen to be extremely ambitious, with fingers in pies unrelated to his immediate job description; coupled with his swift professional rise, it makes him a controversial figure.

Tel: (011) 407–7303

Tillet, Edward The spokesman of the Inkatha Freedom Party Information Centre, Tillet (27) has catapulted into the political limelight in a short space of time: in 1991 he was a journalism student at Rhodes University in Grahamstown. He has also occupied several political homes: the African National Congress aligned National Union of South African Students (Nusas) (1985–87) and the liberal Democratic Party (1989–91) before he joined the IFP to monitor political violence in Natal/kwaZulu and act as the organisation's media spokesman. Based in Durban, he argues that independent violence monitors issue reports biased in favour of the ANC.

Since Tillet emerged on the scene, the IFP's propaganda machinery has sharpened: the organisation now responds swiftly to ANC claims and often goes on the offensive by referring to casualties within its own ranks.

Tel: (031) 309–6803

Tshwete, Steve His role as 'Mr Fixit' during the difficult unification of racially divided sporting bodies, and his keen personal interest in sports, took Tshwete, now national organiser for the African National Congress, to national prominence. He has brought a range of sectors into the organisation's sphere of influence and his department will play a key role in enabling the ANC to fight the election.

Tshwete (55) has been active in politics and sports since his school days. In 1964 he was sentenced to 15 years for Umkhonto weSizwe activities. He was released in 1979 and four years later played a major role in the formation of the United Democratic Front. In 1985 he went into exile and was later co-opted on to the ANC's National Executive Committee; he also served as MK political commissar. After the ANC's unbanning he returned to South Africa to help re-establish the organisation.

Tel: (011) 330–7279/7000

Tutu, Desmond Mpilo The Most Reverend Desmond Mpilo Tutu, archbishop of Cape Town of the Church of the Province of South Africa, was awarded the Nobel Peace Prize in 1984 at the age of 53.

Ordained as a priest in 1961 after studying at St Peter's Theological College in Rosettenville, he worked as a part-time curate in London, returning home in 1967 to become chaplain at Fort Hare University in Alice. He lectured in Lesotho, worked for the World Council of Churches in London and returned permanently in 1975 when he was named dean of Johannesburg, then bishop of Lesotho and general secretary of the South African Council of Churches, bishop of Johannesburg and, in 1986, archbishop of Cape Town.

Tutu was demonised by the media during the apartheid years and the State of Emergency, a legacy which white South Africa has had difficulty in shrugging off.

He is, however, held in high regard by the rest of the country and much of the world for his peace-making efforts, his conciliatory gestures and his ability to separate party politics from the church's role in seeking justice and truth. In a controversial move, he banned his priests some years ago from belonging to political parties, which enhanced his credibility 'on the ground' and with a range of rival organisations. Tutu is the great conciliator and, while he has had the knack of getting it right politically, he is motivated by his religion and an absolute sense of ethics and justice. He has another important quality scarce in South Africa: a sense of humour, useful in defusing potentially explosive situations.

Tel: (021) 761–2531 or (021) 797–5476

Van den Heever, Randall General secretary of the biggest non-racial teachers' union in the country, Van den Heever matriculated from Athlone's Alexander Sinton High School in 1969 and, after earning a BA degree and secondary teacher's diploma from the University of the Western Cape, began teaching at Spes Bona High School, rising through the ranks to become principal in 1983. Along the way he earned a BEd from UWC and a BA (Hons) from Unisa, but his chief focus was working within the Cape Teachers' Professional Association (CTPA), campaigning for improved working conditions for teachers and a unitary, non-racial education system.

He served as president of the CTPA from 1989 but, unable to bring the organisation into the fold of the new, non-racial South African Democratic Teachers' Union, left and was elected general secretary at Sadtu's launch in 1990. Apart from running the union and negotiating on behalf of its members with 15 education departments, Van den Heever is involved in the National Education Committee and the National Education and Training Forum, bodies involved in forging a new education system for the country.

Tel: (011) 331–9589

Van der Merwe, Johan The commissioner of police gives the impression of someone who finds the current attention to community policing — a concept which is still alien to the paramilitary style he grew up with — just a little painful. But Van der Merwe is still very much in control, and is likely to stay in the top job as commissioner of police at least until the elections, although during the transition he will share control of the police with the Transitional Executive Council. The challenge to the SAP during this period will be to keep leadership and command functioning, ensuring the force responds coherently to the challenges of transition.

Van der Merwe (56) headed the Free State security police during the 1970s and was credited with overseeing cross-border raids on anti-apartheid activists in Lesotho. He later moved up to the former South West Africa where he played a key role in anti-terrorist strategies. He was promoted to commissioner of police in 1990.

Tel: (012) 310–1911

Van der Westhuizen, Joffel The head of the defence force's Department of Military Intelligence is one of those acrobatic establishment soldiers who has managed to slip on several banana peels and nevertheless land on his feet. After years as the military's 'dirty tricks' chief, when his organisation took a no-holds-barred approach in active destabilisation measures against the African National Congress, he has managed in the last several months to court the organisation so successfully that he is likely to stay on as MI boss for the foreseeable future.

The ANC does not have much choice: like the country's other intelligence agency heads, the general holds the key to information the ANC needs if it is to govern successfully. And retiring him would simply push him into the arms of the other maverick rightist generals who are already causing political headaches.

But Van der Westhuizen is unlikely to enjoy the freedoms of old, when MI was all about — often very bloody — covert operations and had little to do with its classic military role of information-gathering on potential external threats to the country's security. He will probably find himself reporting to a civilian intelligence co-ordinator who is in turn responsible to Parliament, which is sure to set much narrower parameters for MI's activities.

Tel: (012) 315–0911

Van Graan, Michael A playwright and arts administrator, Van Graan turns the cliché of dour, earnest cultural worker on its head. For although he is among the most effective administrators in the country, he also writes funny, sharp satires.

He is a Capetonian, born in 1959, with a BA English and drama degree and an HDipEd from the University of Cape Town. For several years he worked in theatre and administration for church bodies. In the mid-1980s he organised Cape Town's Arts Festival 86: Towards a People's Culture, which was banned the day before it was scheduled to open.

He returned to university, emerging in 1988 as theatre co-ordinator of the Community Arts Project in Cape Town, then as chairperson, then director. When funding dried up, he went to work for the Congress of South

African Writers (Cosaw). While there he became involved with a broad range of discipline-based art groups — film-makers, writers, musicians and others — in a two-year campaign to lobby for the independence and survival of the arts. At the end of 1993 his position was formalised by his election as general secretary of the National Arts Coalition. The NAC has demanded, among other things, the replacement of the provincial performing arts councils by a British-style independent national arts council.

Some observers see the NAC as a challenge to the African National Congress Department of Arts and Culture; the coalition is calling for independence for the arts, while the DAC appears to favour a measure of state control in a future South Africa.

Van Graan's latest project is the establishment and direction of a major new community centre, the Bartel Arts Centre, in Durban.

Tel: (031) 25–4661

Van Schalkwyk, Marthinus The National Party's answer to the African National Congress's Carl Niehaus, both in debating style and appeal to young Afrikaners, Van Schalkwyk acts as his party's media spokesman.

With a reputation as a verligte dating back to his student days as national president of the Afrikaanse Studentebond, he has developed into the ANC's severest and most public critic, releasing press statements slamming the organisation at every possible opportunity.

Van Schalkwyk (33) succeeded Wynand Malan as MP

for Randburg in 1990. He holds a BProc degree as well as an MA in political science.

Tel: (021) 461–5833 or (012) 348–3100/342–2050

Van Zyl, Olaus The man in charge of the National Party's election campaign, Van Zyl has never won a parliamentary election himself; he is an indirectly elected MP. Van Zyl (49) holds a BSc in civil engineering and a Masters in transport engineering (from the University of California, Berkeley). He was a member of the President's Council for four years until 1988, when he became a member of the Transvaal executive committee — a post he held until March 1993 when he was named executive director of the NP's Federal Council. A month later he became an MP.

He is married to the popular Afrikaans singer Carike Keuzenkamp.

Tel: (012) 348–3100

Verwoerd, Wilhelm The 29-year-old grandson of apartheid architect Hendrik Verwoerd joined the African National Congress early in 1992 and has since become one of the movement's major assets in the Western Cape.

Verwoerd's wife Melanie serves in the executive of the ANC's Western Cape region. Although he maintains a lower political profile, the symbolism of the family name and his obvious sincerity and integrity have made him a drawcard at public meetings.

His 'conversion' followed after his studies in Holland. He joined the ANC at about the same time his grandmother, Betsie, trekked to the fledgling Boerestaat of Orania where other members of the Verwoerd clan live out the old patriarch's vision of a white state in Southern Africa.

The family divisions run deep, and Verwoerd's father, right-winger Professor Wilhelm Verwoerd, a retired geology professor, reportedly refuses to talk to his son. The younger Verwoerd is a lecturer in philosophy at the University of Stellenbosch.

Tel: (021) 808–4515

Viljoen, Constand Thrust into prominence as the prime symbol of the right wing's resurgence, the general may still be trying to reconcile his new role with that of a cattle farmer and a former chief of the South African Defence Force.

He commands an almost mythical following among the right white, although he has not adopted the belligerent rhetoric of his colleagues, at times striking a conciliatory tone out of place in right-wing circles. In December, an armed band of far right-wingers occupying Pretoria's Fort Schanskop refused to leave, even though troops surrounded the fort. They ignored the entreaties of other leaders, but Viljoen succeeded in talking them out, averting almost certain bloodshed.

Viljoen was born 60 years ago in Standerton. He had intended to study agricultural engineering but a lack of funds forced a switch of career and he joined the SADF, which paid for his university studies. In 1956 he was commissioned as an artillery officer.

Twenty years later he was appointed chief of the Army. It was while holding that post that he personally took part in several military incursions into Angola. This gave birth to his reputation as a soldier's general.

In 1980 Viljoen was appointed chief of the SADF. He retired five years later to breed cattle in the Ohrigstad area, only recently becoming active in right-wing politics.

Tel: (012) 342–2872

Von Stülpnagel, Paul Joachim The role of chief observer for the European Community in South Africa (Ecomsa) requires endless patience and tact, as well as a thorough understanding of how to go about de-escalating conflict and weapons levels, which makes Von Stülpnagel, with years of experience as Germany's representative to the Geneva conference on disarmament, a good choice.

Von Stülpnagel (66) had retired from the German foreign ministry when he was asked to come to South Africa. He is an active participant in Ecomsa's almost daily efforts to defuse tense situations and encourage dialogue between the police, the Inkatha Freedom Party, the African National Congress and a myriad of other groupings. The EC observers, along with their United Nations, Organisation of African Unity and Commonwealth colleagues, have been playing a key role in the run-up to elections — not just defusing situations which threaten the peace, but also training local peacekeepers such as monitors and marshals.

Tel: (011) 476–1297

Wessels, Leon The first cabinet member seen on TV lifting a clenched fist and calling 'Viva' ('Viva negotiations!' he shouted while addressing demonstrators outside the World Trade Centre), Wessels embraces the new South Africa wholeheartedly. He was the first senior Nationalist to apologise publicly for his party's racist past.

What makes the 47-year-old Manpower minister's liberal pronouncements even more remarkable is the fact that he represents the working-class constituency of Krugersdorp, normally not a haven of progressiveness.

Born in Kroonstad, Wessels was president of the Afrikaanse Studentebond in one of its most conservative phases, from 1971 to 1973, while earning his law degree. But since joining the cabinet in 1988 as deputy minister of Law and Order, he has become progressively vocal in his rejection of racial discrimination. After the failure of Codesa II, he joined Roelf Meyer in the government's negotiating team, bringing debates back on track when negotiators wandered off on side issues.

Before the present round of negotiations, Wessels took on the mighty farming industry, finally winning a protracted conflict to ensure basic employees' rights for farmworkers.

Tel: (012) 322–6523

Williams, Abe One of the first coloured politicians to join the National Party, Williams was soon promoted to minister of Sports in the last white-dominated Parliament.

The jovial Williams was born at Saldanha in 1940 and qualified as a teacher at Athlone Training College in Paarl, before obtaining a BA degree from the University of the Western Cape and a BEd from Stellenbosch University.

Williams became known as a sportsman and sports administrator, particularly in the rugby sphere. For many years he was organiser and secretary of the South African Rugby Federation, and in the early 1980s acted as assistant manager to the last official Springbok rugby team to visit New Zealand before the country's sportspeople were finally isolated by the rest of the world.

In the 1984 elections for the first tricameral Parliament, Williams won the Mamre seat in the House of Representatives (HoR). Five years later he was appointed the HoR's deputy minister of Education and Culture, and in 1991, HoR deputy minister of National Education and Culture; he also holds the Welfare portfolio.

In April 1993 he joined President FW de Klerk's cabinet as sports minister.

Tel: (012) 21–1781

Yengeni, Tony Sithembiso Ousted in 1993 as regional secretary of the African National Congress in the Western Cape, Yengeni retains significant support among disaffected youths and homeless people in the region whose cause he continues to champion on the basis that World Trade Centre negotiations have come dangerously close to selling them out.

Accused Number One in one of the country's longest running political trials, Yengeni, born in October 1954 to a working-class Cape Town family, signed up with the ANC's underground in 1976 after earlier involvement in the Black Consciousness Movement.

He underwent training in ANC camps in Botswana, Zambia and Angola and earned a diploma in social science after studying in Moscow before becoming regional secretary of the South African Council of Trade Unions, based in Lesotho, from where he was sent to take over control of ANC underground activity in the Western Cape. He was arrested soon afterwards. Indemnified in 1991, he was elected to the national executive of the South African Communist Party and still serves on its Central Committee. While elected to the ANC's regional executive as an additional member, he is likely to spend more time on SACP activities.

Tel: (021) 448–5651

Zama, Linda Zama is an executive member of the African National Congress and sits on the Natal regional executive of the ANC. She shot to prominence in 1993 when she was appointed to the board of South African Posts, the first black woman to hold that position at the parastatal.

Zama (42) made her ANC name as a human rights lawyer who defended political trials in the eighties, soon after qualifying as an attorney in 1983. Zama served articles at the office of the assassinated Griffiths Mxenge, where she honed her interest in public interest law.

She is also largely credited with stamping out the problematic peoples' courts in Natal in the 1980s, when she spent a lot of time explaining the law to youths. Her law firm, Linda Zama and Associates, is the Durban and Districts leader of the National Association of Democratic Lawyers and a trustee of the Street Law Project.

Said not to be one to stand on platforms and give fiery speeches, Zama is something of a political dove.

Tel: (031) 301–0821

Zuma, Jacob Close colleagues tell the story of Zuma's long uphill battle against illiteracy and the lack of any formal schooling as an indication of his intelligence, tenacity and flexibility, traits which continue to serve him well as deputy general secretary of the African National Congress. As one of the most senior figures of Zulu origin within the organisation, he is regarded as having a pivotal role in attempts to break Inkatha's stranglehold over King Goodwill Zwelithini and the traditional leaders and, through them, rural Zulus. Zuma (50) is the only senior Zulu in the ANC's national working committee at a time when the ANC is struggling to disprove Inkatha's claim that the IFP alone represents the Zulu people.

He is no longer formally involved with ANC intelligence, which he headed in exile after joining MK at its inception, but is said to have kept several regional information networks going. Although he is favoured for high office by Nelson Mandela, criticism by the Motsuenyane commission of his failure to prevent human rights abuses in ANC camps may prove a stumbling block to his further political rise.

He is married to Nkosazana Zama, an ANC activist in Natal.

Tel: (011) 330–7000

Zwelithini, Goodwill Since his installation as the eighth monarch of the Zulu nation in 1971, Zwelithini has been faced with the onerous task of steering his people into the modern era amid changing racial and ethnic relationships in South Africa. However, a seat on the royal throne at Nongoma is not what it used to be, as

Zwelithini found out the hard way after his uncle, Chief Mangosuthu Buthelezi, wrote the monarchy out of politics in both the kwaZulu and Inkatha constitutions.

Zwelithini's flirtation with rebellion so vexed his powerful elder that, in 1979, Buthelezi castigated the 'Isilo' (lion of the nation) in front of the entire kwaZulu legislative assembly, accusing him of conspiring to form an opposition party and of urging support for violent revolution. Buthelezi threatened to cut his stipend and, by 1982, Zwelithini was convinced he had no future — and certainly no income — without his uncle.

In the 1980s, as tensions flared between Inkatha and the United Democratic Front, Zwelithini found himself increasingly dragged through 'the heat and dust of politics' by the same man who had argued for his exclusion from it. Now courted by the African National Congress as one hope of ending the conflict, Zwelithini (45) has become the Inkatha Freedom Party's most closely guarded asset — and an essential key to electoral support among rural Zulus.

Tel: (0358) 310–300

2

Organisations and Institutions

An A-Z of what's what in South African politics

African National Congress

It would be a real surprise if the ANC did not win a clear, if not absolute, majority in the election for South Africa's constituent assembly.

Founded in January 1912 as the South African Native National Congress, the organisation is Africa's oldest liberation movement. It began as a gathering of intellectuals — led by Pixley ka Izaka Seme, John Dube and Sol Plaatje — seeking to unite their people across tribal lines. Their representations against, for example, what was to become the 1913 Land Act went unheard, and over time it became little more than a talk shop.

This changed in the post-war ferment of the late 1940s, when a new generation of more radical and impatient Youth League leaders — Nelson Mandela, Oliver Tambo, Walter Sisulu and Anton Lembede — galvanised the organisation into a more militant stance and pushed it into a programme of action involving the 'new weapons' of protest, boycott, strike and civil disobedience.

Their successful takeover of the ANC led to the passive resistance and stayaways of the 1950s. It was also during this period that the Congress Alliance was formed, bringing the ANC together with parallel coloured, Indian and white organisations. In 1956, a Congress of the People, an informal Parliament-like gathering, adopted the Freedom Charter, which was to define the ANC's credo for three decades after this: non-racialism, equality, democracy and a soft socialist demand for social reform through redistribution and nationalisation.

In 1959, Robert Sobukwe led a breakaway of those disgruntled with non-racialism and the influence of white communists and Indians to form the Pan Africanist Congress. For decades in exile, the ANC and PAC — both recognised by the Organisation of African Unity and the United Nations — competed for recognition as the primary liberation movement.

The 1950s also brought the first wave of serious government repression which was to last, and grow steadily more brutal, until 1990. The process began with the lengthy Treason Trial of 156 leaders, saw the banning of the ANC and PAC in 1960 and the decision of both organisations to abandon peaceful resistance and take up armed struggle. It also brought the 'dirty war' of the 1980s when ANC members were detained, jailed and assassinated.

The first few, rather ineffectual, bomb blasts led to the arrest in Rivonia of the ANC military leadership, including Sisulu, Govan Mbeki, Ahmed Kathrada and Dennis Goldberg. With Mandela, already serving a sentence for leaving the country illegally, they were tried and sentenced to life imprisonment.

Tambo led the organisation into exile and many years of frustration in London and Lusaka. His steady, unifying leadership saw the organisation through the relatively inactive and militarily unsuccessful 1960s and 1970s, but the organisation was rejuvenated by the new influx of young radicals after the 1976 uprising. The next few years saw some spectacular, if isolated and infrequent, displays of military action in line with a policy of 'armed propaganda' — the use of high-profile military activities to boost morale and resistance inside the country.

Tambo's greatest success, however, was in the field of diplomacy where, with current national chairman Thabo Mbeki at his side, he quietly worked to establish the ANC as the primary voice of the liberation struggle in the international community and to encourage the political, economic, sporting and cultural isolation of South Africa.

The ANC's fortunes also grew with the shift inside the country away from the black consciousness organisations of the 1970s to bodies such as the United Democratic Front, which were essentially ANC-front organisations.

By the time the government moved to reform and negotiation in the late 1980s, the ANC was established strongly enough, both internally and internationally, to make it impossible for changes to take place without them. Talks with the still imprisoned Nelson Mandela began in 1988 and public contact with the ANC in exile — such as by businessmen who visited Lusaka in 1985 and Afrikaners who met them in Dakar in 1987 — broke the ice. The ANC, meanwhile, had succeeded in getting its blueprint for negotiations, known as the Harare Declaration, adopted by most international bodies.

This reputation as the leading liberation movement

was confirmed after the ANC's unbanning in 1990 and its return home to open up a head office in downtown Johannesburg. That the ANC survived the changeover intact from a militant liberation movement to a political organisation engaged in pragmatic negotiations with the government is an indication of the flexibility of the organisation.

If it achieves its expected majority and becomes the dominant force in the government of national unity, its next challenges will centre on dealing with the high expectations of its supporters and keeping its parliamentary wing and its mass membership in step. The ANC's greatest strength and weakness is that it remains something of a 'people's Parliament', representing the broadest cross-section of interest groups across ethnic, class and age barriers. Its members and leaders range from moderate liberals to hardline Stalinists, though Mandela's moderate and flexible leadership is unchallenged.

The ANC is the leader of what is now called the Tripartite Alliance, with the Congress of South African Trade Unions and the South African Communist Party (and latterly, the South African National Civic Organisation). It also heads the Patriotic Front, a loose association of anti-government organisations. It has opened its election lists to nominations from anyone in the loosely defined 'mass democratic movement', re-emphasising its attempt to address a broad popular constituency.

Its major problem, however, is the simmering disgruntlement of radical elements who believe that too much has been conceded in negotiations and who have the potential to whip up popular disappointment with the failure of the process to deliver significant changes in their everyday lives. At the moment, the organisation is firmly in the hands of a pragmatic leadership — headed by Nelson Mandela, secretary general Cyril Ramaphosa and Thabo Mbeki — though a challenge from radicals such as Winnie Mandela, Peter Mokaba and Harry Gwala can be expected, fuelled by the difficulties of meeting the high expectations lodged in the organisation.

The ANC has a formidable national structure, broken into nine regions and hundreds of branches, led by a National Executive Committee of 52 members. Its head offices in Johannesburg house departments dealing with, among others, education, health, international affairs, intelligence and security, culture, information and publicity, legal affairs and elections.

Tel: (011) 330–7000

Afrikaner Broederbond

Established in 1918 to promote the interests of poor and newly urbanised Afrikaners, the Afrikaner Broederbond was initially a cultural movement which acted in the open; it even fielded a rugby team that played against other clubs. But it quickly transformed itself into a highly secretive organisation manipulating politics behind the scenes.

The Broederbond was instrumental in promoting the racially discriminatory system of apartheid, which was implemented when the National Party came to power in 1948. Throughout the years that followed, most cabinet members, including President FW de Klerk, were Broederbond members.

For many South Africans the Broederbond came to symbolise the sinister source of white domination — a small extra-parliamentary think-tank consisting of elitist Afrikaners who accorded to themselves the power to determine the political destiny of millions of people.

The Broederbond was subjected to a series of bruising exposés in the 1970s and 1980s.

As the country changed after 1990, with a new move towards democracy, the Broederbond also had to change. Nowhere was the predicament of its members displayed as publicly as during open hearings for the new SABC board early in 1993. Where membership of the Broederbond in the past had assured a shortcut to senior, lucrative jobs, especially in the civil service, it now became a distinct disadvantage.

In the face of the new South Africa, Broeders started resigning in droves. Their desertion was ironic when one considers that the Broederbond served as a think-tank during the 1980s for the political changes that were coming, after its leaders conceded in a confidential document that 'the greatest risk facing Afrikaners was not to take any risk at all'.

Traditionally, people could only join the Broederbond on invitation, and only if they were white, male, Afrikaans-speaking members of one of the three Dutch Reformed churches in the country. But towards the end of 1993 the Broederbond opened its membership both to women and to people other than whites. Under its new chairman, businessman Tom de Beer, it has undertaken to continue its activities in the light of day, although 'privacy' will now replace the former insistence on 'secrecy'.

Its aims will still be the promotion of Afrikaans interests, including a legal aid system, an economic advice bureau and international linkage with Dutch-speaking countries.

Afrikaner Volksfront

The AVF is probably the most important development in right-wing circles since the advent of the new South Africa. Under the direction of four former security force generals, it is the first umbrella organisation that has achieved a measure of success in realising the long elusive ideal of right-wing unity.

It was formally founded in May 1993, but the initiative that led to its formation had started almost two years previously with the establishment of the EK 25 (Unity Committee of 25) and the Volkseenheidkomitee (Vekom, or National Unity Committee). Former South African Defence Force General Tienie Groenewald was the central driving force in both these groups, which consisted exclusively of volkstaat visionaries.

In April 1993 this initiative combined with the Conservative Party's 'mobilisation programme', which had started several months earlier, when CP leaders realised that the era of white parliamentary politics had effectively come to an end. The CP's initiative had been formally launched under the chairmanship of yet another former SADF general, Koos Bischoff, a former SADF chief of operations. But this effort 'to mobilise on all fronts to ensure self-determination of the Afrikaner' never really got off the ground.

Soon after the assassination of Chris Hani and the

accompanying militancy and polarisation across the political spectrum, a Committee of Generals (later to become the AVF's directorate) was formed, consisting of Groenewald, Bischoff, ex-SADF chief Constand Viljoen, and a former chief of the South African Police CID, Kobus Visser.

Marshalling the emotions of right-wingers around the highly respected Viljoen, the AVF was soon seen as the new driving force of the right, with the CP having no choice but to join forces — which it did a month after the 'night of the generals'. An executive council was elected, with CP leader Ferdi Hartzenberg as chairman. But although the nine-member executive of the AVF is heavily laden in favour of the CP, the generals of the directorate are very much in the driving seat.

The lack of a single, clear leadership and the ensuing duality is the cause of continuous internal friction among volkstaters, white supremacists, CP hardliners, those willing to negotiate and those who refuse. An added cause of internal tension is the membership of Eugene Terre'Blanche and the Afrikaner Weerstandsbeweging.

However, while these tensions are often seen as signs of an impending split, they are more often the manifestations of a dynamic organisation that will continue to play an important role (albeit one of a spoiler) in the run-up to the elections.

Tel: (012) 43–7793

Afrikaner Weerstandsbeweging

Founded in 1976 by Eugene Terre'Blanche and six others, the AWB is by far the most prominent of paramilitary right-wing movements.

The AWB propagates the concept of an independent volkstaat with a form of state similar to that of the old Boer republics, but it is not willing to further this cause at the ballot box or in negotiations. Terre'Blanche has stated on numerous occasions that the borders of such a volkstaat will be drawn in blood.

The AWB has become increasingly radical in tone and content, and several members over the last few years have been implicated in acts of sabotage. In 1993 the commander of its Wenkommando (WK) was arrested in connection with planned acts of sabotage against the Koeberg nuclear power station. The AWB was also centrally involved in the June 1993 storming and forceful occupation of the World Trade Centre at Kempton Park, bringing negotiations to a halt for several hours and causing a fair amount of damage.

In January 1994 another key military commander, 'General' Japie Oelofse, was arrested in connection with bomb blasts.

Since 1991 the AWB has become almost completely militarised in structure and organisation with 'ordinary' membership being supplanted by membership of the Wenkommando. As part of the WK structure, the country is divided into 30 regions which are subdivided into four commands under a commandant. These units are further subdivided into platoons with a veldkornet (lieutenant) in charge. Other ranks include brigadier, captain, sergeant and corporal.

The Wenkommando itself is divided into the elite Ystergarde (Iron Guards), Rooivalke (Red Falcons), Witkruisarende (Black Eagles), Penkoppe, Stormvalke, the Underwater Unit and 'ethnic' units such as exclusively Portuguese commandos in Johannesburg. In 1993 an air wing was also introduced and parachute training initiated.

The Ystergarde is a much more polished fighting unit than ordinary Wenkommando units, with several of its people former members of the South African Defence Force and South African Police Special Forces.

At one stage new members were inducted at a rate of 20 per month, but it seems the Ystergarde has reached a ceiling of about 200 men. Previously led by Leon van der Merwe, a protégé of Terre'Blanche, the Ystergarde is now under the control of Keith Conroy, an Irish expatriate with wide experience in training. The Rooivalke is the female counterpart of the Ystergarde and under the command of Ansie Cruywagen, wife of a Wenkommando chief of staff, Alec Cruywagen. The Witkruisarende seems to be a battlefield medical team consisting of female members of the Wenkommando with paramedical training. The Penkoppe can be regarded as the Wenkommando Youth League and consists almost exclusively of the children of active AWB members.

The Stormvalke was founded in late 1979 as the first paramilitary wing of the AWB. It has, however, never been more than a motorcycle gang wearing AWB insignia. Dormant in the mid-1980s, the unit was revived again in 1992 under the leadership of a Roodepoort motorcyclist.

Three men clad in diving gear made their first appearance at a May 1992 rally as the Underwater Unit of the Wenkommando. They surfaced again a year later at a joint rally of the AWB and the AVF. No other information is available.

In March 1993 Terre'Blanche released a press statement on the formation of the Vergeldingseenheid (VE), or 'reprisal unit'. Alleging that the VE consists of a hard core of AWB members who keep their identities secret even from Terre'Blanche, the statement also claimed that the unit was founded to retaliate whenever terrorists launched attacks against whites. No verification of the existence of this unit can be found.

AWB spokesmen, including Terre'Blanche, put the Wenkommando membership at between 34 000 and 36 000, but this figure is widely regarded as being optimistic. In September 1992 an official police assessment put the WK membership at 15 000, but even this figure may have been inflated at the time. However the WK expanded rapidly during 1993. Political violence and concurrent polarisation played into the hands of the AWB, and an estimated 2 000 recruits joined up in the first two weeks following the assassination of Chris Hani. Current membership could be 20 000.

Although the AWB's Wenkommando has a relatively large membership compared with other 'private armies', a distinction must be made between active members and those who at one stage in their lives signed up but are not active in the movement any more. Indications, such as attendance figures at rallies, suggest an active membership of not more than 5 000 countrywide.

Terre'Blanche is the AWB's greatest asset because of his powerful oratory, and its worst liability because of his reputation for womanising, drunkenness and buffoonery.

Tel: (01480) 2005/7

Anglo American Corporation
The tentacles of giant conglomerate Anglo American (AAC) stretch into every area of South African life, from the mining of precious metals and diamonds to motoring and wine.

Closely tied to international diamond cartel De Beers, Anglo's history mirrors the colonialisation and subsequent industrialisation of South Africa, growing from a mining house into a colossus with dozens of investments, associates and subsidiaries.

With a market capitalisation of around R20-billion and with assets of around R48-billion, according to the *Finance Week* Top 200, Anglo dominates South African business, controlling between 30 per cent (Anglo's calculations) and 45 per cent. The AAC empire also spreads throughout the globe, from mines in South America to a high-tech battery project in Germany.

Slightly aloof even from the stock exchange near its architecturally understated headquarters in Johannesburg's Main Street, Anglo American corporate culture has been moulded by three generations of the Oppenheimer family.

AAC has always combined the determined pursuit of its harsh core business, mining, dependent on the use of migrant labour under tough conditions, with support for liberal causes and reform. It is currently headed by Julian Ogilvie Thompson but the presence of Nicholas Oppenheimer in the wings signals the ultimate control of the family.

Tel: (011) 638–9111

Azanian National Liberation Army

Following the rejection by the Black Consciousness Movement of Azania and the Azanian People's Organisation of a negotiated settlement, Azanla has pledged to continue with its military operations.

Azanla is the smallest and least prominent of South Africa's resistance armies. Formed in 1984, it is unlikely to number more than 2 000 soldiers. It received training from some Islamic states and also trained with the Eritrean People's Liberation Army. Azanla's activities have involved the sabotage of electric pylons and the killing of policemen and white civilians.

Azanla's commitment to armed insurrection may attract other rejectionists among disenchanted cadres from the African National Congress's Umkhonto we-Sizwe and the Pan Africanist Congress's Azanian People's Liberation Army. But its ability to sustain such a campaign and also withstand state suppression will be weakened by the fact that after April its cadres will be fighting a regime which has legitimacy in the eyes of the population.

The chairman of the BCMA, Mosibudi Mangena, is commander in chief of Azanla and can be reached in Harare.

Tel: (092634) 28187

Azanian People's Liberation Army

Apla was formed in 1961 as a peasant resistance force in the Cape. Then a loose formation of Pan Africanist Congress supporters, it called itself Poqo — which means 'pure' in Xhosa — and attacked whites, policemen and suspected collaborators. It was formally constituted as Apla in 1968.

Apla received training and assistance from China and several African countries, most notably Egypt. This army was, however, inactive for much of the past three decades, despite an influx of recruits in the aftermath of the 1976 student uprising.

It was not until 1990, following the African National Congress's suspension of the armed struggle, that Apla shot into prominence. Its activities have been concentrated on the killing of policemen and white civilians. Attacks on white civilians, coinciding with rising levels of violence in black townships, did much to boost the PAC's standing in the black communities, who felt the police were not doing anything to halt the carnage. It was felt that these attacks were in some way 'evening the score' — that not only blacks were dying, but also whites.

Estimates of Apla's size range from a few hundred to 5 000. Although it is to be integrated into the new National Defence Force, there are indications that some of the more militant factions of the PAC opt to continue the armed struggle against a government of national unity.

Tel: (011) 836–0442

Azanian People's Organisation

Azapo is at its most critical juncture since its founding in 1979 by black consciousness activists. With a strong socialist agenda and a puritan stance on every issue, it faces a struggle against marginalisation both of the organisation and of the ideology it espouses.

Azapo has its roots in the late 1960s resurgence in resistance activity. After nearly a decade-long lull in political activity following the bannings of political organisations, black students broke away from the white-dominated National Union of South African Students and under the leadership of Steve Biko formed the South African Students' Organisation (Saso). Together with the urban strikes of 1973, this reactivation precipitated the 1976 student uprisings.

Following the death of Biko in detention and the banning of political organisations, including the Black People's Convention and Saso, in 1977, there was again a downturn in political activity.

Black consciousness activists regrouped in 1979 to form Azapo. But much of the cream of this generation had gone into exile. Some joined the armed wings of the Pan Africanist Congress and the African National Congress, and others established the Black Consciousness Movement of Azania in exile.

Some of those who stayed behind were later to defect to the United Democratic Front when it was formed in 1983. The emergence of the powerful, Freedom Charter aligned UDF led to a serious contest of black political support which often resulted in clashes between the two organisations.

Azapo's refusal to take part in constitutional negotiations and its failure to provide an alternative has effectively pushed it to the edges. Polls indicate a maximum of one per cent in mass support for the organisation. Furthermore, the armed wing of its exiled BCMA, the Azanian National Liberation Army (Azanla), has not posed much of a threat to the state.

Azapo will none the less remain a constant extra-parliamentary voice in the years to come.

Tel: (011) 333–0132

Black Sash

The Sash was formed in 1955 — as the Women's Defence of the Constitution League — by an ad hoc group of six women outraged by the Senate Bill, which artificially enlarged the Senate to allow for the removal of coloureds from the voters' roll. It derives its current name from the distinctive sash worn by its protesting members.

Black Sash picketers were familiar sights throughout the country during the 1970s and 1980s, voicing liberal concerns about human rights abuses of all kinds. It became, under the forceful leadership of Sheena Duncan and Joyce Harris, an often lonely voice of conscience in the face of state repression and abuses. In particular, it led the campaign to expose and stop the forced removals of this period.

While it is best known for these protests, the organisation spans a number of activities, such as research, monitoring, education and advice through a nationwide network of voluntary advice offices. It has been outspoken on issues of land reform, pension inequalities, gender discrimination, the treatment of domestic workers and detention without trial.

The president is Capetonian Jenny de Tolly.

Tel: (021) 685–3513 or (011) 834–8361

Boereweerstandsbeweging (BWB)

Although quite small when compared with other private

armies of the right, the BWB has since 1991 established itself as one of the most radical and potentially most violent groupings.

One of numerous splinter groups founded after the Paardekraal purge in the Afrikaner Weerstandsbeweging, the BWB is led by Andrew Ford, a farmer from the Rustenburg area. Ford is strongly influenced by the ideas of Boerestaat Party leader Robert van Tonder and under this influence and the auspices of the BWB has also formed the so-called Boere-Inligtingsdiens (Boer Intelligence Service). Part of its brief seems to be compiling lists of those policemen who are involved in the torture of right-wing detainees. Ford also lays claim to the Boere Republikeinse Leër which, in late December 1993, claimed responsibility for a bomb blast on a Soweto railway line and was linked to a document listing possible targets for sabotage, ranging from political to multi-national offices.

The BWB is organised into cells, with different cells supposed to have no knowledge of each other. BWB cells have been associated with several bombings. In October 1993 a bomb, apparently planted to damage shops in the Indian business area at Bronkhorstspruit, killed a policeman who went to investigate a suspect parcel. Those implicated in the bombing allegedly belonged to the Cullinan cell of the BWB.

Towards the end of 1993 it was also revealed that the BWB was training mentally handicapped recruits in the use of arms and explosives and moulding them into a special unit called 'Soldiers of Jesus Christ'. Shortly afterwards, one of the commanders of this unit was arrested in connection with the theft of more than three tons of weapons and ammunition from the South African Defence Force.

Tel: (0142) 25277

Chamber of Mines

The mouthpiece of the mining houses and defender of the interests of the oligopolistic mining industry has been swathed in controversy throughout its more than 100 years of existence.

Its direct intervention in politics in the early days of the Witwatersrand meant some of its members were involved in the infamous Jameson Raid and the attempt to overthrow the government of Paul Kruger.

The Chamber has a notoriously conservative profile, whether defending the mines' safety record, setting its face against affirmative action, or, in the 1980s, standing in the forefront of the South African business campaign against sanctions.

Yet while facing down the National Union of Mineworkers, it has also been constantly in conflict with the government of the day, successfully lobbying for the removal of the policy of reserving key mine jobs for whites.

Its motivation here, as in its formation of a centralised labour recruitment system, has been to keep down labour costs. This recurring theme in the Chamber's history led to the importation of cheap Chinese labour after the Boer war at the turn of the century and the bloodily suppressed white mineworkers' Rand Revolt of 1922.

In recent years the Chamber's influence has diminished along with the importance of the gold mining industry in the economy. Although mining, particularly gold mining, is still the most important earner of foreign exchange for South Africa, and contributes a sizeable chunk to gross domestic product, tax revenue from the mines has gradually been overshadowed by other sources. Industrial policy has with ever more urgency looked at turning the economy towards exports of manufactured goods rather than commodities whose prices in world markets are fickle.

The Chamber, however, remains an important lobbying force. During the tenure in 1993 of enlightened Anglo American director Bobby Godsell several profit-sharing deals between mine labour and management were struck which bode well for a more progressive attitude by the Chamber. Current president is Jurie Geldenhuys.

Tel: (011) 838–8211

Congress of South African Trade Unions

Cosatu, with just over 1,3-million members, is the largest trade union federation in the country and was until 1992 the fastest-growing federation in the world.

It has set itself the goal of increasing its membership to 1,5-million by its 1994 congress. The federation has 14 affiliate trade unions. Its metal union, National Union of Metalworkers of South Africa, is the biggest while the mineworkers' union, National Union of Mineworkers, comes a close second.

The federation is headed by Sam Shilowa, a former security guard, who last year took over as general secretary from Jay Naidoo, who left to pursue a parliamentary career. Naidoo and 20 other Cosatu leaders were seconded to the elections process and will be included on the African National Congress's lists.

The 1993 September congress also voted in a host of worker leaders — workers who have made their way up trade union ranks — to head the federation for the first time since its establishment in 1985. Shilowa is assisted by the youthful Zwelinzima Vavi, who is in charge of organising new members and trade unions into the federation.

Cosatu has moved from being a socialist organisation to one which is showing itself increasingly codeterminist in outlook. The federation is involved in a number of tripartite negotiating forums with business and the government. Its work in two such forums — the National Manpower Commission and the National Economic Forum — is likely to form the crux of its activities for the next few years.

In 1994, much of the federation's time and resources will be spent on electioneering and voter education. As one of the ANC's partners in the Tripartite Alliance, it is campaigning for an ANC victory and is calling on its members to vote for that organisation.

Tel: (011) 339–4911

Conservative Party

The CP was founded in March 1982 under the leadership of Dr Andries Treurnicht, who had been Transvaal leader of the National Party and a minister in PW Botha's cabinet. After serious differences of opinion between Treurnicht and the cabinet on issues such as mixed sport on school level and indications that Indian and coloured representatives might become part of the decision-making process, Treurnicht and fellow cabinet minister Ferdi Hartzenberg resigned their posts. Eight days later they were expelled from the NP and a few days afterwards, with 15 other right-wing MPs, they founded the CP, which soon became the white right's most important representative body.

The CP's first test at the ballot box came in the 1983 referendum. Although voters could not vote for political parties, the 'no-vote' advocated by the CP eventually constituted 35,5 per cent of the total.

During the (all-white) general election of September 1989, the CP won 39 seats (or 31 per cent of the vote) to become the official opposition in Parliament.

The right-wing cause was dealt a devastating blow by the pace of reforms instituted from 1990 by President FW de Klerk and the 1992 referendum on negotiations. The CP seemed to be losing not only supporters but also momentum. Largely contributing to this was the lack of a clear policy, a fact exploited to the hilt by the effective NP propaganda machine. Originally stating its policy to be a return to the constitutional proposals of 1977, the CP gradually moved further back towards a vague Verwoerdian concept of partition between the races.

The failure of the CP to spell out the practical details of such a policy caused some dissent among certain MPs, notably Andries Beyers, CP MP for Potchefstroom and formerly chief secretary of the party.

In August 1992 Beyers led a breakaway group of five MPs to form the Afrikaner Volksunie, a group propagating a smaller homeland for the Afrikaner. Not being able to capitalise on a large amount of grassroots support, the party is for all practical purposes defunct, its policy having been taken over by a transformed CP.

That transformation was the result of several factors, combining after February 1993, when the CP officially launched its 'mobilisation programme' in order to mobilise 'on all fronts for freedom'. With official policy still vague and vacillating, this project never really got off the ground, apart from the creation of a wide-ranging administrative structure.

But the formation of the Afrikaner Volksfront later that year, the general acceptance in right-wing circles of the volkstaat ideal, the death of Treurnicht and the election of the more assertive Hartzenberg as new leader, plus a new militancy right across the political spectrum, flogged the ailing horse into some kind of life once again.

The new CP is a member both of the Afrikaner Volksfront and the Freedom Alliance.

Tel: (012) 342–3408

Constitution

The Constitution of the Republic of South Africa, which will apply until April 1999, is a product of more than two years' negotiations between South Africa's major political parties and movements.

It provides for a non-racial, multi-party democracy under the rule of law, three-tier government and a justiciable Bill of Rights in a united South Africa, including the homelands. An electoral system of proportional representation — or a 'list system' — will be followed, allowing parties to nominate members to Parliament proportionally to the number of votes they receive.

Parliament will double as a constituent assembly

responsible for the final constitution of the country. It will consist of a National Assembly of 400 members and a Senate of 90 members. The National Assembly will consist of 200 members proportional to the various parties' national candidate lists and 200 proportional to their provincial candidate lists.

Executive powers will reside with a government of national unity, which means that there will be enforced coalition government. The president will be elected by Parliament and will act as chairperson of a cabinet which will be constituted of all parties with at least 20 representatives in the National Assembly.

Parties with more than 80 seats will be allowed to appoint an executive vice-president to assist the president. If no party has more than 80 seats, the second biggest party will appoint a vice-president.

For the first time in its history, South Africa's constitution will be paramount and entrenched; it can only be changed with special majorities. This means that Parliament will not be sovereign: laws will be subject not only to the Bill of Rights but also to a list of constitutional principles agreed to by the Kempton Park negotiators. A Constitutional Court will have the final say on whether laws comply with the set criteria.

Provision is made for nine provinces with considerable autonomy. Each of the provinces will be allowed to nominate 10 members for the Senate, proportionally to the votes the different parties receive in the elections. The provinces will have no exclusive powers, however, only concurrent powers with central government. But they will be allowed to adopt their own constitutions, providing that these comply with the principles of the

South African Constitution and fall within the policy framework of the central government. Although the Constitution contains federal elements, it is not a federal constitution in the classic definition.

Individual rights — including freedom of religion — are protected by the Constitution, and 11 languages are recognised as official languages.

Congress of Traditional Leaders of South Africa

Contralesa brings together traditional authorities, like chiefs and headmen, who identify broadly with the liberation movement. It is officially non-aligned, insisting traditional rulers are above party politics.

Started in 1990, it has more than 2 000 members in all four provinces. Contralesa has not gone unchallenged, with difficulties among its members in Natal and conservative rival groups springing up in Transkei and Ciskei.

Presenting itself as a powerful sector of the rural community, Contralesa has been fighting for a place for traditional leaders in the new government. Umtata advocate Chief Patekile Holomisa is the long-serving president of Contralesa.

Tel: (011) 838–5802. Chief Patekile Holomisa (0471) 31–0437

Democratic Party

The party was founded in Johannesburg in April 1989, when the Progressive Federal Party (PFP), the Independent Party (IP) and the National Democratic Movement (NDM) joined forces. Of these, only the PFP had a history of resisting apartheid, going back to the breakaway of a group of liberals from the United Party in 1959 to form the Progressive Party. The Progressive Party had been associated with the redoubtable Helen Suzman who for many years was its only representative in Parliament, maintaining a lone but influential liberal voice that earned her universal respect and international honour.

The IP and NDM were formed shortly before the 1987 general elections, and consisted mainly of a so-called 'fourth force' of Afrikaners disenchanted with the refusal of then prime minister PW Botha to implement inevitable political reforms.

Initially the Democratic Party, combining the full spectrum of left-wing forces in Parliament, was led by a triumvirate of leaders: the PFP's Zach de Beer, the IP's Denis Worrall, and the NDM's Wynand Malan. De Beer was later elected sole leader.

Espousing liberal values and predominantly representing English speakers, the DP never really threatened the power monolith of the Afrikaner-dominated National Party. In the 1989 general election the DP could only attract 20 per cent of the white vote. But it played an important role within Parliament as a moral watchdog over the excesses of the NP's policies, and many of its members were involved in monitoring both the state's oppression and the popular groundswell against the NP apartheid policies.

The NP's fast pace of reform in the last two years created a dilemma for the DP. Some of its members joined the African National Congress, but others are adamant that the party still has an independent role to play in safeguarding liberal principles in a democratic

South Africa. It still draws substantial corporate support and is often seen as the voice of the liberal business community.

The DP was represented at the multi-party negotiations by party stalwart Colin Eglin and Ken Andrew, who both played an important role in the drafting of the transitional constitution.

Tel: (021) 45–1431

Development Bank of Southern Africa

The bank began life as an institution closely associated with the National Party government plans for Grand Apartheid. Set up by South Africa and the independent homelands in 1983, it was envisaged as the banker of the 'constellation of states', ie the homelands and other actually independent countries in the Southern African region, such as Lesotho. Hence the 'Southern' in its title.

Under the leadership of the late Dr Simon Brand, however, the DBSA, as it is commonly known, fought hard to redefine its role, in the process undermining the homeland concept. This probably informed the thinking behind the bank's division of South Africa into nine 'development regions' which overlapped the somewhat ridiculous jigsaw puzzle maps of the homelands and the Republic of South Africa.

Nevertheless, it is viewed with suspicion by some, who hark back to its apartheid past.

While the appointment of the respected Professor Wiseman Nkuhlu as chairman goes some way towards changing the racial profile of the bank, its chief executive is a white Afrikaner, André la Grange.

The World Bank's formal appointment of the DBSA

as its 'counterpart agency' seems to have angered the left, and its recent macro-economic policy model for human development in South Africa attracted a charge from the major union grouping Cosatu that it was trying to hijack the development process.

The DBSA has tried to ensure its survival by throwing its weight behind the transition to democracy, advocating co-operation among those involved in development work, and actually becoming involved in joint projects with the other two big players, the Kagiso Trust and the Independent Development Trust.

The DBSA has so far advanced around R5-billion in development money.

As a lending institution, as opposed to one that influences policy, it has had a tough time actually getting money out into the community, because of what it calls a 'lack of capacity' among recipients and the continuing violence, though critics charge it is not as efficient as it should be. In the year to end March 1993, for instance, it disbursed only R448,6-million out of a total of R1 754-million committed to new projects.

Tel: (011) 313–3911

Eastern Transvaal Boerekommando

The right-wing ETB consists mostly of former members of the Afrikaner Weerstandsbeweging. Although its influence extends, to some extent, into Northern Natal and parts of the Free State, its power base is centred on the Hendrina/Middelburg area, and it is strongest in the Eastern Transvaal.

This group split the AWB's Wenkommando in two when it broke away towards the end of February 1992. It is led by teacher Gawie Volschenk, who rose from obscurity when he was implicated in the sabotage of a platteland school in January 1992. However, lacking the charisma and oratorical powers of a Eugene Terre-'Blanche, he may not be a leader in the accepted sense, but rather a front man for disillusioned ex-members of Terre'Blanche's pre-Paardekraal executive council.

The Boerekommando runs a particularly tight ship; those in charge do not accept any new recruits unless they are vouched for by a trusted member and cleared by an advisory committee. Depending more on the calibre of individual members than on sheer numbers, the ETB is unlikely to consist of more than 400 members. Plans to sabotage power installations have been pushed around for some time, with members even conducting 'dry runs' over weekends, but at the moment it seems the organisation is waiting for Volschenk's court case in connection with the 1992 sabotage incident to run its course before deciding on any specific action. It is perhaps for this reason that the authorities keep post-poning the case. Man for man, the ETB can probably field a much better calibre 'soldier' than any other right-wing army, except for the Ystergarde. It may also be significant that several arms caches have been uncovered in the area where the ETB is active.

Tel: Not available

Freedom Alliance

The FA is a political pressure group consisting of the Afrikaner Volksfront, the Inkatha Freedom Party, the Ciskei and Bophuthatswana homeland governments, and the Conservative Party. It is viewed by many as a rather tenuous alliance of spoilers bonded by the maxim that 'an enemy of my enemy must be my friend'. All the members have at one stage or another pulled out of the multi-party negotiations process at the World Trade Centre, stating as their central reason the perception that the National Party and the African National Congress were pushing a predetermined agenda rough-shod past the other parties.

The founder members of the FA were originally all members of the Concerned South Africans group, which was disbanded in October 1993 only to re-emerge shortly afterwards with a new name.

Pushing a strong regional agenda, with some of its members subscribing to confederalism and others to federalism, the FA rejects the notion of a unitary state. Its founding manifesto states the following principles: the recognition of the right of self-determination; the protection and promotion of free-market enterprise and ownership; entrenched limitations of the power of the central government; and that Southern Africa be organised in member states which are primarily responsible for governance.

Herstigte Nasionale Party

Although negligible in terms of its small membership and proven voters' support, the HNP is significant in so far as it represents a viewpoint still adhered to by a large number of ostensible Conservative Party supporters. But uncharismatic leadership and a rather staid and old-fashioned image have prevented the party from capitalising on this support.

The HNP was founded in October 1969 when Dr

Albert Hertzog, a former cabinet minister, and three other MPs were expelled from the National Party. After Hertzog's death one of them, Jaap Marais, became HNP leader. Polling between 3,5 and 3,3 per cent of the total vote during the 1970, 1974 and 1977 elections, the HNP looked set to take off when its support jumped to 14,1 per cent in the 1981 general election.

But with the newly formed Conservative Party contesting the election in 1987, the HNP's support dwindled once again to 2,9 per cent, reaching an all-time low in 1989 when it could only attract 0,25 per cent of the vote.

Although not as militant in tone as the CP, the HNP has since its founding in 1969 hardly budged from stated policy. Refusing to negotiate with anybody to the left of the National Party government, it wants a return to grand apartheid with black people relegated to bantustans.

Its opposition to a smaller homeland for the Afrikaner has also meant it cannot be a member of the Afrikaner Volksfront.

Tel: (012) 342–3410

Human Rights Commission

An independent organisation, it came into existence in September 1988, seven months after the banning of a number of anti-apartheid organisations and restricting of others, including the Detainees Parents' Support Committee (DPSC).

Among other functions, such as providing counselling for released detainees and lawyers and advice for detainees' families, the DPSC had been monitoring human rights violations, especially detentions. Its restriction created an information vacuum, only partially filled by regional monitoring projects and the Democratic Party's violence monitoring group. The HRC took up the slack.

The HRC gathers information from numerous sources including community structures, lawyers, the media and the government itself. National coverage is assured by a network of collection points located in Johannesburg, Cape Town, Port Elizabeth and Durban, and with a small staff, the HRC provides a vital service in gauging violence in South Africa. It is led by commissioners Dr Max Coleman (national chairman), Brigalia Bam, Rev Denny Chetty, Chris Dhlamini, Fr Smangaliso Mkatshwa, Silas Nkanune, Adv Dullah Omar, Wesley Pretorius, Dr Faizel Randera, Jeremy Sarkin and Howard Varney.

The information collected by the HRC is collated in publications which are distributed nationally and internationally. In addition, the HRC submits evidence to bodies inquiring into human rights violations. Its findings are made available to anyone requesting them.

Tel: (011) 403–4450

Independent Broadcasting Authority

The IBA was due to come into operation on 13 January 1994, taking the airwaves for the first time out of direct government control, but was postponed because of a lack of nominations. The result of agreement at the Multi-Party Negotiating Council, the IBA will be responsible for the planning and management of all the broadcast frequencies. It will determine which frequencies will be assigned, in which areas, and for which type of broadcasting service — public, private or community.

It will award broadcasting signal distribution and broadcasting licences, including those for the SABC.

It will limit foreign control of private broadcast licences, and prevent the concentration of ownership of licences and cross-ownership of broadcast and other media. It will also prevent political parties from obtaining a broadcast licence. It has the power to require a minimum local content on radio and television stations and subject licensees to a code of conduct and a code of advertising practice.

The first IBA was appointed by the state president on the advice of the Transitional Executive Council and, later, it will be on the advice of the National Assembly. It is run by a chief administrative officer and will establish a Broadcasting Technical Committee and a Broadcasting Monitoring and Complaints Committee. In the run-up to elections, it overlaps with the Independent Media Commission, which is charged with ensuring the equitable treatment of all political parties by the broadcast media.

Tel: c/o TEC (011) 328–5490

Independent Development Trust

The IDT was founded in 1990 with R2-billion set aside in the national budget. The importance the government placed in the project was clear when the state president asked Jan Steyn, a former judge and longtime head of the Urban Foundation, to head it. He handed over the reins in early 1993 to Professor Wiseman Nkuhlu.

The independence of the IDT was under suspicion from the beginning because of the source of its seed money. But the controversy didn't stop there. A look at the criticism of two of the IDT's best-known programmes can be instructive for those seeking an understanding of development in South Africa.

Its R800-million capital subsidy scheme came under criticism from non-governmental organisations, including service organisations, as overly prescriptive and heedless of the real needs of the homeless for community facilities and sites close in to major cities. Under the programme, the IDT earmarks R7 500 for servicing each site in areas it develops for site-and-service schemes. These settlements are among the best of their kind in the country, and there is no shortage of applicants.

The IDT also writes loans for students at universities and technikons — R30-million-worth in 1993. That scheme came under attack by student activists early in 1993 for allocating only two-thirds of the money to 'historically black universities' and for letting universities decide how bursary money should be spent.

Despite the controversy, the IDT continues to spend massive funds on development. By October 1993, it claimed it had spent R1,2-billion on 641 projects, with another R1,2-billion allocated. It is directing its money — largely interest in investments from the original R2-billion — into building schools and rural clinics, rural water and sanitation programmes — it is a major funder of the National Consultative Forum on Drought and Rural Development, for example — and teacher upgrading.

Tel: (021) 23–8030

Independent Electoral Commission

The main task of the IEC is to arrange the country's first democratic elections and decide afterwards whether they were free and fair.

According to agreements reached by the country's negotiators — and passed into law by Parliament — the IEC must administer, organise and conduct elections. It must also take the necessary steps to prevent intimidation and violence and will be responsible for voter education.

Within 10 days after the elections, the IEC must declare whether the elections were essentially free and fair, a judgement that must have the support of 75 per cent of the members of the commission.

The IEC can reject or accept the results of the elections in total or in part. The results may not, however, be declared null and void on the grounds only of wrong actions, mistakes or non-compliance to the stipulations of the Election Code or the Election Act.

The IEC's findings will be final. No appeals will be allowed, not even by the special elections court.

The IEC may consist of between seven and 11 South African and five international members who 'do not have a high party political profile'. Its staff consists of an international advisory committee, an election administration directorate, regional electoral officers, presiding officers at voting stations, counting officers, chief election agents, regional and district election agents, voting agents, an election monitoring directorate, monitors, observers, international observers, and an election adjudication secretariat.

The first members of the IEC, nominated by the Transitional Executive Council and appointed by the state president, are Judge JC Kriegler (chairman), Adv Dikgang Moseneke (vice-chairman), Rev Frank Chikane, Dr Oscar Dhlomo, Helen Suzman, JH Heyns, R Jager, D Mokhobo, C Nupen, B van der Ross and Adv Z Yacoob.

Tel: (011) 928–1000 or (011) 397–5000

Independent Forum for Electoral Education

Ifee was formed in April 1992 and is committed to non-partisan voter education.

Its objective is to draw together organisations at national and regional level to provide a co-ordinated and nationwide electoral education and monitoring programme, based on both existing and supplemented organisational resources.

The forum consists of over 30 non-governmental, development, education, church, civic and other organisations. Members, who sign a code of conduct committing them to independence and non-partisanship, include such groups as the Black Sash, Consultative Business Movement, the Institute for Multi-Party Democracy, Independent Mediation Service, Matla Trust, the South African Council of Churches and Lawyers for Human Rights.

Ifee is funded mainly by the European Community and the Dutch government, while each of the individual organisations has its own funding.

Four working commissions meet regularly on a range of specific issues. These are the Media Commission, which co-ordinates media projects; the Lobbying Commission, responsible for liaison with the Independent Electoral Commission and other bodies; the Voter Education and Training Commission, which co-ordinates training activities; and the Monitoring Commission, which co-ordinates a large-scale independent national election monitoring programme.

Tel: (011) 484–2984

Independent Media Commission

The IMC has a crucial role to play in the 'levelling of the playing fields' in the run-up to the elections. Created by the Multi-Party Negotiating Council, it is responsible for regulating broadcasting and state-financed publications and information services during the election campaign, to ensure the equitable treatment of all political parties. State-financed publications will not be allowed to publish advertisements or reports aimed at promoting the interests of any political party. Independent publications, including newspapers, will also have to comply with certain rules; a clear distinction must be made, for instance, between party political advertising and political reporting.

The IMC is appointed by the state president on the advice of the Transitional Executive Council and consists of no more than seven people; the chairman must be a judge, retired judge, practising advocate, lawyer or magistrate. Two members must have broadcasting experience and one must have experience in the print media.

It will enforce the Independent Media Commission Act and the Electoral Act as far as they relate to broadcasting or state publications, including the prohibition on party election broadcasts and political advertisements on television, and on radio except during the election period; ensure the equitable treatment of political parties on all broadcasts, private or public; set the regulations for election broadcasts on public radio; ensure political parties can exercise a right of reply; and monitor compliance with the Act by private broadcasters who carry election material. The IMC has considerable powers to ensure the implementation of its code, which includes a stipulation that no party-political broadcasts will be allowed in the 48 hours preceding polling.

IMC members are Mr Justice John Trengove (chairperson), Dr Namane M Magua, Raymond Louw, Willem J de Klerk, Jenny Malan, Zubeida Jaffer and Libby Lloyd.

Tel: (011) 928–1111 or (011) 397–2186

Inkatha Freedom Party

The ruling party in kwaZulu was formed in 1975 as Inkatha Yenkululeku Yesizwe, a Zulu cultural organisation, and named for the coil heirloom representing Zulu unity and used to soften the weight of goods carried by women on their heads. It was originally formed with the blessing of the then banned African National Congress, since its founder Chief Mangosuthu Buthelezi was an ANC member with a close relationship with Nelson Mandela. The two organisations fell out, however, in the late 1970s and a steady deterioration in their relationship has led to bloody conflict in many parts of the country.

Inkatha claims a membership of 2-million, but it has always been plagued by allegations that it has used its control of pensions, houses and education in the homeland to force people to become members. In practice, it is a top-heavy organisation with Buthelezi occupying an unchallenged leadership, allowing little dissent or debate. Although he has always pictured it as a non-racial, non-tribal and national organisation, it has always been at root a Zulu speakers' organisation and in recent years has resorted to an increasingly militant nationalism and ethnocentricism to bolster its traditional support in rural kwaZulu/Natal. Inkatha also portrayed itself as a liberation organisation, but this was undermined by its links with the homeland and the fact that most of its bile and activity were directed at other liberation organisations and seldom at the government.

Buthelezi was long viewed as a moderate alternative to the ANC, since he rejected violence, sanctions, socialism and boycotts. For many years, the government wooed him, but he consistently refused to negotiate with them while Mandela was in prison and repeatedly called for his release and the ANC's unbanning.

But Buthelezi and Inkatha's image has taken a severe battering in recent years. This began with the 1991 revelations of covert security police and military intelligence support for the organisation, but reached a head in recent months with Buthelezi's belligerent attitude towards his opponents and his stubborn refusal to accept the terms of the constitutional negotiations. This led Inkatha into thinly veiled threats of secession and a loose alliance with the far right wing, thus alienating many of his middle-of-the-road, international and business supporters. Although all the opinion polls give him a small percentage of the vote, he has a loyal, traditional constituency in rural areas and growing support among right-wing whites. He also makes a good deal of political capital over his relationship with the Zulu king.

Inkatha was long headquartered in the isolated kwaZulu capital of Ulundi, a factor which helped its local ethnic constituency but cost it support in the urban areas of Natal. Its head office is now in Durban.

Tel: (031) 307–4962 or (031) 29–3614

Institute for Multi-Party Democracy

Launched in 1991, the IMPD is closely involved in preparations for the elections. Under the leadership of former Inkatha general secretary Oscar Dhlomo, the IMPD has held a series of workshops on voter education and plans to be involved in election monitoring as well. Widely regarded as non-partisan, the IMPD is spearheading a national initiative in conjunction with several other non-governmental organisations to launch an independent election monitoring agency.

The IMPD has also initiated a R2,25-million project, Launching Democracy, to observe political trends in the run-up to elections. Opinion surveys are commissioned and networks of observers have been set up to report on political trends and events at grassroots level.

Head office of the IMPD is in Durban and regional offices are in the Transvaal and Western Cape.

Tel: (031) 306–3744 or (031) 304–3863

kwaZulu Police

Formed in 1980, the 4 000-member kwaZulu Police (KZP) force is at the heart of the political violence ravaging Natal/kwaZulu. With Chief Mangosuthu Buthelezi as its minister of Police, the KZP is seen by critics as the 'private army' of the Inkatha Freedom Party, attacking African National Congress supporters in a bid to prevent the organisation from making inroads in the strife-torn province.

The KZP's credibility hit rock-bottom recently when the Goldstone Commission released a report in December 1993 saying a hit-squad exists within its ranks. This confirmed an earlier exposé of *The Weekly Mail* that KZP members had received military training at the hands of the South African Defence Force (SADF) in the Caprivi strip in the 1980s.

While the ANC and the government are pushing for the KZP to be absorbed into a national peace-keeping force, Buthelezi is resisting the move. The IFP leader is determined to keep it under his control and use it to fight moves to disband the kwaZulu homeland. In a speech in December 1993, he said the KZP would be 'in the front lines of the battle' against the Transitional Executive Council and it would 'protect the citizens of kwaZulu against the ANC'. Based in Ulundi, the KZP commissioner is Lieutenant General Roy During.

Tel: (0358) 20–2017

Lawyers for Human Rights

The organisation grew out of a key meeting held in 1979 at which the present chief justice and some of his colleagues spoke out strongly in favour of a Bill of Rights and the need to protect human rights. However, a full-time LHR directorate was established only in 1987. Since then, LHR has played an important role helping ensure that human rights issues are kept at the forefront of national politics.

Among the work which brought LHR to national prominence was the organisation's death row monitoring. Staff members kept themselves informed of planned executions and a group of lawyers became specialists in bringing last-minute applications for a stay of execution. This led to their action on behalf of Almond Butana Nofomela, a former policeman sentenced to death for murder. Nofomela told LHR lawyers about police hit-squads and alleged police involvement in the murder of several political opponents of the government. The successful stay of execution won by LHR on behalf of Nofomela led to a major political scandal about hit-squads, to the Harms Commission of Inquiry and to several court cases.

More recently, during the negotiations for the interim constitution, LHR national director Brian Currin brought an urgent application against the state president and various government departments asking that they be ordered not to destroy classified documents. In an out-of-court settlement, the government agreed not to shred any further material.

During the run-up to elections, LHR has undertaken to make its staff available to serve on various tribunals which will be established to ensure the elections are free and fair. LHR members around the country will also be encouraged to make themselves available.

After the elections, LHR will involve itself in Bill of Rights litigation and is already planning test cases. Among the first is likely to be a challenge over prison conditions, based on the right not to be subject to cruel, inhuman or degrading treatment.

LHR employs 120 staff in 14 centres. Its projects include penal reform, legal training, housing and disability rights, and a farm workers' project.

Tel: (012) 21–2135

Legal Resources Centre

The LRC has been operating since 1979. Its head office is in Johannesburg, and staff run six regional offices around the country, employing 40 full-time lawyers as well as a number of paralegals and support staff. LRC offers full client services in those cases it accepts, focusing more on trend-setting public interest litigation than on public education and campaigning. Most of the LRC's work deals with human rights issues, land, housing and development, and the abuse of power by state officials.

Best-known LRC cases include three major pass law cases heard by the Appellate Division in the 1980s. The decisions in these cases, including the most famous Rikhoto case, helped ensure the end of the hated pass laws. A brace of legal actions involving forced removals — the Mfengu, Goedgevonden and Oukasie cases — also helped stop that practice and the LRC is now claiming land of behalf of people who were forcibly removed. The LRC is also acting in the current inquest into the 1985 death of Eastern Cape activist Matthew Goniwe, trying to establish that the state was responsible for political murders during the 1980s.

During the pre-election period the LRC has agreed to help with tribunals and boards involved in monitoring the run-up to the elections. Staff also expect to be taking complaints about unfair election procedures to these tribunals and election courts.

After the elections LRC's existing human rights work will continue, although helped with the powerful weapon of the new Bill of Rights. The LRC focus on housing and development in both rural and urban areas will also continue. Given its past record, the LRC will be a key body to watch. For many years under the highly respected directorship of Adv Arthur Chaskalson, it is now led by another well-known lawyer, Geoff Budlender.

Tel: (011) 836–8071

Matla Trust

Matla is a Sesotho word which means empowerment. The trust was started with money raised by the president of the African National Congress but claims to be a non-partisan organisation trying to uplift South Africa's disadvantaged and promoting the development of a democratic society.

Besides running education and skills programmes, the trust has thrown much of its financial weight behind 'education for democracy' and has emerged as a major player in voter education. It is seen to be the driving force behind the Independent Forum for Electoral Education (Ifee), an alliance of over 30 organisations involved in democracy education. Matla, through Ifee, also made substantial submissions to the negotiations forum on how the elections should be run.

Factoring in the fear that a low turnout and a high number of spoilt votes could have a significant impact on the outcome of the election, Matla's work has become politically loaded. Its director is Billy Modise, formerly the African National Congress's representative in Sweden.

Tel: (011) 836–8061

Military Intelligence

Countless 'dirty tricks' episodes through the years have

given the lie to the old adage which claims that Military Intelligence is a contradiction in terms. The organisation proved itself ruthlessly effective in several counter-propaganda operations, and its role in setting up or supporting organisations like Mozambique's Renamo and Inkatha's Caprivi-trained force of urban warfare experts has left a bloody trail across Southern Africa. Yet despite the unmasking of many of its most unsavoury operations, MI is still a shadowy organisation skilled at keeping its true role and reach out of the public eye.

A new government faces the unenviable task of getting the organisation back to work at its real job — providing ongoing assessments of the military threat to the country's security, and preparation for operational readiness. The intelligence wings of the four services — army, navy, air force, and medical — already perform many of the tactical information gathering functions, such as map updating and counter-intelligence/internal security for the forces. Because of the close association of MI chief General Joffel van der Westhuizen with the dirty tricks side of MI, it will be difficult to remove him without provoking him — or those he is leaving behind — to take up ultra-right cudgels.

Tel: Public Relations Directorate (012) 428–4201

National Council of Trade Unions

Nactu is the second largest trade union federation of black workers in the country. It has about 327 000 members in 24 affiliate unions and is strongest in the chemical, construction and transport sectors. Nactu plans to streamline its affiliate unions to 14 through a series of mergers, in line with its campaign of one union in each industrial sector.

It is headed by feisty general secretary Cunningham Ngcukana and his more conservative assistant, Mahlemola Skosana. The federation eschews political alliances (like that between the African National Congress and Cosatu) and preaches a doctrine of trade union independence, although some Nactu leaders are close to the Pan Africanist Congress and to the Azanian People's Organisation.

Nactu is also involved in the National Economic Forum and the National Manpower Commission, but its policies are less well honed than Cosatu's. Nactu launched a women's unit in 1993. The federation is affiliated to the Organisation of African Trade Union Unity.

Tel: (011) 29–8031

National Intelligence Service

Apparently never directly involved in the 'dirty war' against the African National Congress, the NIS has managed to craft an image of itself as the country's intellectual intelligence service, a sort of ivory tower think-tank wisely advising enlightened politicians on how to abolish apartheid and unban the enemies of old. The truth is more complex. Those familiar with the agency say that NIS has not achieved its potential, despite the enormous resources available to it. But it has been an important adviser to government, both under founding director Neil Barnard, an academic brought in from the University of the Orange Free State, and under current director Mike Louw, a career intelligence officer trusted by NIS staffers because of his intimate knowledge of the service.

Modelled on British and American intelligence agencies, NIS has a wide network of informers inside the country and an active, if smaller, group of cloak-and-dagger operatives outside, often based at South African embassies and hitherto involved in keeping tabs on anti-apartheid activists. Their role is likely to increasingly become that of gatherers of economic and technical information, supplying the NIS's analytical staff.

Numbers are a closely guarded secret, but NIS is believed to employ between 5 000 and 10 000 operatives in a full or part-time capacity.

If it is to fit into a new intelligence network currently under discussion, the organisation will face mounting pressure to change, not least because it is a white, male-dominated institution.

A complete reorganisation of South Africa's intelligence services — besides the NIS there are those attached to the military and the police — is likely to take some time. But whatever form the new services take, they will find themselves on a much shorter leash than before. Parliamentary control via a senior government official who carries political responsibility for their doings seems certain, as policy-makers show determination to avoid the past pattern in which a single agency dominated government thinking by virtue of its direct access to the state president.

Tel: (012) 317–5911

National Party

The National Party was founded by General JBM Hertzog in 1914 in an effort to unify Afrikaners politically. The aim right from the start was to achieve a more prominent role for Afrikaners in society and in government, to resist British imperialism, to develop the country and to keep blacks, coloureds and Indians socially and politically apart from whites.

In 1924, with the assistance of the (white) Labour Party under Colonel FHP Creswell, the NP came to power for the first time, ousting Jan Smuts's South African Party (SAP). The NP had the active support of the African National Congress, which in May 1924 had urged the black electorate to 'vote solidly for changes in government'.

Having secured equal language rights for Afrikaans and English, and sovereign independence for South Africa, the NP and SAP were fused into the United Party. Afrikaner ideals were now subject to broader national interests — which led in 1934 to a breakaway by Dr DF Malan and his followers, who formed the Purified National Party.

The present NP grew from the Purified NP, a very different party from Hertzog's NP; it was strongly republican and ethnically exclusive, and it openly set out to uplift Afrikaners materially and promote their group interests at the cost of other communities.

When Malan's NP came to power in 1948, it immediately set out to implement its policy of racial separation, or apartheid, aimed at entrenching white minority rule to the exclusion of all other population groups. A plethora of racist Acts followed.

In 1949 the Prohibition of Mixed Marriages Act was accepted by Parliament, followed by the Population Registration Act (1950), the Group Areas Act (1950), the Separate Representation of Voters Act (1951) which stripped coloured voters of the franchise, the Bantu Authorities Act (1951), Bantu Education (1953), Natives' Resettlement Act (1954), Reservation of Separate Amenities Act (1953), the Preservation of Coloured Areas Act (1961), and the Urban Bantu Councils Act (1961). There were other Acts, ranging from the barring of blacks from 'white' universities to legislation allowing for the independence of black homelands. During the 1960s, under the premiership of Dr HF Verwoerd, the apartheid structures were further entrenched. In 1961, the great Afrikaner ideal of an independent republic was realised.

The racist policies of the NP led to increasing internal resistance and international isolation. When PW Botha came to power in 1978, the state was beginning to lose legitimacy. A 'total strategy' was developed against what was perceived as a 'total onslaught', with the security establishment playing an increasingly prominent role.

The 'total strategy' was supplemented by limited reforms to apartheid laws. Trade unions were legalised, the prohibition of mixed marriages was scrapped, limitations on the movements of blacks were lifted.

Botha's political reforms were supported by verligtes in the NP, including Afrikaner cultural leaders, academics, business people and senior civil servants. They were rejected, however, by both the NP's right wing — which broke away in 1982 to form the Conservative Party — and by those who were supposed to have benefited from the reforms: the majority of black people.

In 1983 a new constitution was forced through Parliament, allowing for an executive state president. Power-sharing with coloureds and Indians was introduced, allowing these groups a minority share in two of the three new chambers of Parliament. The exclusion of blacks led to a countrywide popular revolt, precipitating a State of Emergency.

Parliament became increasingly less important as power shifted to the National Security Management System and the security establishment in general. By May 1987, when Botha called a general election, it had become clear that the new state president had lost his will for further reform. However, Botha succeeded in broadening the NP's base beyond its ethnic origins: as right-wing Afrikaners flocked to the Conservative Party, the NP polled more English votes than ever before in its history.

In 1989, after suffering a stroke, Botha was succeeded by FW de Klerk, following an unsavoury behind-the-scenes power tussle. Previously known as a conservative member of the NP caucus, De Klerk promised a 'new South Africa' free from racism and domination. At its federal congress in Pretoria in June 1989, the NP accepted a 'five-year plan' towards democracy. 'Groups' still formed the basis of the new plan and no allowance was made for negotiations with banned organisations.

On 2 February 1990, De Klerk astounded friend and foe by announcing the unbanning of the African National Congress, the Pan Africanist Congress and the South African Communist Party. The rules of the political game were changed fundamentally. Negotiations with black-dominated organisations which had been excluded from power started later in 1990.

Indications are that the NP thought it would be possible to co-opt the ANC. The negotiations at Kempton Park soon showed that it had seriously underestimated its erstwhile enemies.

The NP has now committed itself to democracy and is promoting an image of itself as a party of reform for the whole country, claiming that its principles are based on capitalism and 'Western thinking'. Although its traditionally formidable election machinery has been damaged in recent years, the NP showed its teeth in the early days of the campaign with a ruthless advertising campaign.

Tel: (012) 348–3100

National Peace Accord and Secretariat

Launched amid great hope and fanfare, the Peace Accord and Secretariat has had limited success in stemming the political violence which has claimed thousands of lives in South Africa.

The accord, signed on 14 September 1991 by all the major political organisations, aims to create peace in South Africa and help rebuild communities which have been ravaged by political violence.

The accord commits the signatories to adhere to political tolerance and prevent their members from taking part in acts of violence or intimidation. It upholds freedom of speech, conscience, belief, association, movement, peaceful assembly and political activity, and a multi-party democracy. It sets out codes of conduct for political organisations and the security forces, especially the police force.

It is overseen by three national structures staffed by

independent volunteers, lawyers and businesspeople who act as peace monitors and watch for contraventions of the accord. The National Peace Committee, headed by businessman John Hall, oversees the working of the Peace Accord and mediates disputes; the National Peace Secretariat, under Dr Antonie Gildenhuys, establishes and co-ordinates regional and local dispute resolution committees; and the National Peace Commission, under Justice Richard Goldstone, investigates the violence and recommends ways to remove the causes of conflict.

Although political violence continues to ravage South Africa and most parties have ignored the accord's provisions at some time, it is difficult to measure the impact of the accord and the secretariat in containing the fighting. 'If nothing happens, then we have been successful,' explains a peace monitor.

Individual campaigns for peace launched by the Peace Secretariat — like National Peace Day held on 2 September 1993, and National Peace Month, September 1993 — have received overwhelming support from the public, but they have had little effect in stemming the long-term pattern of violence. Still, says Gildenhuys, the objective of peace campaigns is to make the public aware of peace and participate in these campaigns.

Tel: (011) 339–3709

National Peacekeeping Force

Announced with much fanfare at the beginning of 1994 by the defence subcouncil of the Transitional Executive Council (TEC), the Peacekeeping Force faced massive personnel and legitimacy problems from its inception. Equipped with police riot gear and trained in riot control techniques but organised along essentially military lines, the force is likely to become the nucleus of a new public order police service replacing the Internal Stability Unit of the South African Police in the post-election period.

The force was envisaged by multi-party negotiators as a prime public order agency in the run-up to the elections, but it has been criticised because of the brief training afforded its members, the absence of important political organisations from its ranks and command structures, the small size of the force, and the timetable for its deployment. Critics have called the organisation 'the national peacekeeping farce'.

At the head of the force is the NPKF Command Council, with representatives of all formations contributing cadres, including SAP Major General Wynand van der Merwe, the deputy commander of ISU and Umkhonto weSizwe's chief of operations, Lombert Moloi.

Introducing the force in January, deputy Defence minister Wynand Breytenbach, who chairs the TEC subcouncil on defence, admitted it would 'be difficult to train the force adequately', but he was adamant that there would be no repeat of the 'kitskonstabel' fiasco, when ill-trained SAP special constables were let loose on the public. Breytenbach said that he hoped the force would be deployed by the end of March, just three weeks before the election. But he was sceptical the force would be at its envisaged strength of 10 000 by then.

One of the big things the new force has going for it is greater legitimacy in the townships than is enjoyed by the police. But just how well the NPKF is accepted by warring political groups will ultimately depend on who has agreed to join it.

At its inception, only 12 of a potential 17 armed formations had opted to participate. Notable among those absent from the force are the kwaZulu Police, the Azanian People's Liberation Army, and the Azanian National Liberation Army, as well as several military organisations of the white far-right, all of whom have been under the spotlight in recent weeks in connection with acts of violence.

In a report to Secretary General Chief Emeka Anyaoku in late 1993, the Commonwealth Observer Mission to South Africa (Comsa) expressed a series of reservations in connection with the NPKF.

Concerns include:

- a 'shift in emphasis . . . from a service organisation to a force trained along military lines';
- a danger that it could become as discredited as the ISU if the NPKF used guns as its first line of defence;
- the limited time within which to mould the new force: 'if the force is to be deployed before elections in April 1994, training would be restricted to (between) six weeks to two months. In our assessment, to mould these diverse forces, a longer training period would have been desirable';
- the expected size of the force, 10 000 strong, compared with the original proposal of 30 000. 'Assuming three shifts a day, only some 3 000 of these troops would be on duty at any given time in the country. Even if these were concentrated in the most violent areas, they would still be a thin force on the ground';
- and the composition of the NPKF, raising questions about its credibility in areas where the IFP, far right and Apla, who haven't joined, have support.

Some observers believe that the primary function of the NPKF may be to draw criticism away from the police and the defence force by handling the dirty work of township public order, control of demonstrations and other political policing. The defence subcouncil, it seems, is looking to the period after the elections, when the new National Defence Force will be born. By drawing the heat for unpopular measures — and what are certain to be failures in public order policing and an inability to stop the bloodshed — the NPKF will serve to legitimise the NDF, the real prize for the military men on the TEC defence group.

At the end of January 1994 the TEC announced that Venda president Brigadier Gabriel Ramushwana would be appointed NPKF commander.

Tel: (021) 328–5490 (TEC)

National Union of Metalworkers of South Africa

The country's biggest trade union has about 273 000 members in the metal and engineering, tyre, automobile manufacturing and motor sectors.

In 1993 the trade union unveiled a three-year bargaining strategy, setting a new mould for wage bargaining in the country and moving away from the annual round of wage offers, demands and disputes. Instead it set a goal of securing a 15 per cent wage increase over three years as well as a plan for the restructuring of work organisation and training schemes for members.

The union also increased its subscription costs in an effort to wean itself off foreign funding.

Numsa is active in a number of negotiating forums and the union was instrumental in the establishment of the electrification forum. The metalworkers' union is the most militant of Cosatu's affiliates and maintains its commitment to socialism and nationalisation.

In 1993, Numsa sent shock waves through the country when it resolved at its congress that Cosatu's alliance with the African National Congress should end and that a working class party should be formed.

Moses Mayekiso remains Numsa's general secretary though he will vacate his position late in 1994 after the election.

Tel: (011) 832–2030

National Union of Mineworkers

With 270 000 members, the NUM is Cosatu's second largest affiliate (after the National Union of Metalworkers). Formed in 1982 under the auspices of black union federation the Council of Unions of South Africa (Cusa), the NUM broke with Cusa to become one of the founder members of the non-racial Congress of South African Trade Unions in November 1985.

Under the inspired leadership of general secretary Cyril Ramaphosa, the NUM grew rapidly in size and militancy. In 1987 its members staged the biggest strike in South Africa's labour history, lasting three weeks and at its height involving over 300 000 miners on 44 mines. The strike, broken by mass dismissals, seriously weakened the NUM: the failure of miners to give significant support to Cosatu's 1988 campaign against the Labour Relations Amendment Act was an indication of this.

In recent years the union has been more moderate and 'co-determinist' in its approach. In response to massive retrenchments on the mines, it pushed hard for a 1991 industry summit, involving representatives of black and white labour, management and the government to map out the future of mining. It also broke new ground by entering profit-sharing agreements with employers.

The union has campaigned strongly for improved health and safety conditions on the mines and for adequate compensation for mineworkers. It was instrumental in the Chamber of Mines' appointment in April 1992 of a judicial inquiry into laws affecting mine safety, in pushing for compensation for the families of 177 miners who died in a fire at the Kinross gold mine in 1986, and in the government's appointment in June 1993 of a commission of inquiry into health and safety in the mining industry.

Politically the union has always been close in spirit to the African National Congress and the South African Communist Party. One of the first of Cosatu's unions to adopt the Freedom Charter as a guiding document, the NUM supported a unified front between labour and other mass-based anti-apartheid organisations, in contrast to other Cosatu unions wishing to restrict a broad front to working-class organisations. Later it was to argue against separate representation for Cosatu at constitutional talks, on the grounds that this was the proper domain of the ANC.

Ramaphosa moved effortlessly from the union's leadership to the post of ANC general secretary. The NUM's assistant general secretary, Marcel Golding, was one of the Cosatu unionists elected to the ANC national list for the April elections.

The union, under general secretary Kgalema Mothlanthe, has been at the forefront of innovative retrenchment agreements and has announced its intention to lobby for a social plan to assist retrenched miners. But the NUM's support for a national minimum wage and its participation in the union Community Growth Fund (a unit trust fund which invests workers' pension and provident funds in socially responsible companies) have also put it at odds with other unions in Cosatu.

Tel: (011) 833–7012

National Women's Coalition

Formed in April 1992, this coalition consists of about 60 national organisations. Together they have written a women's charter and successfully participated in negotiations at the World Trade Centre. They have lobbied for a 30 per cent quota for women in government and during negotiations succeeded in winning the battle against customary law, where the rights of black women would have been overridden by tradition.

Tel: (011) 331–5958

Pan Africanist Congress of Azania

The PAC is an unknown quantity in the 1994 elections. Although membership is minute compared with that of the African National Congress, there has none the less been a groundswell in pro-PAC sentiment in townships since its armed wing, the Azanian People's Liberation Army (Apla), began attacks on white civilians, and with growing disgruntlement in certain sectors with the ANC's moderation. Opinion polls put PAC support between five and 10 per cent, but observers say its showing at the polls could improve significantly if it were to conduct an effective election campaign.

This Africanist movement was formed in 1959 when a faction of the ANC, led by lawyer Robert Sobukwe, broke away, suspicious of growing white, Indian and Communist Party influence within the ANC. The PAC played a key role in organising the 1960 anti-pass campaign which led to the Sharpeville massacre. The State of Emergency that followed and the outlawing of the PAC and other resistance organisations ensured that it did not have time to consolidate itself on the ground. Its armed wing, Poqo (which means pure), attacked state institutions, white civilians and black collaborators, but was soon crushed by the state.

For almost three decades the PAC in exile was wracked by internal wranglings which included assassinations. Lacking a substantial following inside the country, it did not feature much in the uprisings of the 1970s and 1980s. The political stage was left to the ANC-aligned United Democratic Front and the Azanian People's Organisation.

The resurgence of the PAC inside the country only came in 1989 with the formation of the Pan Africanist Movement (PAM), following the successful 1988 takeover of the National Council of Trade Unions by Africanists.

While the PAC will probably be a junior partner in a government of national unity, it is gearing itself up to make a bigger impact in the second democratic elections. PAC strategists are already banking on an ANC government being unable to deliver sufficiently to an impatient populace. Coupled with this is a marked resurgence in Africanist sentiment in some urban centres and forcibly uprooted communities.

But unless the PAC drastically improves its organisational capacity, it faces no chance of translating sentiment into support. Prospects of this movement posing any real threat to the ANC as the major black political grouping are therefore slim.

The organisation has failed to grapple with policy-making and often relies on individual portfolio holders to deliberate and pronounce on various positions — an exercise which sometimes reflects personal opinions.

Tel: (011) 836–0442/0407

Pretoria Boerekommandogroep (PBKG)

The PBKG is closely linked to the Volkseenheid Komitee (Vekom), a forerunner of the Afrikaner Volksfront, and the Boerevryheidsbeweging (BVB). A central figure in the PBKG is Jan Groenewald, brother of Volksfront strategist Major General Tienie Groenewald.

Lieut General Cobus Visser, a former South African Police chief of detectives, was initially asked to head the commandos, with Eric Barnard in charge of training. Visser later became one of the four generals heading the directorate of the Afrikaner Volksfront, and Commandant Willem Ratte, a former intelligence officer/operator with 32 Battalion, has taken over command of the PBKG. It is also linked to similar Boerekommandos, such as the Donkerhoek-BKG and the Behou Pretoria Aksie.

Ostensibly, the PBKG is organised along the lines of a community watch but, if one scratches the surface, it becomes obvious that the organisation is very politicised, with the volkstaat ideal central to everything else. Pretoria is not only seen as their base of operations but as the shrine of Afrikanerdom and the future capital of a volkstaat.

The rationale behind the PBKG appears to be more the laying down of a structure that can be activated in times of crisis.

The PBKG has grown rapidly since its inception at the beginning of 1992 and towards the middle of 1993 boasted more than 1 000 members divided into 14 different commandos in the Pretoria area.

They have similar structures to other right-wing armies with a chief commandant, 14 commandants, veldkornets (about 20) and corporals (about 100). There have been schemes for establishing two different elite corps, one for the protection of VIPs and the other acting more in a ceremonial capacity. The end of 1993 saw the establishment of the 'Reaction Force'. Members of this unit are regularly seen guarding ranking Volksfront members.

In December 1993 Ratte led an estimated 40 PBKG members in occupying Pretoria's Fort Schanskop as a symbolic protest against the first session of the Transitional Executive Council. The PBKG and Ratte were also centrally involved in the establishment of the rebel radio station, Radio Pretoria.

Tel: (012) 335–6840

South African Chamber of Business

As the official voice of organised, white South African Business, Sacob faces new pressure as black business shoulders its way into the limelight. An organisation constrained by the many diverse people who make up its members, it manages to speak for business as well as any business organisation could under the circumstances, lobbying for lower taxes and the like.

It was formed in January 1990 from the merger of the Association of Chambers of Commerce, representing largely commercial interests, and the Federated Chamber of Industries, who represented industry. Under director general Raymond Parsons it has played a constructive role in supporting negotiations. It has also actively supported the National Peace Accord and generally adopted a conciliatory attitude while opposing mass action.

Tel: (011) 482–2524

South African Communist Party

The situation has changed considerably since the SACP banner paraded during the 1922 Rand miners' strike called on the workers of the world to 'unite and fight for a white South Africa'. Soon thereafter, the party was the first political organisation in the country to open its membership to all-comers. It is this multiracialism which ever since has been a cornerstone of the party's policies and its attractiveness to intellectuals and workers alike from across South Africa's ethnic spectrum.

Banned in 1950 under the Suppression of Communism Act — which provided for the office of the liquidator, whose task it was to assemble an official list of communists — the party was forced to operate underground for the greater portion of its history. Those named by the liquidator were effectively banned from active participation in politics, although many found ways of circumventing the restrictions, some legal and others not.

Those communists who remained politically active inside South Africa continued through the 1960s to suffer detention, bannings, and torture at the hands of the state. Among the most prominent victims was advocate Bram Fischer, the offspring of a highly regarded Afrikaner family who became chairman of the underground party and was sentenced to life imprisonment; he died in prison after serving only a few years.

The SACP has emerged intact, organisationally and intellectually, if not without significant bruises, from its period in the underground. These self-inflicted injuries are the result of the SACP's propensity through the decades for toeing Moscow's line faithfully, supporting the invasions of Hungary, Czechoslovakia and Afghanistan, the doubts of individuals notwithstanding. Whether principled or pragmatic, the proximity to Moscow however also served a concrete purpose, greasing the gears between the African National Congress and the Soviet Union in the days before the liberation movements found much support in the West.

The defence of socialism as an economic and social model despite its failure in practice — the party says the Soviet Union collapsed because of a lack of democracy — which has emerged from the party leadership since 1990 has been called opportunist by sceptics and interpreted as a breath of fresh air by those willing to give the SACP the benefit of the doubt. Whatever the case, the real challenge facing the party will come when it is forced to recruit members and voters on its policies alone, rather than as an element of the ANC-led Tripartite Alliance. But that prospect is some years away yet, because the SACP is not fielding an electoral list of its own. For now, it remains a voice for non-racialism and workers' rights within the ANC-led grouping.

Tel: (011) 339–3621

South African Council of Churches

Founded in 1968, the SACC became a spearhead of anti-apartheid activity. A succession of outspoken general secretaries helped make the SACC one of the foremost opponents of apartheid during the years political organisations were banned. It has 23 full and observer members, with Methodist Bishop Khoza Mgojo as president. The current general secretary, Frank Chikane, has been seconded to the Independent Electoral Commission until after the 1994 elections.

In addition to creating closer ties between different denominations, the SACC also brings together the top leadership of its member and observer churches, providing a joint platform from which they have been able to speak about injustice and violence. Key leaders of the SACC around the country have been detained, banned, brought to trial and even, in some cases, killed. In 1988 the SACC building in downtown Johannesburg was bombed and so extensively damaged that the organisation had to move to new premises.

The SACC has played an important role in helping promote negotiations — even though a strong lobby within the delegates at recent conferences called for this role to be replaced by the 'prophetic' role of denunciation which the SACC played for many years. It also has a strong involvement in voter education and the promotion of democracy, and has helped facilitate a series of ecumenical peace monitors who have visited the country.

Tel: (011) 492–1380/9

South African Defence Force

Still recognisably organised on the British model despite efforts over the last three decades to 'Afrikanerise' the forces, the SADF has been a willing servant of the apartheid regime, ruthlessly going into action against the National Party's foes and South Africa's neighbours. The year 1975 saw the forces in Angola in a desperate attempt to prevent the MPLA from taking over. The result was the internationalisation of the conflict and the stationing of Cuban troops in the former Portuguese colony. Content to hold the line for many years, the Cubans finally gave the SADF a thrashing a decade later at Cuito Cuanaval, sometimes called the SADF's Stalingrad. Army officers deny having lost the battle to this day, but South Africa's withdrawal from Angola and Namibia — and some say the end of apartheid — can be dated to the battle.

Conventional warfare has been only one aspect of the SADF's fight against anti-apartheid forces. In a series of bloody cross-border raids in the 1970s and 1980s which affected Botswana, Lesotho and Mozambique, SADF commandos killed and maimed ANC guerrillas, their families and, often enough, innocent locals. The misnamed Civil Co-operation Bureau, formed as a unit of the SADF's special forces, specialised in the assassination of apartheid's opponents both within and outside the country.

And despite battle honours gained in faraway places

such as North Africa and Italy during this century's world wars, the South African Defence Force has always been first and foremost an instrument of domestic policy, from its role in ending the 1922 miners' strike to its deployment today on patrols in townships in support of the South African Police.

The role is unlikely to change in the foreseeable future, with the country's first democratically elected government facing secessionist tendencies on several fronts and an internal security situation which could get worse before it gets better. But in order to serve what is sure to be a less than perfect democracy, the SADF will have to resist the common third-world temptation to take the country over, promising to give it back to the politicians once order has been restored.

The SADF is currently made up of 95 000 full-time uniformed and civilian members, 120 000 Citizen Force members, and more than 130 000 members of commandos, which are largely rural.

Only a culture change within the military, argue critics, can ensure that it remains the servant of democracy and individual human rights. The SADF, they say, must make the transition from a technically proficient army which sees itself as a separate caste to an organisation integrated into the mainstream of society, ready to defend the values upon which a democracy is based. The SADF will have an opportunity to cast off its baggage of old as it integrates with the ANC's military wing Umkhonto weSizwe and the homeland armies to form the new National Defence Force in the months following the election.

Conscription was ended in 1993.

Tel: Chief Directorate Communications: (012) 428–4201

South African National Civic Organisation

Sanco was established in March 1992 to co-ordinate and represent civic associations on a national level at a time when these bodies were changing from forums of anti-apartheid struggle, which they had been since the early 1980s, to vehicles for development and local government reform.

The key phrase in any successful application for funding for a development programme is 'community participation'. With affiliated civic associations in nearly every township and village, all of which claim to be non-partisan, the participation and approval of Sanco or its local affiliate has become vital to any local or national development project and the organisation has representation on a range of development and local government forums.

Sanco's broad base of support has made its stamp of approval vital to the African National Congress's election campaign. After Sanco officially decided, at its national conference in November 1993, to throw its weight behind the ANC, it was informally co-opted into the Tripartite Alliance, which is now known as the 'Tripartite + One'.

At the national conference in November 1993, Winnie Mandela, who had been building a power base among informal settlers in the PWV, won election as deputy president. Mandela's election was the first indication of her comeback, confirmed not long afterwards when she was elected president of the ANC Women's League.

Sanco has regional offices in 13 areas throughout the country. Its national office is in Johannesburg.

Tel: (011) 838–2038

South African Police

What's in a name? Attempting to adjust to the demands of a participatory democracy, the SAP is adding the word Service to its title. The suffix is an attempt to signal a move away from the old style of paramilitary law enforcement on behalf of a hated regime and towards a style of policing which satisfies community requirements. But the addition is perhaps more telling than many senior officers would like to believe, signalling as it does that the old force remains intact, if amended.

As with South Africa's military and intelligence organisations, real change can be expected to come slowly to the police, with the old guard still firmly in the saddle for some time to come and old military habits and thought patterns refusing just to disappear.

There is growing hope that the SAP will, with time, become more responsive, setting public order priorities which encourage co-operation from communities as yet loath to assist the police. A new brand of police officer does exist within the force, at junior levels among black policemen and women who have formed a union, the Police and Prisons Civil Rights Union, and at very senior levels among white officers. Both groups are making efforts to develop a doctrine of service capable of striking a chord with communities used until now to being harassed and maltreated by the police rather than protected by them.

But the problems of the SAP go beyond questions of

doctrine. At 115 000 serving officers, the force is seriously understaffed. European policing experts familiar with the SAP believe it should grow by up to 50 per cent, with civilians taking over many administrative functions so that more uniformed officers can be put back on the beat. The Waddington report, written by an English policing expert following the 1992 Boipatong massacre, was particularly critical of the SAP's professional shortcomings. Standards of detective work, scene of crime techniques, and other specialist areas are said to lag years behind the current international norm.

Perhaps most important in the short term will be how the senior officer corps, with its roots in apartheid, responds to direction from a legitimate government.

The SAP will itself only gain legitimacy if its officers are able to accept that the force exists to serve all South Africans and no ideologies.

Tel: Public Relations Directorate (012) 21–1040

Southern African Catholic Bishops' Conference
Based in Pretoria, the SACBC is an executive body, carrying out decisions of Catholic bishops in South Africa, Namibia, Botswana and Swaziland. It was founded in 1947.

For many years, the SACBC spoke out strongly against apartheid, and joined with church leaders of other denominations in supporting protest action to end minority rule. During the worst days of repression, in October 1988, its headquarters was bombed and had to be rebuilt. Its one-time secretary general Father Smangaliso Mkhatshwa was repeatedly detained and banned and eventually won a damages claim against the government for torture while in detention.

Leading SACBC figures based in the nominally independent homelands continue to play a prominent role in opposing oppression and breaches of fundamental rights in those regions. During the run-up to elections, the SACBC will be supporting election and peace monitoring, encouraging Catholics to vote and those who wish to do so to become part of the monitoring process; 25 full-time staff are involved in voter and democracy education around the country. The SACBC also played a key role in establishing the Independent Forum on Electoral Education which brings together non-governmental organisations and most of the churches involved in voter education.

In the longer term, the SACBC is likely to follow the example of its equivalent organisation in Zimbabwe and maintain a watchful eye on political developments, speaking out against what it perceives to be injustice, regardless of who is in power.

The secretary general is Brother Jude Pieterse.

Tel: (012) 323–6458

Thebe Investment Corporation

Thebe is an investment company started at the end of 1992 as a means of channelling the African National Congress's foreign funding and promoting black economic empowerment.

Thebe's major shareholder is the Batho-Batho trust whose trustees include Nelson Mandela and Walter Sisulu. One of its board members is the leader of the organisation's PWV region, Tokyo Sexwale, and its managing director Vusi Khanyile headed the ANC's Department of Finance before leaving to start Thebe.

Media revelations early in 1993 suggested that the company was promising 'privileged access to a future government' in a joint venture publishing deal with Macmillan Boleswa. This was followed by a string of controversial exposés of deals and practices the organisation was involved in, including the fact that a number of its subsidiary companies were insolvent.

Despite this, Thebe has mushroomed into something of a black business empire. Together with a Canadian consortium, it will launch a regional airline — SA Express — in March 1994.

Other wholly owned and joint venture companies in the Thebe stable include: Nolwazi Publishing, an educational book publishing venture with Macmillan Publishers and Skotaville; Bheki Computer Systems, a joint venture deal with American computer giant Digital Equipment Corporation; Oriole Travel; Sizwe Car Hire; Thebe Trading — an import company; Dakawa Properties; Thebe Properties — which deals in metropolitan, residential, commercial and industrial properties; and Movement Marketing Enterprises which, set up to market ANC souvenirs, has branched into the hawking trade as a distribution centre. Thebe also has interests in the cellular telephone industry.

Tel: (011) 29–2741

Transitional Executive Council

The TEC represents the first grip on state power for the extra-parliamentary liberation movements of South Africa. During the run-up to the elections, it entails — for Parliament and the government — the first abdication of some of their areas of authority.

The basic purpose of the TEC, as agreed to by the country's negotiators in Kempton Park, is to 'promote the preparation for and transition to a democratic order in South Africa'. In layman's terms, it means that the TEC will level the political playing fields and create a climate for free political activity in the run-up to the elections in April 1994.

The initiative for the establishment of the TEC came from the African National Congress, which argued that the white-dominated government could not be both referee and player in the elections. It also insisted that the TEC should have joint control over all armed forces in the country.

To achieve this, wide-ranging powers have been extended to the TEC and its seven subcouncils.

Represented in the TEC is one member of each of the parties that participated in the multi-party negotiations. Parties who walked out of the talks, notably the members of the Freedom Alliance, have declined membership of the TEC, while the Pan Africanist Congress has also decided not to participate. In the end, 19 of the original 26 negotiating partners are represented in the TEC, which has its head office in the Saambou Building in Andries Street, Pretoria.

Eight of the 19 members serve in a management committee, which normally meets a day ahead of the full TEC meetings on Tuesdays to prepare the agenda. Controversy surrounded the exact role of the TEC after it was established by an Act of Parliament in September 1993, with the ANC insisting that it had substantial powers and the NP government arguing that it had only a supervisory role to play.

There is no doubt, however, that the TEC has the powers to restrict the government's competence severely in important areas, specifically in the areas demarcated to the TEC subcouncils.

The subcouncils are: law and order, stability and security, defence, intelligence, foreign affairs, status of women, finance, and regional and local government and traditional authorities.

The first three subcouncils have eight members each, and the rest six. Represented in the subcouncils are members of various political parties with specific knowledge of their areas of competence. The subcouncils get their instructions from the TEC and have wide powers to curtail government actions as well as access to all information relevant to their tasks.

According to the TEC Act, each government and administration in the country — including the independent homelands — must keep the Council informed of all its proposed legislation. If the TEC or one of its subcouncils has reason to believe any proposed legislation is likely to have an adverse effect on the attainment of democratic elections, it may instruct that government or administration in writing not to proceed. These governments and administrations will then, according to law, be obliged to comply. The same applies to political parties.

Tel: (012) 328–5490

Tripartite Alliance

The Alliance, which is putting up one election list in the name of the African National Congress, consists formally of the ANC, the Congress of South African Trade

Unions and the South African Communist Party. In late 1993 the South African National Civic Organisation was also co-opted on to the team.

Although its historical and ideological roots go back to the 1950s, with the Congress Alliance that brought together the ANC and its coloured, Indian and white counterparts, the Alliance continues because of a happy coincidence of present political interests. The ANC needs the organisational skills, material support and membership of the country's largest trade union federation. Many of its best strategists and election prospects belong to the SACP and the party's reputation for militancy has given it a powerful base in the ANC's constituency.

Cosatu needs a political organisation which can win the election for the constituent assembly and represent its interests in government.

The SACP does not have enough popular support to be a powerful political force on its own, so it must remain in an alliance with its more powerful partners and try to get them to incorporate its political and social objectives in their agendas.

No matter what critics might wish, it is unlikely that the Alliance will fragment while its members are jointly able to mobilise the majority of South Africans behind them.

Tel: c/o ANC (011) 330–7000

Umkhonto weSizwe

Founded in December 1961 as a response to the government's intransigence in the face of peaceful anti-apartheid protests, Umkhonto weSizwe (MK) was rarely an effective military force, much to the chagrin of the thousands of young men and women who spent significant portions of their lives in the difficult conditions of the training and transit camps. Taught to think and act like soldiers, they were often condemned to long periods of waiting for an opportunity to go into action against apartheid. For those chosen for infiltration back into the country the attrition rate was very high, the strategic effectiveness of their operations — with few exceptions, such as the 1980 rocket attack on Sasol — limited. The Sasol attack, which sent white South Africa into a state of deep shock, was part of a 1980s strategy of armed propaganda, designed to respond to the township militancy which had become apparent starting with the Soweto uprising in 1976. The idea was to raise morale and militancy among township youth fed-up with the political vacuum created by the banning of the ANC and other organisations in the early 1970s.

MK commander Joe Modise and chief of staff Siphiwe Nyanda nevertheless take one significant element into the new defence force: despite the torture and execution of cadres in Angola during the 1980s following mutinies, their army is South Africa's most democratic armed formation, its cadres drawn from all of the country's ethnic groups, its rationale the struggle against an unjust and undemocratic system.

Since its unbanning in 1990, and the return of many cadres from exile, MK has battled to keep its forces together and to avoid unrest. With little financial support from the ANC, and experiencing difficulties finding jobs, cadres have found the wait for slots in a new military very burdensome. Some have turned to crime, others have tied their colours to the masts of other political parties, even that of the erstwhile enemy, the National Party.

Whatever MK's shortcomings, both technical and political, its formal dissolution and integration into the South African Defence Force when the new National Defence Force is formed after the election is bound to contribute to a change of culture within the military. The challenge for MK's cadres will be to absorb the conventional training which will be the prerequisite of command within the integrated SADF.

Tel: (011) 330–7000 (direct number)

Urban Foundation

Created in the wake of the 1976 uprising to try to improve urban living conditions, the Urban Foundation, well supported by business donors, has been active ever since in housing, education, urbanisation issues and community enablement activities. Any number of projects begun under UF auspices, from group credit schemes for low-income homebuyers to resource centres in informal settlements, have been spun off over the years and function now as independent NGOs. A UF unit established in mid-1992 deals with development strategy and policy; strategy and policy formulation is also a major portion of the work of the housing and education units.

In housing, the UF has devised a loan guarantee initiative, acts as project manager in upgrading informal settlements, trains members of communities involved in development, and does substantial research in areas such as housing's role in the economy, minimising conflict between longtime residents of an area and their new, low-income neighbours and the development of a framework for promoting low-income housing. It supports the concept of market-driven housing provision with key state intervention — in targeted subsidies, for example, loan guarantees and regulation.

In education, the UF's education policy unit (Edupol) is looking at new ways to finance education efficiently and soundly. It has also been doing research into educational reconstruction, teacher salaries and capacity-building among parents, teachers, students and others for the restoration of a culture of learning.

Tel: (011) 403–5500

Western Cape Community Organisation

A new umbrella civic federation launched in October 1993, Wecco brings together a diverse body of affiliates, ranging from squatters' associations to an alliance of white ratepayers' organisations. The rationale for its formation appears to have been a bid for more leverage by some parties who felt themselves under-represented in the Local Government Negotiating Forum.

However, in some quarters it is seen as positioning itself as a counter to the ANC-aligned South African National Civic Organisation with concomitant potential for destabilising the region. Wecco president Joe Marks, a former United Democratic Front stalwart who later defected from the African National Congress to join the Democratic Party, of which he is now regional deputy leader, defends it as a non-party political, community orientated organisation and denies it is Inkatha aligned, an accusation made after it emerged that IFP officials attended its launch in Stellenbosch.

Tel: (021) 75–9973

Western Cape United Squatter Association
Formed by squatter leaders in 1989, Wecusa is headed by Jeffrey Nongwe, the Crossroads warlord who ousted former Witdoek leader Johnson Ngxobongwana in a bloody power struggle. While many of the squatter leaders claim allegiance to the African National Congress and some even head their local ANC branches, the relationship between the two organisations has repeatedly become strained, particularly in the face of challenges to the squatter leaders' authoritarian style of leadership by younger ANC members who have criticised them for acting undemocratically.

Dependent for their political survival on their ability to deliver land and other resources to their followers, Wecusa members have been identified as key players by the state and private developers. However, their failure to consult properly with their followers over the implications of development has fuelled bloody conflicts, most notably in Crossroads.

Wecusa makes no bones about its antagonism towards the South African National Civic Organisation (Sanco), with whom it is engaged in a long-standing feud over the right to organise among shack-dwellers. Talk of Wecusa becoming a national squatter association has raised concerns that it could lead to a head-on confrontation with Sanco and possibly split the ANC. What is clear, however, is that whoever commands the loyalty of those living in the densely populated squatter settlements will hold considerable leverage at election time.

Tel: (021) 34–8638

3

Forums

An A-Z of who's talking to whom in South Africa's negotiating forums

The development of a range of national negotiating forums dealing with socio-economic issues has been one of the most unusual and important phenomena of contemporary South Africa.

The forums arose because, beginning in about mid-1992, any government attempt to deal with these issues was met with the charge that it was acting unilaterally and without legitimacy. There was also a concern that crucial issues — such as housing and electrification — could not wait until constitutional negotiations were finished.

The membership of each forum is determined by its focus, but all of them bring together a range of interest groups including non-governmental organisations, business, trade unions, political parties, special interest groups and — sometimes reluctantly — government, which participates in the major ones.

In many cases, the government can no longer make decisions without the consent of the relevant forum. In effect, the forums are forcing a process of consultation and negotiation in dealing with most of the major socio-economic issues. They also have the virtue of drawing interest groups into the policy-making process; instead of sitting outside and sniping away, they have to engage with forum partners in the complexities of the issues under discussion.

Devised as an interim measure, forums may continue to function well beyond the elections, for the organisations that serve on them are not likely easily to relinquish the power they have achieved for civil society.

Local Government Negotiating Forum

The aim of this unelected, non-statutory body, founded in March 1993, is 'to contribute to the bringing about of a democratic, non-racial, non-sexist and financially viable local government system'.

At its inception it consisted of 60 members, equally divided between statutory and non-statutory bodies involved in local government; its 12-member management committee was divided along the same lines.

Three working groups deal with legal and constitutional issues; services and finance; and management, administration and training.

The forum was established after resistance erupted to the government's interim measures for local government. A number of organisations argued that the Interim Measures for Local Government Act (1991) placed too much power in the hands of the authorities and called for the needs of local government to be re-negotiated at a representative forum. At the end of September 1992 a task group which included the South African National Civic Organisation, the central government, provincial governments and organised local government met to prepare the way for the forum.

Among priorities — along with the Interim Measures for Local Government Act — were rent and service charge boycotts and guidelines for local negotiations.

The forum has agreed on a draft Local Government Transition Bill to replace the Act as enabling legislation providing for local government during the transition period, and it contributed to the chapter on local government in the new transitional constitution.

It has resolved that the transition to non-racial local government be implemented in three phases:

- A pre-interim phase, in which existing local authorities are replaced by nominated local and metropolitan councils;
- An interim phase in which elections are held for interim councils; and
- A final phase in which a final constitutional model for local government is unveiled.

According to its secretary Dirk Strydom, statutory and non-statutory sides are also represented through a number of umbrella organisations. The statutory side includes the Council for the Co-ordination of Local Government Affairs, the Municipal Executive of South Africa (and its four provincial affiliates), the four provincial administrations, the National Committee of Local Government Associations, the Urban Councils' Association of South Africa, the United Municipalities of South Africa, the Major Cities Association, the South African Association of Municipal Employees, the Transvaal Local Government Association, the Transvaal Municipal Association, the Department of Finance, and the central government.

The non-statutory side includes the South African National Civic Organisation, African National Congress, Congress of South African Trade Unions, and the

South African Municipal Workers' Union, the latter three being part of the Sanco delegation. According to the co-ordinator of the ANC/Sanco bloc, Andrew Boraine, the Pan Africanist Congress and Azanian People's Organisation were also invited by Sanco to form part of its delegation but they refused to participate.

Tel: Linda Kruger (012) 42–4482

National Economic Forum

The National Economic Forum (NEF) has been a working prototype of a social concord between labour, business and government which may be the foundation for future South African economic prosperity, forging consensus between normally adversarial stakeholders.

It was launched in October 1992, a year after the Congress of South African Trade Unions first called for its formation as part of its protest against Value Added Tax. Its primary objective is to ensure that any 'major economic restructuring undertaken, particularly during the period of transition, should have the support of all economic stakeholders'.

It is organised into short-term and long-term working groups, a plenary and a process committee, which is the co-ordinating body.

The short-term working group's projects include:

- Job creation, including public works programmes, retrenchment and ways of reducing unemployment;
- Public sector restructuring; and
- Human resources development, including skills training and education.

By mid-1993 it had achieved some success. Agreement had been reached that the Unemployment Insurance Fund should receive compulsory state funding and be restructured to benefit workers temporarily laid off or on extended short time, and that a national job creation programme and small business development programme should be established.

In December 1993 the NEF approved the allocation of R45-million to 195 new job creation projects.

The long-term working group identifies issues for policy research and negotiation, focusing on:

- Finance, including the role of financial institutions in mobilising and allocating savings;
- Foreign trade, including the establishment of a task force to address all aspects of policy;
- Investment, with the major emphasis on private fixed investment; and
- Labour markets, including job creation and productivity.

It has reached agreement on a policy framework for foreign direct investment and agreed to the establishment of a task force to investigate all aspects of trade policy.

The NEF has had successes and setbacks. In 1993 the forum put forward to the General Agreement on Tariffs and Trade a sophisticated proposal on protective tariffs which carried the stamp of approval of all NEF participants. But shortly afterwards an agreement by the NEF on delaying the implementation of an unpopular fuel price hike was ignored by the government.

The NEF has no statutory powers, although this is under discussion. It has avoided conflict over government measures which, in the context of the fragile consensus politics of the transition to democracy, could have been seen as 'unilateral' — a signal to the union movement and the tripartite alliance to take to the streets in mass protest.

One of its weaknesses is a failure to represent all economic stakeholders. Missing are representatives of small business, the informal sector (including subsistence farmers), the unemployed, and consumers.

Fears have also been expressed that the NEF could represent corporatism, a kind of cosy cronyism between powerful interest groups, shutting out smaller communities and groups who are not well organised, like the rural poor.

Each category of membership — business, labour and government — is responsible for one-third of the costs of the forum, although labour has argued that its portion should come from public funds because workers are taxpayers. In fact foreign embassies have settled some of labour's costs.

Membership of the forum includes the Afrikaanse Handelsinstituut, Building Industries Federation of South Africa, Chamber of Mines of South Africa, Cosatu, Council of South African Bankers, Federation of South African Labour Unions, Federated Hospitality Association of South Africa, Foundation for African Business and Consumer Services, Institute of Retirement Funds of Southern Africa, Islamic Business Chamber, Life Offices Association, National African Federated Chamber of Commerce and Industry, National Council of Trade Unions, South African Agricultural Union, South African Association of Consulting Engineers, South African Chamber of Business, South

African Consultative Committee on Labour Affairs, South African Federation of Civil Engineering Contractors, South African government, South African Property Owners' Association, and the Steel and Engineering Industries Federation of South Africa.

Tel: (011) 614–2251

National Education and Training Forum

In May 1993, the government agreed to the establishment of an education forum. Agreement followed negotiations with the National Education Conference and business organisations as well as strike action and class boycotts conducted by teachers and pupils in protest against the government's 'unilateral restructuring' of the education system.

A facilitating committee was established to negotiate a founding agreement; a draft was published in early July and the National Education and Training Forum (NETF) was launched formally in August 1993.

The objectives of the NETF as stated in the founding agreement are to seek agreement on:

- How to resolve education crises about which effective action can be taken immediately;
- The restructuring of the education system (at the time of founding, fragmented into 14 different departments) into a national system capable of correcting imbalances and of meeting the development needs of South Africa; and
- Core values and broad policy frameworks for a future system, as well as a process to achieve an integrated approach to education and training.

The forum consists of a plenary, an executive committee (which is responsible for planning, co-ordinating and guiding the work of the forum) and specially appointed working groups.

Two working groups have focused on restructuring the education system and short-term crisis issues. The first has identified education policy issues which need to be addressed by technical subcommittees and devised a framework and terms of reference for those committees.

The second working group is a crisis committee and, says Peninsula Technikon rector Franklin Sonn, chairman of the education forum, it has played an important role in helping to resolve disputes over salary increases, the payment of matric exam fees and the rationalisation of teaching staff in House of Representatives (coloured) schools.

Although responsibility for the management of education rests with the government, the director general of National Education, Dr Johan Garbers, has conceded that since the government is represented on the forum, it would be impossible, if consensus is reached, for recommendations not to be implemented.

Membership of the forum includes the Afrikaanse Handelsinstituut, Chamber of Mines, Committee of Colleges of Education, Committee of University Principals, Department of Education and Training, Department of Education Co-ordination, Department of National Education, Federal Committee of Technical College Principals, House of Representatives, National Education Co-ordinating Committee, National Professional Teachers' Organisation of South Africa, National Training Board, Private Sector Council, South African Chamber of Business, South African Democratic Teachers' Union, Steel and Engineering Industries Federation of South Africa, Teachers' Federal Council, and Union of Teachers' Associations of South Africa.

Tel: Dr Franklin Sonn (021) 959–6201

National Electrification Forum

The National Electrification Forum (NELF) was launched in May 1993, eight months after the first attempt failed following disagreements over who should serve on it. Its aim is to develop a strategy leading to access to affordable electricity for the population, and to implement it, as rapidly as possible. The NELF's success will ultimately be judged by the extent to which electricity is spread from beyond the 2,4-million consumers who have it to some 30-million still without it. It expects to be ready to make recommendations to a new government by May.

The NELF says it is committed to transparency in the forum's proceedings and in implementing agreements reached. It has also undertaken to involve electricity consumers in the forum, particularly women and rural communities. The plenary has some 170 delegates.

The NELF's plenary chairman, Dr Johan Kruger, says it is significant that the government is a fully fledged participant. The deputy chief executive of Eskom, Allen Morgan, says Eskom will not undertake any unilateral changes without consensus in the forum.

Seven working groups are focusing on:

- A regulatory framework, structure and policy for the electrification process;
- A human resources strategy;
- A supply technology strategy;

- An industry database;
- Policies and strategies for finance and tariffs;
- Policies and strategies for reorganising electricity supply structures; and
- Environmental policy and affordable electrical appliances.

The plenary group agreed in November 1993 that generation and bulk transmission of electricity should remain with Eskom and the number of distributors should be rationalised. This should, theoretically, make electricity cheaper, although local authorities are complaining that the new policy will cost them a lucrative source of income. The forum has also decided to set up a body to monitor the electrification process and has agreed that a national electrification fund should be established to finance development projects, particularly in rural areas.

The forum is funded by the Development Bank of Southern Africa, Eskom and a trust fund for groups needing assistance.

Membership of the forum's management committee includes the African National Congress, Association of Municipal Electrical Undertakings, Department of Mineral and Energy Affairs, Development Bank of Southern Africa, Eskom, National Union of Metalworkers of South Africa, National Union of Mineworkers, South African Chamber of Business, South African National Civic Organisation, and United Municipal Executive.

Tel: (011) 313–3027

National Health Forum

Founded in August 1993, it aims to reach consensus on restructuring the South African health system and to identify priorities for development, especially in communities which currently have no access to health care facilities. Membership is open only to organisations concerned with health issues on a national basis. Political parties per se are excluded, although among the membership of the Patriotic Health Front, which is represented on the forum, is the African National Congress, as well as civic associations and trade unions. Also among the membership are representatives of government health departments (including those in the 10 homelands). There are other stakeholders with observer status.

Chairman of the forum is the ANC secretary of health, Ralph Mgijima.

The forum is funded by the Department of National Health and Population Development.

Tel: Ralph Mgijima (011) 330–7000

National Housing Forum

The National Housing Forum (NHF), formally launched in August 1992, aims to negotiate a practical future direction for the housing sector. It grew out of an urgent meeting in August 1991 convened by the Independent Development Trust and the Development Bank of Southern Africa, in response to requests from the Kagiso Trust and South African National Civic Organisation, to discuss the problems surrounding hostels countrywide. The parties involved decided the hostels issue could not be dealt with in isolation from the broader housing crisis.

The government withdrew from the forum in January 1992, while it was still in the planning stage, arguing that it would not allow interim government by stealth. Since then, however, the NHF and the Department of Local Government and National Housing have established a joint housing initiative which aims for a more efficient application of state housing funds to facilitate housing delivery. The government has made R500-million available. In addition, the NHF and the government have agreed to take joint responsibility for the hostel upgrading programme.

In December 1993 the NHF and the government replaced the National Housing Commission with a National Housing Board of six members nominated by the forum, six chosen by the government, and seven decided jointly by both. The board's task is to deliberate on policies negotiated between the NHF and government and advise the government on what action to take.

When the minister of Housing announced last year that a subsidy of R7 500 to buyers of houses built before 1983 by the government would be extended to houses built after 1983, the forum said it had not been consulted and suspended negotiations, which were resumed after the minister agreed to consult the forum before making any decisions.

The forum is currently examining:

- Overall housing policy and strategy;
- Functional housing policy and strategy, looking at practical approaches with regard to land, finance and institutional structures. It is examining a proposal by the minister that R1-billion be allocated to insure banks against risks associated with low-cost loans; and
- A set of overall housing programmes.

The forum is funded by the Independent Development Trust and the United States Agency for International Development.

NHF membership includes the African National Congress, Association of Mortgage Lenders, Azanian People's Organisation, Construction Consortium, Cosatu, Development Bank of Southern Africa, Independent Development Trust, Inkatha Freedom Party, Kagiso Trust, Life Offices Association, Pan Africanist Congress, South African Consultative Committee on Labour Affairs, South African National Civic Organisation, South African Housing Trust, material manufacture and supply sector, and the Urban Foundation.

Tel: (011) 838–2822

National Legal Forum

Although one of the youngest of the country's legal organisations — it was still being formally established at the time of going to press — this forum has the potential to be extremely important. It is likely to play a significant role before and after the elections.

It was originally conceived by the National Association of Democratic Lawyers (Nadel) but has now drawn in almost every other establishment and non-establishment legal group.

Nadel's plan for a body representative of all sectors of the legal community grew out of the organisation's unwillingness to be involved in any of the legal structures set up before a democratic government was in power. It followed years of a strict policy (honoured somewhat in the breach) that its members should not hold office as judges, or on any Bar or Law Society. Eventually Nadel decided to ease its non-participation rule and call for a forum which would satisfy its criteria of representivity, at least until the elections; its vision was that the government should take no major decision on legal issues before the elections without consulting and reaching consensus with the forum. Some forum members want the body to continue after elections, but in an advisory capacity.

The forum is not without its own difficulties: members cannot agree on the role the government, and in particular Justice minister Kobie Coetsee, should play; sections of the legal community have indicated disquiet about a more radical role for the forum proposed by some members. These include suggestions for disbanding the Bar Councils and Law Societies and reconstituting them in a completely different form.

At a maximum of 1 500, Nadel's membership is tiny compared with the total number of lawyers, legal academics and para-legals in the country. The forum is something of a coup for Nadel, allowing it to play a greater role in shaping the future of the legal community than its numbers might suggest.

National Rural Development Forum

This forum was established in June 1992 by the Independent Development Trust and the Kagiso Trust. It was initially called the National Consultative Forum on Drought and its function was to co-ordinate drought relief efforts in the whole of South Africa (including the 10 homelands). However, when participants agreed the root cause of drought-related problems in rural areas was underdevelopment, the name was changed in July

1993 to mark the inclusion of rural development in its activities.

The forum consists of eight regional forums — in the Border region, the Eastern Transvaal, the Orange Free State, kwaZulu/Natal, the Northern Cape, the Northern Transvaal, Namaqualand and the Western Transvaal — and a national forum, co-ordinating the activities of task forces concentrating on employment, nutrition and water supply. A national early warning system is being developed.

The National Rural Development Forum focuses on developing the strength of the regional forums, which have strong representation on the national body. Participation by national organisations on the steering committee is at the invitation of the regional forums.

The national body is working to ensure that rural development is part of the work of other national forums and institutions devoted to economic policy, electricity, health, housing and local government, and not considered separately.

The forum is funded by the Independent Development Trust, the Kagiso Trust and a number of foreign embassies. Moreover, its water supply task force received funds from the government's drought relief package in 1993.

Membership of the forums includes businesses, civic associations, donor agencies, the government, trade unions and welfare organisations. Political parties such as the African National Congress, the Inkatha Freedom Party and the Pan Africanist Congress are represented on the regional forums only.

Tel: (011) 339–5412/7

National Transport Policy Forum

A range of interest groups with a stake in transport came together in February 1992 to establish this forum, whose initial aim was to contribute to the creation of an official and non-discriminatory transport policy. The Department of Transport was initially reluctant to participate but is now a member, according to forum chairman George Negota, and in June 1993 the minister of Transport, Dr Piet Welgemoed, said the department and the forum would jointly formulate a new national passenger transport policy.

The government has agreed to give the forum R3-million for the establishment of local taxi forums consisting of all the taxi associations operating in particular areas, in an effort to curb conflict between taxi associations. These local forums will be represented on a national body, which will in turn be represented on the National Transport Policy Forum.

The forum's long-term aim is to help formulate a transport policy for the entire southern African region.

Membership includes the African National Congress, Azanian People's Organisation, Congress of South African Trade Unions, National African Federated Transport Organisation, Pan Africanist Congress, Road Federation, South African National Civic Organisation, South African Bus Owners' Association, South African Rail Commuter Corporation, Southern African Black Taxi Association, Spoornet, Tolcon, and Transnet.

Tel: George Negota (011) 337–2100

By early 1994, three more national forums were on the way:

The National Telecommunications Forum
Contact: Jim Duncan
Tel: (011) 313–3565

The National Tourism Forum
Contact: Peter Mokaba
Tel: (011) 333–6750

The National Youth Development Forum
Contact: Erron Al-Amin
Tel: (011) 834–6865

There are about 100 local negotiating forums, including the Metropolitan Chamber in Johannesburg, One City initiative in Port Elizabeth, Interim Development Committee in Durban, and others bringing together city and township councils plus civic associations and other relevant groups. There are also 10 regional economic development forums. And the National Manpower Commission qualified as a forum when, in early 1993, it was restructured to include all trade union and employer bodies.

4

Issues

An A-Z of what matters in South African politics

Abortion

The question of whether a woman has the right to terminate her pregnancy has been left open by all the major political parties, who refuse to state where they stand on the matter, except the ANC. The ANC's draft health policy, released in January 1994, proposed the legislation of abortion on demand, but hedged its bets on this contentious issue by saying there should be further consultation and discussion on the issue. The status quo makes abortion unlawful unless the woman has been raped, her life or physical health would be threatened by childbirth, her mental health would be permanently damaged or the foetus has congenital defects.

Legal experts say pro-choice activists are now able to take the route of their American counterparts and appeal to the courts, citing certain clauses in the Bill of Rights in the new Constitution. There are two that have a bearing on abortion. The first is clause 9, which states: 'Every person shall have the right to life'; the second is clause 13 which guarantees an individual right to privacy.

The right to life clause has caused some concern for abortion reform groups, as some lawyers and judges say it precludes abortion. The debate centres on whether a foetus under 12 weeks can be legally defined as a 'person'. Ultimately, this decision will be in the hands of the judges of the Constitutional Court.

It was the privacy clause in the American Bill of Rights that made abortion legal. The judges of the United States Supreme Court ruled that the state could not interfere with a woman's right to make a private decision about her pregnancy. However, parts of this decision were reversed as the composition of the court changed, showing the pitfalls of using a widely defined right for a specific issue. South African advocates of 'choice' would prefer to have a law which entrenches abortion rights.

There is only one pro-choice organisation in South Africa, the Abortion Reform Action Group (ARAG), but chairman Dr Marj Dyer says they are supported by a wide range of women's groups. Anti-abortion lobby groups include Pro-Life South Africa, run by Dr Claude Newbury, and the Saltshakers, a Cape Town group.

Affirmative Action

Black economic empowerment has moved centre stage along with anti-trust policy, while nationalisation has edged towards the wings, as a realistic way for the African National Congress to redress past economic injustices.

Affirmative action has different nuances in the private and the public sectors. In the public sector a new government will have to advance blacks to top posts, while the outgoing National Party government has wanted to calm the fears of anxious white civil servants. This has led to the fear that affirmative action for civil servants will entail expanding the public sector when the world trend is towards leaner government.

Also, the country's powerful labour grouping Cosatu even threatened to strike against assurances of job security for present white civil servants. In the end a deal was struck: tenure for five years, after which all new posts will be subject to affirmative action.

Affirmative action in the private sector, on the other hand, is increasingly seen by organisations as having moved from the area of social responsibility to that of survival. Businessmen fear both community pressure and legislated quotas by the ANC in government. A *Weekly Mail & Guardian* survey in late 1993 showed 97 per cent of business leaders in favour of affirmative action and 84 per cent already implementing it in their firms. Black businessmen have won from the ANC a promise of legislation, though it is not clear how this would work.

Equally, businesses fear rejection by consumers. Among companies which have moved furthest in advancing blacks is South African Breweries' beer division, the bulk of whose customers are black. The most radical policy is that of parastatal Transnet, for long a place of sheltered employment for unskilled whites, which now disallows the employment of any white without the personal authority of the chairman.

The end of apartheid has left many companies scrambling to employ more blacks in senior positions, creating a premium among the relatively small pool of qualified blacks, but also speeding up identification and training within organisations of blacks with potential.

Losers in the game so far have been white women, and to some extent race groups other than Africans. Right-wing white unions have had their membership boosted by resisting affirmative action.

Bill of Rights

For the first time, a Bill of Rights — Chapter 3, entitled 'Fundamental Rights', in the new Constitution — will protect individuals from the power of the state. Many pre-election 'privileges', such as the right to freedom of assembly, to freedom of movement inside the country and to freedom to leave the country, have become fundamental rights to which everyone is entitled.

The Bill of Rights, however, operates only 'vertically', governing relations between the state and citizens, and not 'horizontally', and therefore does not deal with relations between citizens. Critics believe this is a failing since it does not outlaw the practice of apartheid by private individuals.

Other critics have pointed to the Bill's tolerance for detention under a State of Emergency, albeit strongly circumscribed.

The Bill of Rights invites a number of test cases, the most obvious relating to abortion. While the Bill enshrines the right to life, it is silent on the question of capital punishment and abortion. The death penalty is likely to be outlawed anyway, given official African National Congress policy, but the courts will no doubt soon be asked to decide whether or not termination of pregnancy conflicts with the Bill of Rights. In his comments on the Bill, then still at draft stage, the chief justice said the judges anticipated the Bill would outlaw abortion. However, the Constitutional Court in deciding this issue would first consider whether the concept of a right to life as entrenched in the Bill of Rights was identical to that which would be given such a phrase in the common law. Anti-abortion groups, aware of the distinction, fear that without a clause specifically entrenching the right to life of a foetus, some means will be found to declare abortion legal.

Other issues to watch include affirmative action and non-discrimination. Cases testing the limits of the Bill's provision are sure to come to the Constitutional Court early on. The Southern African Catholic Bishops' Conference has already given notice that in staffing its schools, it will not abide by an equality clause outlawing discrimination against gay people. Such a case would have to deal not only with the right to discriminate, but also whether schools or other institutions partly funded by the state are bound by the Bill of Rights. As the Bill is binding only on the legislature and executive, and does not cover judge-made common law, additional laws will be needed to prevent unwarranted discrimination between individuals. Otherwise companies or organisations not using government funds could be free to refuse to employ women or black people. Already a number of lawyers and legal organisations are preparing their arguments for other cases they anticipate.

Constitutional Court

One of the most bitter battles of the whole negotiating process was fought over how appointments to the Constitutional Court should be made. This gives some indication of how important all sides believe this new court will be. It will have the power to adjudicate on the validity of legislation, weighing up whether laws conflict with the new Bill of Rights. The court will also be the final appeal on cases testing rights under the Bill of Rights. Its work will involve 'political' decisions, delivering judgments which comment on the government's actions, and which have the power to halt state programmes.

Appointments to this court will be closely watched, by some for evidence of political bias, by others to see whether the new judges better reflect the composition of society than the present judiciary. The Judicial Services Commission is specially instructed to bear in mind that the court should reflect a cross-section of gender and race, so it is likely to be the first South African Bench not dominated by white males. All its members must be South African citizens, ruling out the possibility of 'importing' foreign judges to join the bench over the transitional period, as has been done in a number of other African countries.

The Constitutional Court, to be headed by the president of the Constitutional Court, will sit in Johannesburg. Its members will include at least four sitting judges. The court will hear cases en banc; that is, all its 11 members will sit together to hear evidence. This ensures the composition of the court hearing a particular matter cannot be selected by the president of the Constitutional Court, as is alleged to have been the case in the Appellate Division in the past. However, this raises the strong likelihood of serious delays in getting matters heard, and in obtaining judgment.

Judges of the Constitutional Court will hold office for a single, non-renewable period of seven years, compared with judges of the Appellate Division and the supreme courts, who hold office until retirement or impeachment.

Customary Law

The term customary law refers to customs and traditions which have historically regulated communities, especially in the areas of marriage and family. The paying of lobola or a dowry, practices surrounding marriage, birth and death, and the duties of individuals to their families all fall within the ambit of customary law, which varies for different communities and from region to region.

Traditional leaders feel strongly that customary law should be recognised in South Africa and pushed hard for this in the multi-party negotiations. Some draft versions of the Bill of Rights did make provision for customary law to have equal status with clauses guaranteeing gender equality. But the provision never made it to the final Bill of Rights, mainly because of opposition from women delegates, who argued that some customary laws restricted women's rights.

They referred to laws which prevent women from owning land, from inheriting their husband's property or from having a say in the community decision-making body, which is composed of male elders.

Customary law has not been codified and placed on the statute books, but it has found its way into formal legal structures through the law of contract. A court hearing a dispute, usually about marriage, divorce, children and maintenance, would take customary law into account if the parties had been married under its provisions.

The Bill of Rights will change this situation. Not only does it guarantee women the right to equality before the law, it also entrenches it in a clause which says that no right may be limited by common law, customary law or any other legislation. However, customary law is likely to become an issue in South Africa, as it has in countries like Zambia and Zimbabwe. Their experience has been that legal rights have little effect on established practices, as individuals do not always know their rights and, if they do, do not have the resources to fight for them.

Education

Social, economic and bureaucratic realities in education will not change with a new political dispensation, however far it goes in enabling the restructuring of 16 racially based education departments into a unitary system open to all. With increasing numbers of black children annually entering schools ill-equipped to cope with them, the erosion of a culture of learning, soaring drop-out rates and increasing militancy on the part of teachers, schools are likely to remain a focus of conflict manifesting in sporadic boycott actions and strikes. At tertiary level, major challenges include the question of how to fund university education for those unable to afford it, the exclusion of students on financial and academic grounds, and student-driven campaigns to radically transform historically white institutions.

While the broader education debate has shifted from resistance rhetoric and state dictate to round-table discussions on how to lift education out of the morass it is in, the crucial question is whether or not the common accord on the need for a single, non-racial education system can be translated into agreement on how to achieve this: what form it should take, how it should be financed and governed and a myriad other complexities. Reviving the South African economy depends on effective education and training, yet massive education spending — 21,4 per cent of the 1993/94 budget — has yet to reap results.

Federalism

Federalism or not — that was one of the most hotly debated issues at the negotiations in Kempton Park. The agreement which was finally reached is expected to be subjected to serious strain in the five years of entrenched coalition government until 1999.

National Party negotiators insist that the basis has been laid at Kempton Park for federalism to develop as cohesion takes root among the new ruling elites in the to-be-created provinces. The South African Communist Party's Joe Slovo hailed the same deal as a victory for a unitary South Africa over federalism. Conflict seems inevitable.

Having abandoned racial categories as 'building blocks' in a future political dispensation, the NP at the negotiating table reverted to federalism as a means of limiting the powers of the central state, which they knew would be controlled by the African National Congress.

The ANC, for the same reason, preferred a unitary state which they could dominate. The movement did agree, however, to the division of South Africa into nine new provinces as a means of — in the words of its chief negotiator, Cyril Ramaphosa — 'bringing government to the people'. But at the same time the ANC insisted that the regional powers should be limited and subjected to the overriding powers of central government.

A strong case for 'true federalism' with highly autonomous provinces was put forward by some members of the conservative Freedom Alliance, notably the Inkatha Freedom Party and the Bophuthatswana government. The Conservative Party, while purportedly supporting federalism, came up with proposals that more closely resembled confederalism in the form of an independent Afrikaner homeland.

In the end an agreement was reached that, while it did not fulfil the conditions of classical federalism, it could not be rejected as *not* being federal.

The nine new provinces — largely based on the economic development regions the country was divided into by the Development Bank of Southern Africa — will take effect over the next five years while the present homeland administrations are being phased out.

The regional boundaries, powers and functions are protected in the transitional Constitution, requiring a two-thirds majority in the Senate to be changed.

The deal does not allow any exclusive powers to the provinces in which central government will have no say. It does, however, allow a long list of 'concurrent powers' between central and provincial governments with most of the original powers residing with the provinces.

Central government will, for the sake of national standards and uniformity, set the parameters within which the provinces can legalise.

Mechanisms — including the Constitutional Court — have been built into the process to ensure that a new government cannot encroach on the functional areas of the provinces. The court will in turn be bound by the constitutional principles agreed to by the Kempton Park negotiators.

The powers of central government to overrule legislation passed by the provinces are strongly qualified. Provision is made in the Constitution for the principle of subsidiarity, which means that decision-making powers are developed to the lowest level possible.

The principle of asymmetry, which allows provinces to choose how much of the available powers they want to exercise, is equally seen as a way of ensuring that those provinces which feel strongly about their autonomy can demand the maximum powers, while others only need to apply those executive functions they deem necessary.

Freedom of Expression

The battle for freedom of speech, of the press and information in South Africa has been a long and arduous one. The country has a long tradition of individuals and organisations which fought attempts to silence them. The years of National Party rule, however, saw the government steadily winning the battle to silence its critics through a battery of legislation, the closure of newspapers and the detention, banning and harassment of journalists.

By the 1980s there were over 100 laws which placed severe restrictions on the publication of information about all the important areas of South African life: military and police activity, prison life, nuclear research and the opinions of opponents to the government. Some of these were infamously ludicrous, such as the Key Points Act which prevented photographs of sensitive security installations which were never identified for fear of alerting saboteurs.

The *World* newspaper was banned in 1977 for its role in reporting the Soweto uprising. A combination of financial and political pressure also saw the closure by proprietors of the country's two leading liberal newspapers in 1985, the *Rand Daily Mail* and the *Sunday Express*.

Information repression reached its height during the States of Emergency from 1985–90, when unprecedented restrictions were placed on reporting of security force action, identifying detainees and expressing the views of banned organisations or individuals. A number of publications were seized or temporarily closed down (in particular, *The Weekly Mail, New Nation,* and *South*) and journalists were detained for lengthy periods.

Despite this, the country constantly spawned outspoken anti-government publications, such as the 'alternative newspapers' of the mid-1980s, including *The Weekly Mail, Vrye Weekblad* and *South,* and a lively bunch of journalists who were prepared to take enormous risks to fight censorship. One notable example was *Cape Times*'s editor Tony Heard, who in 1989 defied the law to run an illegal interview with African National Congress president Oliver Tambo.

There are many critics who blame a lack of media diversity on the domination of the industry by a handful of white businessmen. Afrikaans newspapers have been dominated by sycophantic National Party loyalists, the English media by the conservative mining industry. All broadcasting (excluding only those taking advantage of gaps created by the homelands system) has been in the direct control of the government, but the establishment of the Independent Broadcasting Authority (IBA) in 1994 is due to end this.

Other media — in particular film and literature —

were strictly controlled by the Publications Act, which gave enormous power to faceless bureaucrats to remove material deemed to be offensive or dangerous.

The 1990 unbannings and a sudden, new-found government commitment to press freedom brought a 'Prague Spring' when media enjoyed an unprecedented freedom to publish as they saw fit. Most of the restrictive laws remained on the statute books, but were no longer implemented. The government agreed to review all restrictive press legislation and to hand over control of the airwaves to the IBA. The censors implementing the Publications Act loosened their interpretation of the rules, unbanning a wide range of political publications and soft porn.

The agreement on a Bill of Rights in the new Constitution has also strengthened the ability of the media to defend themselves. The Bill protects freedom of expression and recognises a right to information that affects one's rights.

More recent threats to press freedom have come through violence, intimidation and political intolerance aimed at journalists, which has sometimes restricted coverage of areas of conflict.

The major organisations involved in the fight against censorship include the Anti-Censorship Action Group (Acag) and the Campaign for Open Media (Com), which planned a merger at the time of going to press, and the Media Defence Trust (MDT), which funds the defence of newspapers and journalists under threat from the state.

Tel: Acag/Com (011) 29–4355/6287

Gay Rights

The first South African gay and lesbian pride march took place in Johannesburg in October 1990 — it was also the first on the continent of Africa. Soon afterwards, a programme to collect submissions for a Lesbian and Gay Charter was put into action.

Until then, gay rights had never fully been placed on the national political agenda. The prime mover behind the march was the Gay and Lesbian Organisation of the Witwatersrand (Glow), among the first to display a truly non-racial following, along with such groups as Cape Town's Organisation of Gay and Lesbian Activists (Olga).

South African society has not been tolerant of homosexuals in the past. Apartheid era laws discriminate against them, and black traditional society often displays patriarchal disapproval. Interestingly, while some African National Congress office bearers (like Albie Sachs) have supported the drive for gay rights, others (like Tokyo Sexwale) are still capable of homophobic comments — and groups like the Pan Africanist Congress display antipathy to the idea of gay rights; Benny Alexander is on record as saying homosexuality is 'un-African'.

The 1990 march, which has been repeated annually, is the most public symbol of a campaign that, in the wake of the unbannings of liberation movements, has managed to insert the battle for gay rights into the broader struggle for human rights in a democratic South Africa.

But another event played a rather different part in crystallising gay protest: the 1991 trial of Winnie Mandela, accused of kidnapping and being a party to the murder of teenaged activist Stompie Seipei. He had been among young activists removed from the Soweto Methodist Manse and held at her home; and her defence made much of the testimony of his associate, Katiza Cebekulu, to try to show there had been paedophiliac or at least homosexual misconduct at the manse, as if thereby to justify the abduction of the youths.

The trial brought the issue of discrimination against gay people — and the social attitudes that underlie it — to the public eye.

The gay movement's activities in South Africa are centred on ensuring that the principle of non-sexism is carried out to the fullest: that there may be no discrimination against a person on the grounds of his or her sexual orientation. First included by the ANC in its draft Bill of Rights, a clause outlawing such discrimination has now been enshrined in the Fundamental Rights section of the Constitution. Such a provision will presumably render existing anti-sodomy and other 'indecency' laws — which, for instance, outlaw sexual congress between consenting adult men — illegal.

Although legal protection against discrimination for homosexuals is in sight, the battle against social prejudice in general continues.

There are still debates within the gay movement, however. The black-white split of the apartheid era has not been totally overcome, and the difficulty in settling on one unifying 'gay identity' in a society still riven by class and gender divisions has been demonstrated in various forums. There is also some disagreement over the degree of militancy that is acceptable.

Tel: Glow: Simon Nkoli, c/o Township Aids Project

(011) 982–1016, (011) 982–5621; Association of Bisexuals, Gays and Lesbians (Abigale): Midi Achmat (021) 24–1532

Gender Equality

Equal status in society for men and women is entrenched as a principle in the new Bill of Rights, which declares that 'every person shall have the right to equality before the law' and that no person may be discriminated against because of gender.

However, how to turn this principle into reality is a question which encompasses many issues. These include affirmative action, abortion rights, violence against women, customary law, marriage and maintenance.

Some women's rights activists believe that women can make great strides in all these areas by focusing on one strategy during the transition: getting women into Parliament. They argue that when a significant number of women are involved in political decision-making, they will represent the interests of women and so improve their position in society.

One organisation, The Women's Lobby, works on getting women into all levels of the political process by identifying women in community, church, political and women's groups as possible candidates. It offers workshops to educate them and lobbies political parties, business groups and the media about promoting women into policy-making positions.

Another group — Women for Women in Government — has targeted the transitional phase as a critical time for making a leap in gender equality. The campaign lobbies political parties and the media to promote a gender quota system in the elections. The idea is that candidate lists drawn up by political parties contesting the election should include significant numbers of women, at least 30 per cent.

So far, the African National Congress is the only party that has agreed to the quota, after intense lobbying by the ANC Women's League and some prominent men and women in the organisation.

Initially there was a feeling in gender equality groups that women's rights should be promoted within parties and organisations. But some women's rights advocates have become disillusioned with this approach and are considering supporting a women's party. One has been established in Cape Town and it hopes to raise enough money and support to contest the elections.

The Transitional Executive Council (TEC), whose job is to 'level the playing fields' for elections, may also play a role in gender equality through one of its subcouncils, which is devoted to women's issues. The quota system and other concerns will be canvassed there and the subcouncil can make recommendations to the TEC.

The Women's National Coalition, launched in 1992, represents almost every women's grouping in South Africa — more than 70 — from churches to unions and political parties. Its brief was to produce a women's charter which would ensure the inclusion of women's rights in the new constitution. In January 1994 the Coalition presented a research report outlining the demands of women around the country. It took just under a year to complete and included the results of over 200 focus groups, questionnaires, interviews, rallies, workshops and seminars. It will form the basis of a women's charter which was being drafted at the time of going to press.

The coalition also lobbied for the inclusion of women delegates in the negotiating teams at the multi-party negotiations and promoted discussion on a number of women's issues, particularly violence. The establishment of the coalition was an important development as it can lobby for women's issues with the weight of a huge membership behind it. However, it is sometimes hamstrung by the need to accommodate all its members and widely divergent views. The coalition's mandate from members ends when the charter is finished, and it will reassess its role at that stage.

Housing

The housing backlog of an estimated 1,35-million families is reflected in informal shack settlements springing up around metropolitan areas as urbanisation proceeds at a breathtaking pace. Provinces, local councils and non-governmental organisations have developed some settlements with varying degrees of services, ranging from pit latrines only in some areas to sites for which the Independent Development Trust has paid contractors R7 500 to get it right, with running water, water-borne sewerage, streets and stormwater drainage.

Debates centre on whether schemes should focus on the creation and consolidation of site-and-service, or on the provision of incremental (under R12 500) or starter (up to R47 500) houses. Election promises by the National Party's minister of housing to house every family are unrealistic, says the Urban Foundation, which fears the R2,5-billion currently available will not stretch far enough to meet the needs of the poorest: the 75 per cent of all homeless families who cannot afford a mortgage loan.

The Tripartite Alliance's Reconstruction and Development Programme released in January 1994 promises that 300 000 houses will be built every year for the next five years, but does not specify the level of housing to be supplied. The RDP also promises legislation outlawing redlining, which addresses another crucial issue. Building societies, badly stung in the 1980s, are reluctant to lend in areas where bond boycotts or violence have interrupted payments in the past and made repossession impossible. This makes most areas in most townships out of bounds. Institutions have extended the symbolic red line drawn around no-go areas to inner cities and suburbs where large numbers of low-income black families have moved, as well as some upper-income neighbourhoods whose equity has presumably been devalued by the appearance of shack settlements nearby.

Opponents of redlining say a refusal to lend encourages slumification, and the South African National Civic Organisation (Sanco) has been talking about legislation outlawing the practice. So has the African National Congress, although the ANC also mentions incentives to encourage banks to make credit available in these areas.

Although the UF/Association of Mortgage Lenders home loan guarantee scheme has backed up nearly 15 000 loans in the 'starter' range, more is clearly needed, and the UF, the minister of housing and the Housing Forum are studying schemes which would require the government to take much of the risk in areas in which banks and building societies are reluctant to write mortgage bonds.

Judiciary

After decades of steadily eroding public confidence in the judiciary, judges are among those who stand to gain credibility after the elections. The judiciary has been tarnished by having applied apartheid laws and legislation designed to keep the system intact. Government misuse of the courts and political appointments added to the problem.

The secret judicial appointment system which operated in the past almost invited political interference. After April 1994, however, judges are to be appointed by a Judicial Services Commission (JSC) consisting of representatives from the profession, from the existing judiciary, legal academics and elected politicians. The JSC must still formulate the rules under which it will operate, so it is not yet clear how much of the process will be open to the media and whether the public will be given the opportunity to comment on names being considered for appointment.

The judiciary has also been strongly criticised because virtually all its members are white and male.

The JSC will be very much aware of these criticisms when it begins to make new appointments. On the other hand, Chief Justice Michael Corbett, who will have a seat on the JSC, has made it clear he will not sacrifice the 'quality' he expects of a judge for political correctness. He has said it will take some years before the predominantly white male face of the judiciary is changed because of a shortage of sufficiently senior and experienced candidates who do not fit into the white male category. Others on the JSC could share this view.

The first few appointments of the JSC should give some clues about which view will predominate. After the elections, judges must be chosen for three courts, the Constitutional Court, the Appellate Division and the supreme courts in the provinces, and the JSC will play a decisive role in appointments to all three, although the criteria and procedure for appointments to the Constitutional Court differ somewhat from those to the other courts.

As to the existing judiciary, one of the last decisions of the negotiating council was to permit them to continue into the new dispensation with their jobs guaranteed, although they will be required to take a new oath of office. No provision has been made for the removal of judges seen as racist or too sympathetic to the executive. However, some in this category might take the opportunity to stand down rather than serve under a new dispensation, and decline to take the new oath.

Land

Land hunger among South Africa's rural and urban dispossessed and the political and economic strength of white farmers have turned land into one of the hotly disputed areas of South Africa's transition.

A piecemeal redistribution programme, emerging from a combination of political expedience between the government and black political opposition and solid research by non-governmental organisations, involves the provision of land to the poor and the sale of land on the open market as well as restoration — the return of land to those removed in line with apartheid policies (an estimated 3,5-million people over three decades).

In 1991, after the 1936 Land Act was abolished, the government set up an Advisory Commission on Land Allocation to hear claims from dispossessed communities to parcels of land still owned by the state and to advise the state president on his decision in each case. There was much wrong with the commission: it could deal only with state land, it could advise but not act, and it worked extremely slowly.

There were claims that state land had been hastily sold to white farmers to exclude it from the commission's jurisdiction, and certainly about a million hectares of land belonging to the South African Development Trust was transferred to the control of homelands governments, who now have sole power to decide who gets it.

In 1993, 'advisory' was dropped from the commission's name and instructions and it was given the power to act.

While property rights clauses in the new constitution have effectively ruled out large-scale nationalisation and restoration of land, there is a provision in the constitution calling on Parliament to establish a land claims court.

Organisations involved in the issue are watching closely to see what kind of court it will be and who will serve on it.

In October 1993, the World Bank released its recommendations for redistribution of land. In a report compiled by South African academics and non-governmental organisations with some participation by officials of the African National Congress, it was recommended land be bought from white farmers at fair prices and sold to black farmers, who would pay for it with a combination of government or donor grants, loans and equity.

The Tripartite Alliance's Reconstruction and Development Programme published in January 1994 proposes a combination of market and non-market mechanisms to provide land for redistribution and services to help new farmers use their land productively. Thirty per cent of agricultural land would be redistributed within five years. For restoration, a land claims court would have judged all claims within five years.

Nationalisation

African National Congress economic policy has come a long way since Nelson Mandela, before his release in February 1990, restated unequivocally its support for nationalisation of mines, banks and monopoly industry.

When Mandela said modification of the ANC's views on the subject was unthinkable, he was merely reflecting long-standing commitment to the Freedom Charter, produced in the mid-1950s, long before nationalisation had fallen into its present disfavour in the Western world. In exile, the ANC had stuck to the policy of nationalisation as a means of transferring white control to the majority.

But the 'N-word' proved a powerful invocation of fear and loathing in South African business and media. So fierce was international opposition that it was quickly downplayed if not dropped from ANC policy. In particular, opposition from Scandinavian social democracies and ANC allies in Eastern Europe swayed ANC leadership.

In the most recent ANC economic policy document it is stated that nationalisation will be considered 'if such actions will strengthen the ability of the economy to respond to massive inequalities . . .'

The sidelining of nationalisation is part of a broader shift in ANC policy thinking from strict socialist policies and a change in its attitude to business.

However, while ANC leadership has more or less abandoned the policy of nationalisation, there is some evidence that nationalisation as a concept still commands a good deal of grassroots support. The fear abides in the business community that it will be taken up as a popular cry once again some time in the future.

Political Tolerance

The absence of a culture of political tolerance is one of the most serious issues in the run-up to an election. The habits of state political repression, including the way it legitimised counter-attack by its victims, are proving hard to get rid of. In particular, some organisations and individuals who were previously restricted in their political activities are now challenging — sometimes violently — the right of white political parties to operate in townships. Officials of bodies such as the South African National Civic Organisation argue that the playing fields are not yet level and therefore these parties do not have the right to exercise their political freedom. In particular, the Democratic Party and the National Party have had meetings disrupted by township activists.

In addition, the intensity of the conflict between political organisations, such as between the Inkatha

Freedom Party and the African National Congress, has spiralled to the point where in some areas they do not recognise each other's right to operate. This has been fuelled by the spiral of revenge for previous attacks and has created large 'no-go' areas for certain political parties, particularly in Natal/kwaZulu and the East Rand.

In Bophuthatswana, the ANC and its allies are still severely harassed by the authorities, making it difficult to envisage free political activity during the election campaign.

The Transitional Executive Council is charged with ensuring free political activity during the election campaign, and will be assisted by foreign monitors from the United Nations, the Organisation of African Unity, the Commonwealth and the European Community.

Privatisation

This will be the litmus test of African National Congress economic policy in future.

The ANC has more or less abandoned nationalisation and become much more accommodating of business in its thinking. That it has not embraced privatisation is one sign that it is still far from being a party with whom business can feel entirely comfortable.

Its reasons for distrusting privatisation are manifold. Partly this is the lingering hangover of the objection to privatisation by the Nationalist government in the days when the ANC still favoured nationalisation. Privatisation was seen as a selling off of the family silver before the heir apparent, the ANC, could inherit it.

That then state president PW Botha became an ardent

proponent of privatisation in the dying days of his rule does not endear the concept to those on the left. Indeed, ANC and union opposition has been so bitter that the government has been stalled at the commercialisation stage of the process where — preparatory to privatisation — state corporations become more efficiently run companies, though still state-owned.

At least some in the ANC betray a persistent desire to effect change (or retard it) through direct control. For instance, ANC telecommunications spokesman Andile Ngcaba said the privatisation of telecommunications monopoly Telkom was impossible because jobs would be lost.

There is still a feeling in the ANC that government intervention, albeit of the Far Eastern model rather than the Eastern European, can be relied on to restructure the economy on a new dynamic growth path.

Redistribution

'Redistribution of wealth' has been the rallying cry of the left since other strategies like nationalisation have fallen into disfavour.

A key element originally of ANC economic thinking was 'growth through redistribution', a version of the earlier 'inward industrialisation' advocated by conservative establishment figures during the apartheid era.

Business and those on the right insisted in reaction that 'redistribution through growth' was the correct strategy, and that a trickle-down of wealth would be a better way of uplifting the poor than what they saw as Robin Hood policies.

The redistribution approach assumes policies that will

put money in the pockets of the poor will kickstart the economy without draining money from the foreign exchange reserves of the country. It smacks of the macro-economic populism that ruined Latin American countries and is too inward looking to find much favour with economists.

A focus on growth alone, however, will not address the inequalities created by apartheid and is sure to run into political trouble.

Hence there has been a reassuring tendency by left and right alike to adopt a middle path of 'growth with redistribution'.

Third Force Violence

'The third force' is a vague phrase used loosely to describe those allegedly responsible for violence that, in recent years, has appeared to be professionally organised and politically motivated. Generally, the phrase is used to express concerns that far right wing members or former members of the security forces, particularly those involved in the 'dirty war' against government opponents in the 1980s, are fomenting violence in order to disrupt or prevent political change.

These fears have been fuelled by the Trust Feed Case, in which policemen were convicted in 1992 of undertaking a political massacre and senior officers were implicated in the alleged cover-up; recent accusations by Justice Richard Goldstone that members of Inkatha who received covert military training in the 1980s have been involved in hit-squad activities; Judge Goldstone's 1992 raid on Military Intelligence offices; and President FW de Klerk's dismissal of top generals in a December 1992 clean-up.

The uncertain definition of the 'third force', however, gets to the nub of debate over the causes of recent political violence in the townships. One school of thought is that those responsible for the hit-squads and other covert activities of the past, most notably the Department of Military Intelligence, continued this activity beyond 1990. Recent clampdowns by the government may have driven these units out of formal military structures, but there is a fear that their operations have been 'privatised' and they are now operating as free agents. Another school, led by the government, suggests that the cause of violence is simply ANC-Inkatha political rivalry and it has not needed outside fuelling. A more complex, and highly controversial, suggestion is that the current violence is the long-term outcome of the African National Congress's promotion of ungovernability, boycotts and violence during the 1980s.

Another obvious factor is the social and economic conditions that make groupings, such as squatter camp residents and hostel-dwellers, ripe for manipulation by those who want conflict.

5
Statistics

Vital indicators of the country's geo- and socio-politics

Contents

Population statistics	282
Age	284
Rural:urban proportion	285
Home language	285
Major population centres	286
Level of education (see also Education)	288
Income	290
Employment and unemployment	292
Crime and violence	294
Basic health indicators	297
Education (see also Level of education)	299
Poverty	301

Unless otherwise indicated the term "South Africa" refers to the area within the 1910 Union of South Africa boundaries including the nominally independent homelands of Transkei, Bophuthatswana, Ciskei and Venda (TBVC). Many official and semi-official statistics omit the TBVC territories. The term "coloured" in the South Africa context refers to people of mixed race origin.

Population statistics

Mid-1993 estimates of South Africa's population outside the TBVC are 32 589 000 of which 5.149-million are white, 3.402-million coloured, 1 022-million Asian and 23.016-million black.

Source: *Demographic statistics 1993.* Central Statistical Service.

GRAPH 1: SOUTH AFRICA POPULATION 1991

TOTAL ESTIMATE: 38.9-MILLION

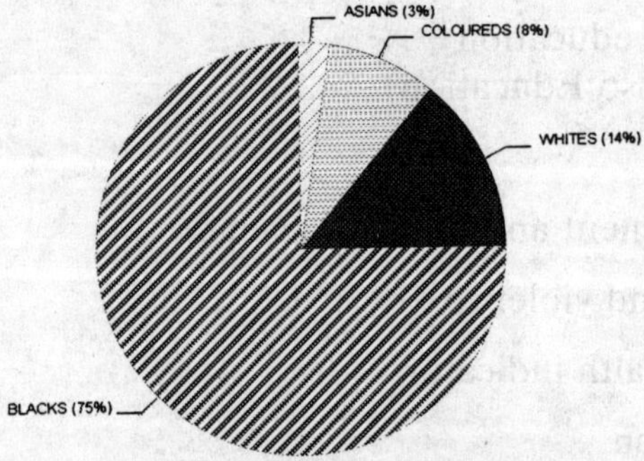

Source: Development Bank of Southern Africa.

Bureau for Market Research estimates indicate the population will reach 47.5-million by 2000. Department of National Health figures for the number of children per woman in 1991 were: whites 1.7, Asians 2.3, coloureds 2.8 and blacks 4.7.

The population of South Africa including the TBVC homelands is some 39.54-million living in a country of about 1.22-million km^2. Some demographic feature comparisons of "white" South Africa and the homelands are as follows:

TABLE I	Area (km^2)	Population (1993 estimate)	Population growth 1985-93 (%)	Density (persons per km^2)	Urbanisation rate 1993 (%)
South Africa total	**1 220 088**	**39 541 954**	**2.06**	**32**	**50.0**
Transkei	43 654	3 330 169	1.85	76	6.0
Bophuthatswana	40 011	2 125 804	2.53	53	17.8
Venda	5 807	598 975	3.38	98	5.1
Ciskei	9 100	887 728	1.54	107	39.2
Gazankulu	7 484	1 042 634	7.12	139	7.1
KaNgwane	3 917	897 382	9.41	229	11.1
KwaNdebele	2 208	445 885	5.69	202	19.9
KwaZulu	36 074	5 880 185	3.96	168	23.6
Lebowa	22 137	2 864 196	3.32	134	7.2
QwaQwa	1 040	379 034	6.67	363	8.7

Source: Development Bank of Southern Africa Development Information Group. November 1993.

Age

Over 10-million of the almost 32-million people living in South Africa outside the TBVC falls in the age group 5-19 years and over 8-million are in the 20-34 year old group.

GRAPH 2: AGE DISTRIBUTION
(EXCLUDING TBVC)

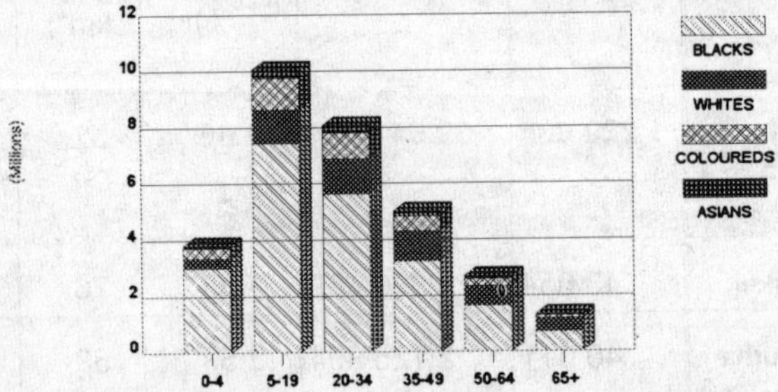

Source: 1991 Population census. Central Statistical Service.

According to the 1991 population census 46.9% of the population outside the TBVC was under the age of 21. A more detailed age breakdown is as follows:

TABLE 2	**Total**	Whites	Coloureds	Asians	Blacks
65 yrs+	**4.3%**	9.4%	3.4%	3.4%	3.3%
<3 yrs	**7.1%**	4.0%	6.6%	5.7%	8.0%
<6 yrs	**14.6%**	8.4%	13.6%	12.0%	16.3%
<18 yrs	**40.8%**	27.3%	40.1%	36.9%	44.2%
<21 yrs	**46.9%**	32.6%	47.1%	43.1%	50.4%
Average	**25.7yrs**	33.2 yrs	25.0 yrs	26.9 yrs	23.9 yrs

Rural:urban proportion

Outside the TBVC, 56.6% of the population live in urban areas and 43.4% in non-urban areas. A further breakdown is as follows:

TABLE 3	Total	Whites	Coloureds	Asians	Blacks
Urban	56.6%	91.1%	83.2%	96.2%	42.7%
Non-urban	43.4%	8.9%	16.8%	3.8%	57.3%

Source: *Demographic statistics 1993*. Central Statistical Service.

According to the Development Bank of Southern Africa annual report of 1993, *functional* urbanisation in South Africa as a whole is 66 percent. See Table 1 for further information.

Home language

The most widely spoken home language in South Africa outside the TBVC is Zulu which has over 8.35-million speakers. Afrikaans comes next with 5.75-million and English fourth as the home language of 3.4-million people.

TABLE 4: Major home languages excluding TBVC			
Zulu	8 354 470	Afrikaans	5 750 814
North Sotho	3 458 638	English	3 436 717
Xhosa	2 513 411	South Sotho	2 240 430
Tswana	1 443 478	Shangaan/Tsonga	1 440 932
Swazi	953 918	Other	1 394 112

Source: 1991 Population census. Central Statistical Service.

Because these rankings exclude the ethnically-based TBVC territories, they are misleading. Xhosa is spoken and has official status in Transkei and Ciskei and the same applies to Tswana in Bophuthatswana and to Venda in Venda. The combined population of Transkei and Ciskei is 4.2-million (Table 1) which, if added to 2.5-million Xhosa speakers in the rest of the country (Table 4), totals 6.7-million. This suggests that Xhosa should rank as the second most widely spoken language after Zulu. Similarly, the number of Tswana mother tongue speakers should rank alongside that of North Sotho with 2.1-million people living in Bophuthatswana and 1.4-million speakers living in the rest of the country.

The small numbers of blacks speaking English and Afrikaans as home languages appear to support this hypothesis:

TABLE 5: Afrikaans and English as home languages excl TBVC

	Whites	Coloureds	Asians	Blacks
Afrikaans	57.5%	83.2%	1.3%	0.4%
English	38.7%	15.0%	94.9%	0.2%

Source: 1991 Population census. Central Statistical Service

Major population centres

According to the 1991 census there were 4 865 827 people living in the Johannesburg/Randburg/East Rand/West Rand (Witwatersrand) urban area. The Pretoria/Witwatersrand/Vereeniging (PWV) area was home to 6 719 578 people on census day, or over 21 percent of the population outside the TBVC. One of every three people live in Transvaal and one in four in Natal/KwaZulu (TBVC excluded).

TABLE 6: Major population centres (1991 census districts)	
Johannesburg/Randburg	1 916 063
East Rand	1 378 792
Far East Rand	700 906
West Rand	870 066
Pretoria/Wonderboom/Soshanguve	1 080 187
Vereeniging/Vanderbijlpark/Sasolburg	773 594
Klerksdorp	321 478
Durban/Pinetown/Inanda	1 137 378
Pietermaritzburg	228 549
Cape Peninsula	2 350 157
Port Elizabeth/Uitenhage	853 204
King William's Town/East London	270 127
Kimberley	167 060
Bloemfontein	300 150
OFS Goldfields	427 569

These are all urban areas in the "white" part of South Africa falling under the jursidication of a formal local authority. As can be seen in Table 1, the homelands are predominantly rural although high population densities may indicate that there are *functionally* urban population concentrations in these areas as well. QwaQwa, for instance, consists only of the Witsieshoek district with a population of 379 034 (Table 1).

Level of education

According to the 1991 census, 84.3% of South Africans over the age of seven outside the TBVC are literate. This is defined as people who can speak, read and write at least one language.The Development Bank of Southern Africa puts adult literacy in South Africa at 73.2% and, according to the Department of National Health and Population Development, the literacy rate is 69% (TBVC included). Estimates of *functional* literacy are as low as 50%. Over 3-million people over 18 outside the TBVC have no formal education at all.

TABLE 7A: Highest level of education (excluding TBVC)

	Total	Whites	Coloureds	Asians	Blacks
None: <6yrs	4 529 354	425 429	447 186	118 847	3 537 892
None: 6-18yrs	1 381 540	93 389	108 961	19 457	1 159 733
None: 18yrs+	3 010 039	31 993	216 175	41 052	2 720 819
None: total	8 920 933	550 811	772 322	179 356	7 418 444
Std 1-5	9 904 739	569 767	1 207 222	232 097	7 895 653
Std 6-10	10 429 754	3 033 963	1 196 393	510 921	5 688 477
Std7-10 +certificate/dipl.	744 722	477 399	53 487	26 517	187 379

According to the census, over 90% of the population over 18 with no formal education are black while 84% of the population with university education are white. Of the people whose highest level of education was a first degree on census day, over 82% were white and of those with postgraduate degrees, 88% were white. Blacks with doctorates comprised a mere 6.4% of the population outside the TBVC in 1991.

Table 7B: Highest level of education (excluding TBVC)
University educated population

	Total	Whites	Coloureds	Asians	Blacks
Bachelor's degree	**305 306**	252 128	9 577	15 816	27 785
Bachelor+ certificate/ diploma	**61 339**	52 750	3 507	3 247	1 835
Master's	**27 349**	25 343	410	952	644
Master's+ certificate/ diploma	**4 835**	4 426	98	129	182
Doctorate	**10 553**	9 100	237	473	743
Doctorate+ certificate/ diploma	**1 870**	1 715	31	67	57
Total with university education	**411 252**	345 462	13 860	20 684	31 246

Source: 1991 Population census. Central Statistical Service.

Income

Per capita monthly income at 1990 prices was blacks R160; coloureds R270; Asians R470 whites R1 300 (Department of National Health). 1991 census information on earners who specified their incomes shows 38.6% of whites and 40% of Asians earned between R10 000 and R29 999 compared with 24.5% of coloureds and 18.5% of blacks in this category. Most coloureds (28.4%) and most blacks (32.8%) fell in the income group R1 000-R2 999 per annum. The following information is drawn from the 1991 population census:

GRAPH 3: ANNUAL INCOME (TBVC EXCLUDED)

ALL RACES: 11 034 660 INCOME EARNERS

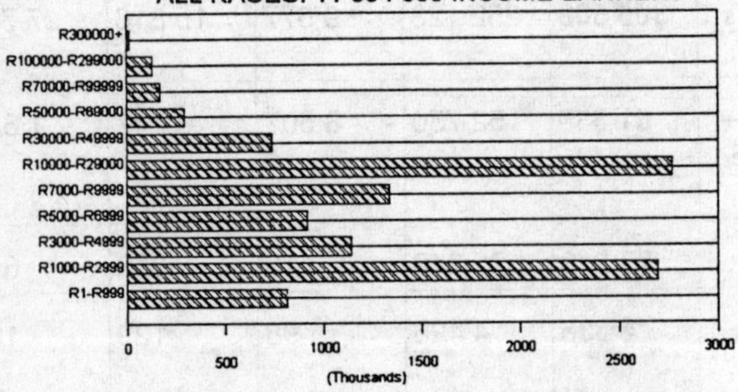

GRAPH 4: ANNUAL INCOME (TBVC EXCLUDED)

WHITES: 2 867 668 INCOME EARNERS

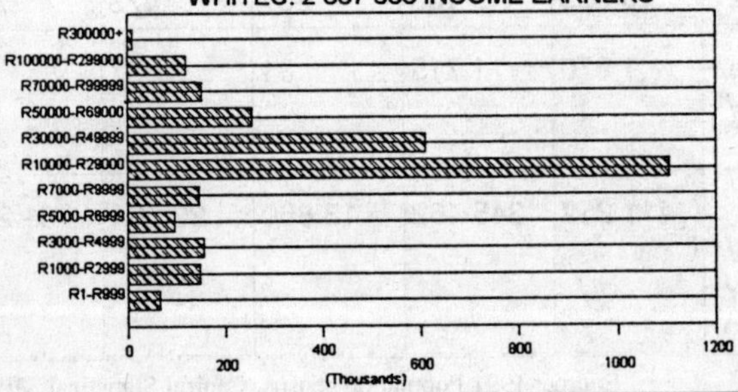

GRAPH 5: ANNUAL INCOME (TBVC EXCLUDED)

ASIANS: 382 585 INCOME EARNERS

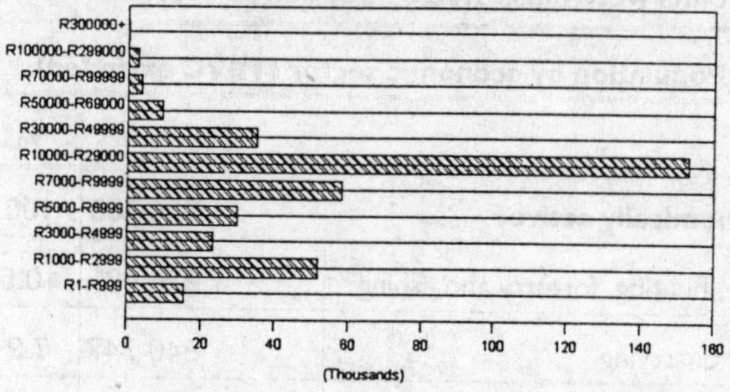

GRAPH 6: ANNUAL INCOME (TBVC EXCLUDED)

COLOUREDS: 1 296 021 INCOME EARNERS

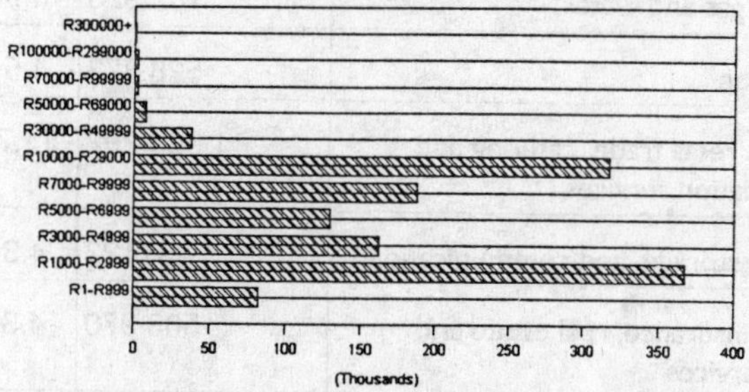

GRAPH 7: ANNUAL INCOME (TBVC EXCLUDED)

BLACKS: 6 488 388 INCOME EARNERS

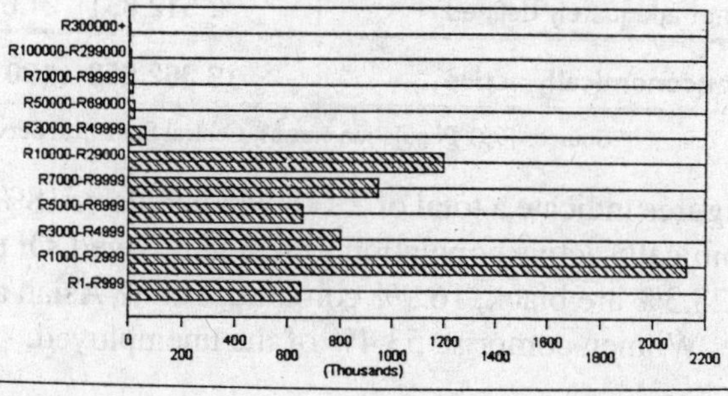

Employment and unemployment

South Africans were classified by economic sector as follows:

TABLE 8: Population by economic sector (TBVC excluded)		
	Total	%
Total economically active	**11 624 368**	**100**
Agriculture, hunting, forestry and fishing	1 224 435	10.5
Mining and quarrying	840 747	7.2
Manufacturing	1 417 127	12.2
Electricity, gas and water	102 928	0.9
Construction	526 373	4.5
Wholesale, retail trade, catering and accommodation services	1 385 292	11.7
Transport, storage, and communication	497122	4.3
Financing, insurance, real estate and business services	503 970	4.3
Community, social and personal services	2 640 521	22.8
Activities not adequately defined	2 512 851	21.6
Total not economically active	**19 362 552**	**100**

Source: 1991 Population census. Central Statistical Service.

Census figures indicate a total of 2 118 648 people or 18% of the economically active population were unemployed. Of this number, 23.3% are black, 16.9% coloured, 12.7% Asian and 4% white. Women comprise 53.4% of the unemployed.

According to the National Manpower Commission (NMC), the real proportion of unemployment (TBVC included) is about 39% of the economically active population (EAP) or 4.9-million people. The NMC says about 300 000 people enter the labour market every year, or 1 200 every working day. Only 15 000 formal job opportunities were created every year between 1981 and 1991, meaning only about 5% of all new entrants to the market are employed in the formal economy every year. Between September 1989 and the second quarter of 1992 at least 250 000 jobs were lost of which 117 000 were in the mining sector, 67 000 in manufacturing and 42 000 in construction.

TABLE 9: Composition of the economically active population (EAP) of South Africa.

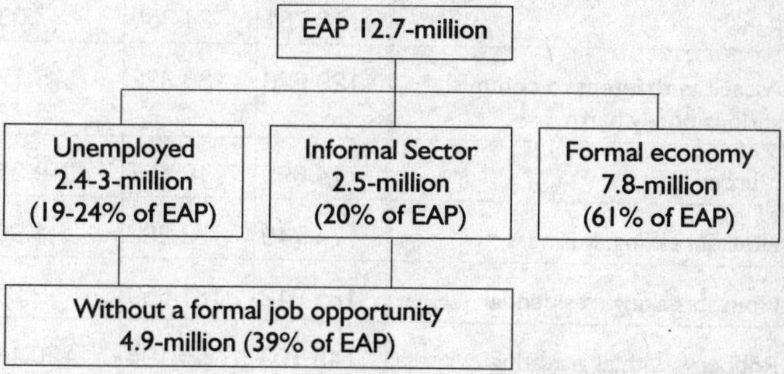

Source: National Manpower Commission Annual Report 1992.

Unemployment in the homelands is significantly worse than in South Africa as a whole. According to the Development Bank of Southern Africa, the participation of economically active people in the economy was 56.9% for South Africa. This figure for the TBVC as a whole was 33.7% and for the self-governing homelands, 40%.

Crime and violence

South African Police (SAP) statistics indicate 1 781 861 cases of serious crime were reported in 1992 outside the TBVC, of which 53.2% were solved. Details of reported serious crimes in 1992 were as follows:

TABLE 10: Serious crime	1991	1992	%change
Illegal strikes	24	50	+108.33
Public violence	2 402	2 250	-6.33
Illegal possession of firearms and ammunition	9 706	10 580	+9
Explosives Act	378	448	+18.52
Rape	22 761	24 360	+7.03
Assault with intent to commit serious bodily harm	129 626	136 322	+5.17
Murder	14 693	16 067	+9.35
Housebreaking: business	74 749	73 282	-1.96
Housebreaking: residential	185 912	181 659	-2.29
Robbery: with aggravating circumstances	45 103	54 194	+20.16
Robbery: other robberies	23 833	24 483	+2.73
Stock theft (excluding poultry)	24 116	26 921	+11.63
Shoplifting	51 658	58 371	+13
Theft: bicycle	25 538	23 524	-7.89

TABLE 10: Serious crime	1991	1992	%change
Theft: motor vehicle	71 120	71 532	+0.58
Theft: from motor vehicles	160 179	154 247	-3.7
Thefts not mentioned elsewhere	251 507	259 690	+3.25
Fraud, forgery, malappropriation, embezzlement etc.	55 280	58 576	+5.96
Arson	23 920*	6 389	-73.29
Malicious damage to property	92 676	96 138	+3.74
Insolvency Act	403	435	+7.94
Driving under the influence of alcohol or drugs	32 073	32 157	+0.26
Crimes related to prostitution	190	210	+10.53
Sodomy	755	777	+2.91
Incest	227	187	-17.62
Indecent assault	2 961	3 180	+7.4
Intercourse with a girl under the prescribed age and/or female imbecile	647	669	+3.4
Child-theft	1 494	1 698	+13.65
Cruelty towards and ill-treatment of children (excluding sexual offences, assault and murder)	1 556	1 465	-5.85

*Including 12 000 "dubious" reported cases of arson in 1991.

Source: Annual report of the Commissioner of the South African Police. 1992.

The incidence of crime increased to 8 500 crimes per 100 000 population in 1992. The SAP blames over 65% of crime on unemployment and deprivation. The number of murders per 100 000 population was 77 with 176 in Natal and 110 in the Soweto/ Witwatersrand area. The rate of armed robbery per 100 000 was 375 and for rape, 116. The SAP say 0.72% of serious crime was committed with a political motive. Of the 16 067 murders in 1992, 2 036 of these (12.67%) were committed with a political motive. Murders of SAP members steadily increased from 71 in 1989 to 224 in 1992.

(Source: Annual report of the Commissioner of the South African Police 1992).

TABLE 11: Deaths in political violence

	HRC	SAP	SAIRR
1985			879
1986			1 298
1987		454	661
1988		653	1 149
1989		659	1 403
1990		2 674	3 699
1991	2 582	2 240	2 672
1992		2 036	
1993	4 364		

Sources: Human Rights Commission, South African Institute of Race Relations, South African Police.

Basic health indicators

Blacks and coloureds are markedly worse off than whites and Asians with respect to basic health:

TABLE 12: Basic health indicators 1990

	Asian	Black	Coloured	White
Life expectancy male	64.5	57.8	57.6	69.4
Life expectancy female (years)	71.2	64.8	65.7	76.5
Birth rate/1000 population	20.4	35.0	22.2	13.7
Crude mortality rate/1 000 population	4.4	8.3	7.7	6.7
Population growth rate/100 population	1.6	2.4	1.4	0.7
Infant mortality rate/1000 live births	10.6	52.8	39.4	8.6
Maternal mortality rate/100 000 live births (excl TBVC)	15	23	30	3
Childhood mortality rate (1-4 years old) per 1 000 population	0.9	1.2	2.6	0.8
Deaths 0-4 years as a percentage of all deaths (excl TBVC)	6.4	17.8	15.2	2.5

Source: *Health trends in South Africa 1992*. Department of National Health and Population Development.

TABLE 13: Incidence of some notifiable diseases 1991				
	Asians	Blacks	Coloureds	Whites
Tuberculosis/100 000 population	57	191	652	15
Measles /100 000 population	2.6	9.3	4.2	2.7
Typhoid/100 000 population	1.8	5.1	1.1	0.4
Meningitis/100 000 population	0.4	1.8	9.4	0.7

Source: *Health trends in South Africa 1992*. Department of National Health and Population Development.

South African National Tuberculosis Association estimates of the extent of tuberculosis are that there are over 100 000 new cases of the disease every year or 235 per 100 000 population, ten times more than the incidence in developed countries and 15% above the African average.

Aids is not a notifiable disease in South Africa and many varied estimates of the extent of full-blown Aids and HIV infection have been published. According to the National Manpower Commission, the disease is most prevalent in the most economically and reproductively active group of 20-39 years old, approximately 400 000 people are already infected and 400 new infections are occurring every day. If no antidote has been found by 2000, South Africa is expected to have between 3.7-million and 4.3-million HIV carriers and a total of between 600 000 and 1.1-million people are expected to have died from Aids.

(Source: National Manpower Commission Annual report 1992.)

Education

The inequalities in levels of education (Table 7) are underpinned by inequalities in the provision of school education:

TABLE 14: Primary and secondary school education 1991.

Department	Pupils	Teachers	Pupil: teacher	Expenditure/ pupil (R)
House of Assembly (Whites):				
Cape	225 894	15 388	15:1	3 553
OFS	115 030	6 780	17:1	3 135
Natal	71 956	5 033	14:1	3 807
Transvaal	515 142	28 989	18:1	2 961
House of Delegates (Asians):	234 550	12 873	18:1	2 961
House of Representatives (Coloureds)	858 774	36 510	24:1	1 521
Education and Training (Blacks outside the homelands)	2 361 403	59 913	39:1	644
Gazankulu	338 611	8 453	40:1	572
KaNgwane	246 816	6 351	39:1	428
KwaNdebele	149 834	3 874	39:1	572

Department	Pupils	Teachers	Pupil: teacher	Expen- diture/ pupil (R)
KwaZulu	1 614 665	32 872	49:1	402
Lebowa	972 743	25 712	38:1	678
QwaQwa	110 937	3 387	33:1	910
Transkei	1 205 713	24 433	49:1	na
Bophuthatswana	579 287	18 781	31:1	na
Venda	243 626	7 520	32:1	na
Ciskei	269 865	6 901	39:1	na
Total	10 114 846	303 770	33:11	940

Source: Spangenberg, JP. *Education in South Africa: a regional overview 1991*. Midrand: Development Bank of Southern Africa.

TABLE 15: Matric results 1991

	Blacks	Coloureds	Asians	Whites	**Total**
Candidates	304 315	22 405	14 258	65 933	406 911
Pass (%)	46%	83%	95%	96%	54%
Exemption	10%	21%	49%	42%	17%

Source: South African Institute of Race Relations.

In 1992 44% of black matric candidates passed and in 1993 the success rate declined to 38.5%. Over R27-billion or 21.4% of the 1993/94 Budget was allocated to education. This is 7.3% of the country's gross domestic product.

Poverty

Bureau for Market Research figures indicate that in 1989 40% of the South African population was living below the minimum living level (MLL). The MLL is a measure of the smallest amount of money on which people can live.

GRAPH 8: PERCENTAGE OF POPULATION

BELOW MINIMUM LIVING LEVEL 1989

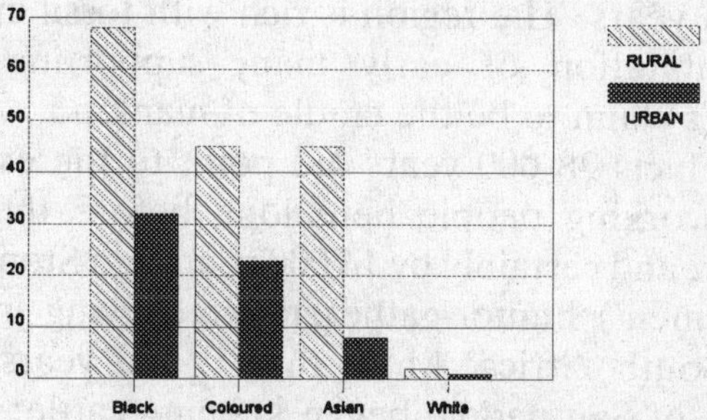

Source: *Health trends in South Africa 1992*. Department of National Health and Population Development.

At least 18-million of South Africa's population fall below the MLL and between eight and nine million blacks are "completely destitute". Achieving minimum living standards for the whole population (basic education, adult education and training, primary health care, housing, electrification, rural development, access to land, small business development, social security, welfare, telecommunication, transport, water and sanitation) will cost R57-billion over the next five years.

(Source: Professor Wiseman Nkuhlu, chairman of the Development Bank of Southern Africa, quoted in *Cape Times*, October 22 1993).

6

History

A concise chronology of what happened when in South Africa

Hunter-gatherers have lived in southern Africa for two million years. The region is rich with fossil evidence of the habitation of early man, supporting southern Africa's claim to be the cradle of mankind.

Artefacts 28 000 years old point to the existence of stone-working people here long before the dawn of history, and certainly by 14 000 years ago Stone Age San ('Bushmen') hunter-gatherers were living in areas all over South Africa. More than 2 000 years ago, one stream of San people began keeping cattle; they were forerunners of the Khoikhoi ('Hottentots'). It is assumed they took to herding after contact with Iron Age Bantu-speaking pastoralists north of present-day South Africa. Archaeological evidence shows Bantu-speaking people settled in Natal and the Transvaal rather later than this encounter — around AD 300 — and in the eastern Cape about 1 000 years ago.

'Bantu' refers to a group of about 300 sub-Saharan African languages to which all indigenous South African languages other than Khoikhoi and San (Khoisan) belong. The Bantu-speaking people are divided into two main groups, the Nguni and the Sotho, based on linguistic and cultural factors.

Traditionally, political units were small, being chiefdoms comprising clans. But some time before 1600 Nguni clans began to expand their power and incorporate neighbouring clans; it was the beginning of a period of formation of larger political units in chiefdoms or kingdoms. The best-known chief in this process was Tshawe, who founded the Xhosa kingdom.

Towards the end of the 18th century, loose confederations began forming among the northern Nguni. The Ndwandwe under Zwide, the Ngwane under Sobhuza, and the Mthethwa under Dingiswayo were the largest of these groupings. Dingiswayo and Zwide drafted men into age regiments (amabutho) to subjugate weaker neighbours and take control of land and access to the Delagoa Bay trade route. A drought and the ensuing famine in 1801–2 put immense pressure on resources and population and set in motion a period of intense conflict.

The term mfecane or difaqane ('crushing') is used to describe the 'reign of terror' of the Zulu king Shaka, deploying conscripted armies to destroy other chiefdoms, steal grain and cattle, kill opponents and absorb survivors into the Zulu kingdom. The effects of this dispersal of many kingdoms were felt far to the north of the present borders of South Africa.

The occurrence of the mfecane is disputed, but it is generally agreed that there was a great deal of conflict and dispersion between 1795 and 1870 which coincided with the expansion of kingdoms and military power and, in its final stages, with the Great Trek, when whites moved into the interior.

There are indications that Table Bay was a port of call for Phoenician trading ships. However, documented trade between Europeans and indigenous people only began in about 1450, with Portuguese explorers looking for a sea route to the East.

Portugal's trade monopoly with the East was broken by 1510, when the Portuguese viceroy of India and 150 men were killed in a clash with Khoikhoi in Table Bay. Not long afterwards, the Dutch moved in to fill the vacuum, and by the mid-17th century, they had established permanent settlements.

Significant dates in a chronology of conflict

1652 The Dutch East India Company sets up a refreshment station at the Cape under Jan van Riebeeck. He refuses to recognise Khoikhoi title to the land.

1658 After the Company refuses to allow Van Riebeeck to enslave the Khoikhoi, a group of slaves arrives from Angola and West Africa, scores of them transferred from a Portuguese slaving ship.

1659 The first of several Khoikhoi wars fails to push the Dutch out of the Cape.

1688 Settler numbers are increased by the arrival of the Huguenots, French Protestants fleeing religious persecution.

c1690 The Trekboers, a class of wandering white farmers, move west into the hinterland. Many of these take land and animals from the Khoikhoi.

1690 A slave uprising at Stellenbosch fails.

1713 A smallpox epidemic decimates the Khoikhoi.

1780 The Dutch 'forcibly remove' Xhosa chiefdoms living east of the Great Fish River; later this is named the First Frontier War.

1795 The British capture the Dutch garrison at the Cape and seize control of the region, ending 150 years of Dutch rule.

1801-2 A period of serious drought in Natal and elsewhere is followed by the Madlathule famine, adding to the pressure for land and resources.

1809 The Hottentot Proclamation, issued by the British in the Cape Colony, introduces pass laws to South Africa.

1815 Shaka succeeds Senzangakona as chief of the Zulu after having led Dingiswayo's Mthethwa army. He builds age regiments into fierce fighting units and carves out the Zulu kingdom.

1819 Shaka defeats the Ndwandwe under Zwide, the last serious rival to his power, and builds a powerful army with which to extend his kingdom. He becomes notorious for his cruelty.

1820 Nearly 4 000 British settlers, attracted by the offer of free land and free passage, arrive at Algoa Bay.

Their recruitment is a plan by British authorities to use them as part-time soldiers on the eastern frontier. Although many try their hand at farming, most eventually settle into towns.

1828 Shaka is assassinated by two of his brothers, Mhlangane and Dingane.

1834 Slaves are freed in the Cape by the British authorities, although the trekkers continue kidnapping black children for use as slaves until about 1850.

1835-6 Louis Trichardt, Hans van Rensburg and Andries Potgieter lead Afrikaner treks to the north in the first of a series of mass emigrations. A series of battles ensues as the trekkers encounter Ndebele, Zulu and others.

1836 Trekkers defeat the Ndebele in the Battle of Vegkop.

1837 A combined trekker, Griqua and Rolong force defeat the Ndebele and drive them across the Limpopo.

1838 In February, Voortrekker leader Piet Retief and his party are stoned to death by warriors on the command of Zulu chief Dingane; days later Dingane's men kill 500 people at a trekker encampment. At the end of that year, on 16 December, fewer than 500 trekkers defeat 10 000 Zulu warriors. The site of the battle is renamed Blood River by the Voortrekkers who hold the day sacred as evidence of a covenant between themselves and the Lord.

1846 Swazi chief Mswati grants trekkers land in the eastern Transvaal.

The British set up a locations commission to divide Natal up among blacks and whites.

1847-8 Victoria East and British Kaffraria are established on Xhosa land.

1852 Transvaal Boers are granted independence in terms of the Sand River Convention.

1854 Boer commandos lay siege to an Ndebele community who have taken refuge in a northern Transvaal cave with their leader Makopane to avoid slave raids; more than 1 000 die.

1858 Xhosa resistance to the British crumbles after numerous wars and the great cattle killing which follows the vision of a young Xhosa woman, Nongqawuse. A famine follows the mass slaughter of cattle and burning of crops which it had been believed would result in the withdrawal of the British.

1860 The first indentured Indian labourers arrive in Natal.

1867 In the first diamond rush, prospectors rush to Hopetown on the Orange River after a stone found on a nearby farm turns out to be a diamond.

c1870 Indian traders, called 'passengers' to distinguish them from indentured labourers, arrive to set up businesses in South Africa.

1870 A hut tax payable only in cash is introduced to force blacks off the land and into the employ of whites.

1871 Gold is discovered in the eastern Transvaal. It ushers in the era of migrant labour as young black men travel to the mines to earn enough cash to pay their hut taxes.

1872 The Cape Colony takes control of the Transkei.

1879 Griqualand East is annexed to the Cape and a combined British-Swazi force crushes the Pedi under Sekhukhune.

The British try to make sure only whites have guns after an ignominious defeat at the hands of the Zulu at Isandhlwana.

A law is passed in the Transvaal forbidding any person of colour to be a licence holder or hold any connection with the mines other than being in the service of a white person.

No blacks are allowed to own land in the Transvaal.

1882 Trekkers declare the republics of Stellaland and Goshen on Tswana land.

1884 Xhosa newspaper *Imvo Zabantsundu* is started under John Tengo Jabavu, providing a voice against pass laws and other racist legislation.

1885 An outbreak of phylloxera destroys vineyards throughout the Cape. Mining companies move to consolidate their land holdings.

1886 The Main Reef of gold-bearing ore is found on the farm Langlaagte, on the Witwatersrand, drawing thousands of miners from Britain, Europe and the United States as well as from other parts of southern Africa.

1887 The Cape passes the Parliamentary Voters' Registration Act to nullify tribal land tenure as a basis for property qualification for the vote.

1888 Cecil Rhodes wrests control of all the Kimberley diamond mines.

1892 The Cape Franchise and Ballot Act triples property qualifications for the franchise, excluding even more blacks. Defiance against headmen enforcing unpopular government regulations starts to take root.

1892-7 Rinderpest sweeps through the country, decimating herds of cattle, forcing many formerly successful subsistence farmers off the land.

1893 Mohandas Gandhi arrives in South Africa and is soon associated with passive resistance campaigns against anti-Indian legislation.

1893-6 Cecil Rhodes forces the Ndebele to pay over 100 000 cattle in 'levies' and uses British South Africa Company police to enforce hut tax collection.

1894 Pondoland is annexed to the British empire. The Glen Grey Act, brokered by Cecil Rhodes, is passed, forcing blacks off the land and providing cheap labour for the mines. The legislation limits the amount of land each family can occupy, changing succession laws to make the eldest son the only heir and forcing payment of a tax on anyone unable to prove he has been in employment for five months of the year.

The Natal Indian Congress is formed to resist attempts to limit the Indian franchise.

1895 The Rhodes-backed Jameson Raid, intended to seize the Transvaal from the Afrikaners who control it, fails.

The Transvaal limits to five the number of black families allowed to live on white farms.

1896 Legislation to limit Indian immigration is passed.

1897 The British annex Zululand, carve the kingdom up into chiefdoms and send King Dinuzulu into exile.

The Transvaal is annexed.

1899 The town of Louis Trichardt is sacked by Venda warriors.

1899-1902 The South African War between the British and the Boers divides the country, laying waste towns and farms and killing thousands of people. In deploying a scorched earth policy, the British burn farms to stop guerrilla tactics and set up concentration camps for Boer women and children and their black farm tenants.

1903 The war over, the British re-establish 31 000

exiles and 110 000 Boer concentration camp inmates on their land and pay war damages.

1904-7 Mining companies start importing Chinese labour in spite of resistance from white miners.

1905 The South African Native Affairs Commission rejects political equality and recommends ways of ensuring that blacks and whites live apart, using the reserves (homelands) as a source of labour. The commission recommends a separate, inferior education for blacks to ensure they do not develop 'white' aspirations.

1906 A passive resistance campaign is begun in Natal to oppose Indian pass laws.

The British crush a rebellion under Bambatha, head of the Zondi clan, against the addition of a poll tax to the existing hut and dog tax. The rebellion fails, and two years later Zulu chief Dinuzulu, whose support Bambatha had claimed, is convicted of high treason, public violence, sedition and rebellion, and imprisoned.

1910 The Union of South Africa is established comprising Transvaal, the Orange Free State, Natal and the Cape. It has a sovereign Parliament and a Senate with limited powers. Blacks are excluded from the vote everywhere except in the Cape and the right of blacks to be represented directly in Parliament is withdrawn. Constituencies are loaded to ensure disproportionately large representation for rural constituencies where Afrikaners are in the majority. Chinese labour is repatriated.

1911 Mine job reservation legislation reserves well-paying mine jobs for whites and it is made an offence for blacks to break a labour contract.

1912 The South African Native National Council (SANNC) is launched. Eleven years later it will change its name to the African National Congress.

1913 The Natives' Land Act, in terms of which blacks and whites can acquire land only in separate designated areas, is passed. Sharecropping is made illegal and the only blacks allowed in 'white' areas are labourers. About 7,5 per cent of the land is allocated for blacks under this Act; the 1936 Natives' Trust and Land Act brings this to a total of 13 per cent.

1914 White miners strike. The SANNC suspends opposition to the government with the outbreak of World War I and offers its services. The National Party is formed to further the interests of whites.

1918 Black miners launch the 'bucket boy' strike against low wages, poor housing, job reservation, poor health facilities and poor education. An anti-pass campaign is launched.

1919 The Industrial and Commercial Workers' Union of South Africa (ICU) is formed under Clements Kadalie.

1920 Black miners strike against low wages, poor housing and poverty and are forced underground at bayonet point. The Native Affairs Act establishes government-appointed councils to represent blacks in 'white' South Africa.

1921 Police shoot dead 183 members of the Israelite religious sect near Queenstown who had declared themselves 'independent'. The Afrikaner Broederbond becomes a covert organisation which starts securing positions of power for its members in every area of social life.

1922 Martial law is declared to put down a violent strike by white miners on the Witwatersrand determined to fight off attempts to abolish job reservation. The Stallard Commission recommends 'natives should only be permitted in municipal areas for as long as their presence is required by whites'.

1923 The ICU begins to play an openly political role. The Natives (Urban Areas) Act gives local authorities the power to establish black townships, to determine access to these, to enforce pass laws, to force blacks to live in townships and to deport people to the reserves.

1924 The National Party and Labour Party form a 'whites first' pact and win the election.

1925 The first of many ICU-organised work stay-aways, used as political and work-related protests, takes place in Bloemfontein.

1927 ICU protests spark off farm strikes and actions of

defiance like refusal to pay taxes and dog licence or cattle-dipping fees. The ICU successfully challenges the eviction of farmworkers from Natal farms in court.

Legislation to control 'unrest' is enacted.

The ANC organises opposition to government attempts at removing the vote of blacks in the Cape, expanding advisory councils and 'redefining' the votes of coloureds.

1928 The Communist Party of South Africa develops a programme for African majority rule with one person, one vote.

1930 A pass-burning campaign is launched by the Communist Party.

1934 The National and South African parties form the United South African National Party. A breakaway faction forms the Purified National Party, a forerunner of the National Party.

1935 The All-Africa Convention is formed to resist the disenfranchisement of blacks in the Cape, but fails, and in 1936 blacks are removed from the Cape voters' rolls.

1939 South Africa joins the war with the blessing of the ANC, although black servicemen are not allowed to fight and are not issued with arms. The pro-Nazi Afrikaner nationalist Ossewa Brandwag is formed. Later, soldiers and civil servants are banned from becoming members of it and leading OB members are interned until the end of the war.

1941 The African Mineworkers' Union is formed.

1948 The National Party under Daniel Malan is voted into power, narrowly beating Jan Smuts's United Party and beginning more than 40 years of apartheid rule.

1949 The Prohibition of Mixed Marriages Act is passed, the first of a decade of restrictive measures.

1950 The Suppression of Communism Act, the Population Registration Act (to underpin race classification), the Immorality Act (to stop sex between people of different races) and the Separate Representation of Voters Act are passed.

1952 The ANC Defiance Campaign starts and the Congress of Democrats and Coloured People's Organisation are launched. The Public Safety Act is passed, as is the oddly-named Abolition of Passes Act, which introduces the dompas, or reference book.

1953 The Reservation of Separate Amenities Act is passed, as is the Bantu Education Act, forcing most mission schools into the government system and changing the syllabus so that, in the words of minister of Native Affairs Hendrik Verwoerd, later prime minister, 'The school[s] . . . equip the Bantu to meet the demands which the economic life . . . will impose on him', severely restricting the subjects taught to black scholars.

1955 Black residents of Johannesburg's Sophiatown

are forcibly removed and the area razed to make way for a whites-only suburb, which is named Triomf.

At a two-day Congress of the People in Kliptown, outside Johannesburg, sponsored by a range of organisations including the African National Congress, the Freedom Charter — calling for equal rights — is adopted.

1956 Coloureds are removed from the voters' roll. One hundred and fifty-six activists are charged with treason; the massive trial ends five years later with acquittals.

1958 Hendrik Verwoerd, considered by many to be the architect of apartheid, becomes prime minister.

1959 The Pan Africanist Congress (PAC) is formed under lawyer Robert Sobukwe as a breakaway from the ANC in rejection of what is seen as the growing influence of communists and Indians in the movement.

1960 Police shoot PAC pass law protesters at Sharpeville. Sobukwe is sentenced to three years' imprisonment. The ANC and PAC are banned. A State of Emergency is declared.

1961 On 31 May, following a white referendum, South Africa leaves the British Commonwealth and becomes a republic.

The ANC adopts the policy of armed struggle.

1963 The government introduces 90-day detention legislation to crush Umkhonto weSizwe and Poqo, the armed wings of the ANC and the PAC respectively. Police swoop on ANC activists at Lilliesleaf farm in Rivonia. Nelson Mandela, Walter Sisulu and others are sentenced to life imprisonment.

1966 A knife-wielding messenger stabs Verwoerd to death in Parliament. BJ Vorster succeeds him as prime minister.

Cape Town's District Six, a prime piece of property near the centre of town and home to a mixture of all races, is declared a white area, its residents removed and its buildings razed. For decades, no one will build on the site.

1969 The South African Students' Organisation is formed under Steve Biko, marking the beginning of the black consciousness movement.

1972 The black consciousness orientated Black People's Convention is formed.

1975 The South African army invades Angola; the government denies its troops are there.

The television age begins in South Africa as the government establishes the SABC.

1976 Protests against the use of Afrikaans in black schools initiate violence, beginning in Soweto on 16 June, in which hundreds are killed.

1977 Black consciousness activist Steve Biko dies in detention. Two newspapers and 17 political organisations, many of them black consciousness orientated, are banned.

1978 Newspapers expose a campaign by the Department of Information to change the country's image by buying media covertly in South Africa and overseas, spending millions of rands. Among the scandals is the covert funding of an English language, government supporting newspaper, *The Citizen*.

1979 In the wake of the Info scandal, Vorster resigns and is replaced by former minister of Defence PW Botha.

The Council of Trade Unions and the Federation of South African Trade Unions are formed. The Industrial Conciliation Act embodies recommendations of the Wiehahn Commission, including official recognition of black trade unions.

1980 Umkhonto weSizwe guerrillas blow up the Sasol refinery in Sasolburg.

1983 In a huge referendum turnout, two-thirds of South African white voters approve the establishment of a tricameral parliament which will include coloured and Indian houses but exclude blacks.

Two major organisations are launched, one on the left — the United Democratic Front — and another on the right — the Conservative Party.

1984 Archbishop Desmond Tutu is awarded the Nobel Peace Prize.

Violence mars the elections for the new tricameral Parliament, but it is duly established. The violence continues into the following year.

1985 The Congress of South African Trade Unions (Cosatu) is formed. A State of Emergency is declared, applying only to parts of the country and for a limited time, in response to outbreaks of violent resistance.

1986 Pass laws and the Mixed Marriages Act are abolished. A countrywide State of Emergency is declared. It is renewed yearly until 1990.

Meanwhile, Justice minister Kobie Coetsee holds secret meetings with ANC leader Nelson Mandela, on Robben Island serving a life sentence, to discuss the possibility of bringing the ANC into the political process.

1987 After a general election, the Conservative Party replaces the Progressive Federal Party as the official Opposition in Parliament.

1988 An attempted coup in Bophuthatswana is put down by South African troops.

The activities of the United Democratic Front, 16 other political organisations and Cosatu are restricted.

1989 After meetings between Mandela, still a prisoner, and cabinet officials, Botha invites Mandela for tea at Tuynhuis, his official residence.

Botha retires as state president following a stroke and is replaced by FW de Klerk, who holds meetings with

Mandela, by now living in a warder's residence in the grounds of Victor Verster Prison. Mandela is allowed meetings with leaders of the UDF, Cosatu and other political organisations.

In the Harare Declaration, the ANC sets out the terms under which it will negotiate with the government. Political detainees go on hunger strikes to force authorities to charge or release them. A new defiance campaign is launched. The first anti-apartheid marches are allowed to take place. The Pan Africanist Movement is launched. Allegations of police hit-squads are made by former police captain Dirk Coetzee.

Late in the year, ANC stalwart Walter Sisulu and seven other long-term political prisoners are released.

1990

February On 2 February President FW de Klerk lifts bans on the ANC, the PAC and the South African Communist Party and removes restrictions on the UDF and Cosatu. Nelson Mandela is released on 11 February after 27 years in prison. Other political prisoners go on hunger strike in support of their demands for their unconditional release.

March The Ciskei government is overthrown by a military coup. The Harms Commission of Inquiry into alleged state hit-squads begins. Marches demanding the release of political prisoners are stopped. The ANC calls off talks with the government because of the police shooting of nine people in Sebokeng.

April The Venda government is overthrown by a

military coup. Right-wingers raid an SADF base and steal weapons. Exiled ANC leaders arrive for talks with the government.

May The government and the ANC sign the Groote Schuur Minute to facilitate the release of political prisoners, the return of exiles and the amending of security legislation. Indemnity legislation is passed. Hospital apartheid is abolished. A massive Cosatu protest against the Labour Relations Amendment Act is held. Several bomb explosions occur and are blamed on right-wingers.

June The State of Emergency is lifted everywhere in the country, except in Natal. The Separate Amenities Act is repealed.

July A massive ANC-Cosatu stayaway is held to protest against violence in Natal. ANC National Executive Committee member Mac Maharaj is detained in connection with 'Operation Vula', allegedly a plot to overthrow the state.

August The Pretoria Minute is signed in which the ANC renounces its armed struggle. Hundreds of people are killed in a wave of ANC-Inkatha Freedom Party violence in East Rand townships.

September The commission of inquiry into security force shootings at Sebokeng declares their action 'unjustifiable'. The Hiemstra Commission report details spying activities by the Johannesburg City Council.

October The State of Emergency in Natal is lifted. The government and ANC agree that people accused of or serving sentences for politically motivated offences committed before 8 October 1990 will qualify for indemnity.

November A coup is attempted in Transkei but does not succeed.

December Amnesty is extended to political prisoners.

1991

January After parents' bodies in scores of white schools vote to admit children of other races, Model C schools begin registering a multiracial student complement. ANC and IFP leaders Nelson Mandela and Mangosuthu Buthelezi sign an agreement to stop violence between followers of the two organisations.

February Prosecutions under the Group Areas Act are suspended. Some political prisoners are released.

March The nine accused in the Operation Vula trial receive indemnity. A judicial commission into the shooting of 42 people at Sebokeng by the SADF finds the action indefensible. The death toll in political violence over the last five years reaches 5 000.

April The ANC accuses the government of being party to ongoing political violence and threatens to withdraw from negotiations unless the government outlaws the carrying of weapons, dismisses the ministers responsible for the security forces and takes control of these forces. The agreed date for the release of political prisoners and return of political exiles passes with neither of these processes being complete. Political prisoners stage a hunger strike in protest.

May Police shoot at right-wingers attempting to evict communities reoccupying a farm from which they were forcibly removed. A partial ban on weapons is announced. Winnie Mandela is found guilty of kidnapping and of being an accessory to assault in a case involving the death of a young activist. The ANC suspends negotiations with the government and announces a campaign of mass action.

June The 1913 and 1936 Land Acts, the Group Areas Act, the Black Communities Act and hundreds of racist restrictions in other laws are repealed. The Population Registration Act is repealed, leaving the constitution as the only major piece of apartheid legislation in place.

July The government and the ANC agree that the process of releasing political prisoners has been finalised. Government funding of Inkatha and its union ally Uwusa is exposed. The government admits it funded parties opposed to Swapo at the time of the Namibian election. President FW de Klerk says all covert operations aimed at political opponents will cease.

August The government allows United Nations participation in the repatriation of exiles. Three right-wingers die in clashes with police at Ventersdorp.

September The National Peace Accord is signed by all major political players other than the right wing. The implementation of Value Added Tax leads to massive ANC-Cosatu protests against the levying of the tax on basic foods and services.

The government, ANC and IFP reach an agreement that opens the door to negotiations.

October The Goldstone Commission, headed by Judge Richard Goldstone, is established to investigate public violence and intimidation.

November A two-day anti-VAT stayaway is held by Cosatu and the National Council of Trade Unions.

December Most of the major political parties assemble at the World Trade Centre near Kempton Park on 20 December to launch the Convention for a Democratic South Africa (Codesa), the first 'real' constitutional negotiating forum. Eighteen organisations participate, including the government, the NP, ANC, Democratic Party and three other parliamentary parties, the 10 homeland administrations, the Transvaal and Natal Indian Congresses and the SACP. Staying away are the Conservative Party, Azanian People's Organisation, the PAC and the right wing.

1992

January Violence continues from both ends of the political spectrum. Right-wing groups embark on a campaign of raiding armouries for weapons and blowing up buildings. Apla, the armed wing of the PAC, continues its armed struggle by attacking police and civilians.

February A Patriotic Front of anti-apartheid organisations is launched, marking the entry of the PAC into negotiations. It includes the PAC, ANC, Cosatu, the coloured Labour Party and some homeland leaders.

March A whites-only referendum gives the government firm support for negotiations, more than two-thirds in a high turnout.

April Former police captain Brian Mitchell and four special policemen are found guilty of murdering 11 UDF supporters at Trust Feed in 1988. A commission is appointed to investigate the possibility of a high-level cover-up.

May IFP leader Mangosuthu Buthelezi refuses to attend the second plenary session of Codesa (Codesa II) because Zulu king Goodwill Zwelithini is refused full status as a negotiator. The negotiating session ends in deadlock after the working group on a constitution-making body fails to reach agreement.

The Goldstone Commission blames ANC-IFP rivalry for most of the political violence in South Africa.

June At least 39 people are killed in a middle-of-the-night attack on shacks in Boipatong, an informal settlement on the East Rand, sparking an international outcry. The ANC suspends negotiations with the government and initiates a 'rolling mass action' campaign with the SACP and Cosatu.

July South Africa participates in the Olympic Games for the first time since 1960.

August The government initiates bilateral talks with Azapo, the CP and the PAC which continue for months in an effort to broaden the base of negotiations.

September At least 24 people are shot dead and 198 are injured by Ciskei Defence Force soldiers in a march on Bisho, sparking massive protests.

The ANC and the government sign a Record of Understanding (RoU) in terms of which 150 political prisoners convicted of murder will be released, the Codesa II deadlock is resolved, certain hostels will be fenced, and the carrying of traditional weapons will be banned. The signing of the bilateral RoU marks the beginning of a process of closed-door negotiations between the government and the ANC, who set agendas and make crucial decisions privately.

Buthelezi, pointing out that decisions affecting the IFP are taken without consulting it, says neither the IFP nor the kwaZulu authorities will be bound by these agreements.

October The government tries to hold talks with the IFP but the IFP is not interested. The IFP, right-wing political organisations and the leaders of Ciskei, kwa-Zulu and Bophuthatswana join forces to oppose negotiations dominated by the government and the ANC. This group becomes known as the Concerned South Africans Group (Cosag) and, by the middle of the following year, as the Freedom Alliance.

President FW de Klerk conditionally apologises for apartheid. An ANC commission of inquiry details human rights violations at its detention camps. Further indemnity legislation is enacted by referral to the President's Council.

November The ANC changes its position on power-sharing, after SACP leader Joe Slovo proposes 'sunset clauses' to move transition forward.

Massive corruption is revealed in Lebowa, in the Department of Development Aid and in the Department of Education and Training. Two extensive SADF projects to undermine the ANC are exposed.

December The government suspends talks with the PAC until Apla attacks on white civilians cease. The first Advisory Commission on Land Allocation adjudications are largely accepted by the government. Twenty-three senior SADF officers are suspended or retired for suspected involvement in illegal activities to sabotage negotiations. The Goldstone Commission maintains that the primary trigger for political violence is ANC-IFP rivalry.

The kwaZulu legislative assembly adopts a constitution for a future state of kwaZulu/Natal as an autonomous member state of a federal republic of South Africa.

1993

January The government proposes a non-racial education system and phases out 'own affairs' tricameral Parliament administrations.

February IFP and ANC members are arrested for arms smuggling. The government and the ANC propose power-sharing and a five-year interim government of national unity after an election.

March A multi-party negotiations planning conference is attended by 26 parties including the kwaZulu government, the Conservative Party, the Afrikaner Volksunie, the PAC and delegations of traditional leaders. The government announces it has dismantled six nuclear bombs built secretly between 1980 and 1989.

April Negotiations resume at the World Trade Centre, with 26 parties, including the CP, the PAC and the IFP, participating.

SACP general secretary Chris Hani is assassinated by a right-winger, sparking violence and protests all over the country.

May Eighteen right-wing groups are brought together as the Afrikaner Volksfront to demand Afrikaner self-determination in a federal state. Azapo confirms it will not participate in negotiations. The principle of a federal state with constitutionally entrenched powers for regional governments is accepted at the negotiating forum.

June The conviction of Winnie Mandela on kidnapping charges is upheld on appeal but that of being an accessory to assault is overturned.

After negotiators use the notion of 'sufficient consensus' to rule that the country's first elections will be held on 27 April 1994, the IFP and the CP walk out of the talks, and are joined by Bophuthatswana and Ciskei, now known as the Freedom Alliance. Another peace meeting is held between IFP and ANC leaders Mangosuthu Buthelezi and Nelson Mandela.

Led by an armoured vehicle, armed right-wingers attack the site of negotiations, the World Trade Centre in Kempton Park, and assault some of the participants.

The PAC refuses to abandon the armed struggle.

July The date for the first non-racial election is set for 27 April 1994.

Eleven white churchgoers are shot dead in Cape Town.

August At least 470 people die in violence in East Rand townships.

September An ANC commission of inquiry describes human rights abuses in ANC detention camps.

The negotiating council accepts the draft Bill for the Transitional Executive Council (TEC) which, with its seven subcouncils, is responsible for creating a peacekeeping force and levelling the playing fields in the run-up to elections.

October The United Nations lifts sanctions against South Africa, with the exception of the arms and oil embargoes.

It is announced that Mandela and De Klerk have jointly won the Nobel Peace Prize.

November Three years of constitutional negotiations come to an end with agreement on constitutional issues. It is decided that South Africa will be divided into nine provinces. Negotiators strike last-minute deals to reach the deadlines they have set for themselves, including controversial concessions, like one ballot paper to count both on a regional and a national level. The transitional constitution accepted in the early hours of 18 November makes provision for a non-racial, multi-party democracy, three tiers of government and a justiciable Bill of Rights applicable in a unitary South Africa, including the homelands. A system of proportional representation will apply, and Parliament will double as a constitution-writing body. These arrangements will be in effect until April 1999.

December A special session of Parliament passes the negotiators' draft Bills into law. The TEC, with representatives of all parties to the negotiations, is installed. The government and ANC continue talks with the Freedom Alliance over whether outstanding issues can be resolved in time for the FA to participate in elections.

7

Office Bearers

The key office bearers of the key political offices

African National Congress (ANC)
Head Office Tel: (011) 330–7000
President: Nelson Mandela Tel: (011) 330–7273/7426
Vice-president: Walter Sisulu Tel: (011) 330–7057
General secretary: Cyril Ramaphosa Tel: (011) 330–7067
Treasurer general: Thomas Nkobi Tel: (011) 330–7070
Deputy general secretary: Jacob Zuma Tel: (011) 330–7064
National chairman: Thabo Mbeki Tel: (011) 330–7286

Departments and department heads
Arts and Culture Tel: (011) 330–7323
Wally Serote Tel: (011) 330–7229
Economic Policy Tel: (011) 330–7285
Trevor Manuel Tel: (011) 330–7267
Education Tel: (011) 330–7326
John Samuel Tel: (011) 330–7241
Election Tel: (011) 330–7291
Popo Molefe Tel: (011) 330–7189
Finance Tel: (011) 330–7252
S Shibambo Tel: (011) 330–7249
Health Tel: (011) 330–7205
Cheryl Carolus Tel: (011) 330–7204

Information and Publicity
Pallo Jordan Tel: (011) 330–7096
Legal Tel: (011) 330–7258
Matthew Phosa Tel: (011) 330–7259
Legal and Constitutional Tel: (011) 330–7186
Zola Skweyiya Tel: (011) 330–7264
Military HQ Tel: (011) 330–7174
Joe Modise Tel: (011) 330–7167
Organising
Steve Tshwete Tel: (011) 330–7279
Political Education Tel: (011) 330–7219
Raymond Suttner Tel: (011) 330–7218
President's Office
Tel: (011) 330–7273/7476
Research Tel: (011) 330–7054
Frene Ginwala Tel: (011) 330–7234
Secretary-general's Office
Tel: (011) 330–7067
Social Welfare
Jackie Selebi Tel: (011) 330–7125
Women's League
Winnie Mandela Tel: (011) 330–7288

Regional offices and chairpersons
PWV Region: Tokyo Sexwale Tel: (011) 29–6066
Northern Transvaal: Ngoako Ramathlodi Tel: (01521) 91–4311
Eastern Transvaal: Matthew Phosa Tel: (01311) 53051
Western Transvaal: Solomon Rasmeni Tel: (018) 464–1080
Northern Cape: Manne Dipico Tel: (0531) 81–2099/13
Eastern Cape: Linda Mti Tel: (041) 55–9618

Western Cape: Dr Allan Boesak Tel: (021) 448–5651
Border: Silumko Sokhupha Tel: (0431) 43–9734
Northern Natal: Aaron Ndlovu Tel: (0351) 921503/10
Southern Natal: Jeff Radebe Tel: (031) 307–5460
Natal Midlands: Harry Gwala Tel: (0331) 94–6558
Northern OFS: Ace Magashule Tel: (057) 357–4779
Southern OFS: Sekhopi Malebo Tel: (051) 48–0441
Transkei: David Ndawonde Tel: (0431) 31–0814

Afrikaner Weerstandsbeweging (AWB)
Head Office Tel: (01480) 2005/7
Leader: Eugene Terre'Blanche
Assistant leader: Ernest van der Westhuizen
Private secretary to leader: Danie Small
Financial administration: Martie Terre'Blanche
Training and security: Leon van der Merwe
Personnel: Marietjie Jacobs
Insurance and pensions: Nico Prinsloo

Congress of South African Trade Unions (Cosatu)
Head Office Tel: (011) 339–4911
President: J Gomomo
First vice-president: Chris Dlamini
Second vice-president: Godfrey Oliphant
General secretary: Sam Shilowa
Treasurer: Ronald Mofokeng

Regional secretaries
Witwatersrand: Amos Masondo Tel: (011) 873–2610
Western Transvaal: S Mokoema Tel: (016) 55–1855
Northern Transvaal Tel: (012) 324–3022
Highveld: JJ Mabena Tel: (0136) 51711

Northern Cape/OFS: Thabo Makweya Tel: (0531) 81–1088
Western Cape: Jonathan Arendse Tel: (021) 462–3673/4
Eastern Cape: Dennis Neer Tel: (041) 43–4024
Southern Natal: Thami Mohlomi Tel: (031) 304–1690
Northern Natal: Sipho Cele Tel: (0351) 92–2354

Cosatu affiliates (including general secretaries of each union)

Chemical Workers' Industrial Union (CWIU)
  Rod Crompton Tel: (031) 25910/9
Construction and Allied Workers' Union (Cawu)
  Matthews Oliphant Tel: (011) 29–4321/3
Food and Allied Workers' Union
  Mandla Gxanyana Tel: (021) 637–9040/4
National Education, Health and Allied Workers' Union (Nehawu)
  Phillip Dexter Tel: (011) 337–8516
National Union of Metalworkers (Numsa)
  Moses Mayekiso Tel: (011) 832–2030
National Union of Mineworkers
  Kgalema Motlanthe Tel: (011) 833–7012/9
Paper, Printing, Wood and Allied Workers' Union (Ppwawu)
  Sipho Kubheka Tel: (011) 834–4661/3
Post Office and Telecommunications Workers' Association
  Mlungisi Hlongwane Tel: (011) 333–4351/5
SA Clothing, Textile and Allied Workers' Union (Sactwu)
  John Copelyn Tel: (031) 301–1351
SA Commercial, Catering and Allied Workers' Union (Saccawu)

Papi Kganare Tel: (011) 331–8716
South African Domestic Workers' Union (Sadwu)
Flourie de Villiers Tel: (021) 47–9621
SA Railway and Harbour Workers' Union (Sarhwu)
Derrick Simoko Tel: (011) 29–5429
South African Municipal Workers' Union (Samwu)
John Ernstzen Tel: (021) 697–1153/4
Transport and General Workers' Union (T&GWU)
Nkosinathi Nhleko Tel: (011) 29–4913

Conservative Party (CP)
Head Office Tel: (012) 342–3408 or (021) 403–2911
Deputy leader: Dr F Hartzenberg

Provincial offices
Transvaal: PF Steinman (chairman) Tel: (01441) 26218
Cape Province: K Janker (chairman) Tel: (0531) 81–1177
Eastern Province Tel: (041) 30–7682
Western Province Tel: (021) 461–1508
Natal: CH Werth (chairman) Tel: (0381) 4241 or (031) 47–8233
Orange Free State: NP Oosthuizen (chairman) Tel: (051) 47–2668

Spokespersons
Administration and Tourism
Adv SC Jacobs Tel: (0148) 294–7274
Agriculture and Agriculture Affairs
AAB Bruwer Tel: (01524) 85665
Communication
Dr PWA Mulder Tel: (01801) 31176

Constitutional Development and Planning
Dr F Hartzenberg Tel: (012) 342–3408
Defence
WJ Snyman Tel: (01521) 91–1741
Education and Training
S Pienaar Tel: (0154) 3619
Environmental, Forestry and Water Affairs
CB Schoeman Tel: (011) 739–7147
Finances and State Expenditure
C Uys Tel: (01344) 3–2825
Home Affairs
HDK van der Merwe Tel: (01213) 4–4235
Justice & NID
Adv JS Prinsloo Tel: (011) 766–3691
Law and Order
DS Pienaar Tel: (0154) 3619
Local Government and Welfare, Housing and Works
HJ Coetzee Tel: (0132) 2–9411
Manpower
FJ le Roux Tel: (011) 744–4457
Mineral and Energy Affairs
PJ Paulus Tel: (011) 753–2801
National Education and Culture
A Gerber Tel: (01211) 2–4100
National Health and Population Development
FH Pauw Tel: (051) 22–6325
Planning and Provincial Affairs/National Housing
JH Hoon Tel: (01471) 2–1803
Public Works, Transport and Telecommunications
J Chiole Tel: (012) 386–0962
Trade, Industry and Economic Co-ordination
DGH Nolte Tel: (01212) 2–0544

Democratic Party of South Africa (DP)
National Head Office Tel: (021) 45–1431
Leader: Dr Zach de Beer
National chairman: K M Andrew
Chairman of the National Council: David Gant
Principal executives
  Executive director: J Selfe
  National director research: Prof N Olivier
  National director finance and administration: J Hart
  National director marketing and communication: C Knott

Regional offices and chairmen
Northern Transvaal: R Harpur Tel: (012) 326–1284
Southern Transvaal: PG Soal Tel: (011) 483–2743
Eastern Transvaal: A Thatcher Tel: (011) 394–6425
Western Cape: J Walsh Tel: (021) 45–1420
Eastern Cape: M Finnemore Tel: (041) 52–1770
Southern Cape: N Bischoff Tel: (0441) 74–2348
Border: Brian Cooney Tel: (0431) 53993
Natal Coast: M Ellis Tel: (031) 309–4920
Natal Midlands: P Barnard Tel: (0331) 42–7692
Orange Free State: Andries Botha Tel: (056) 33033

Government Departments
Agriculture
  Minister: Dr Al van Niekerk; Deputy: AT Meyer
  Tel: (012) 206–2307 / (021) 45–7225
Constitutional Development and Communication
  Minister: RP Meyer; Deputy: SJ Schoeman
  Tel: (012) 341–1380 / (021) 461–0851

Correctional Services
Minister: AJ Vlok
Tel: (012) 207–8268 / (012) 323–8198
Defence
Minister: HJ Coetsee; Deputy WN Breytenbach
Tel: (012) 428–2206 / (021) 45–3880 / Pager (012) 325–8404 Code 8524
Education and Training
Minister: SJ de Beer
Tel: (012) 326–0126 / (021) 45–7350
Environmental Affairs and Water Affairs
Minister: JA van Wyk; Deputy: WN Breytenbach
Tel: (012) 299–9111 / 299–2596
Finance
Minister: DL Keys; Deputy: TG Alant
Tel: (012) 21–8675 / (021) 45–7594
Foreign Affairs
Minister: RF Botha; Deputy: RS Schoeman
Tel: (012) 351–0005 / (021) 45–5848 / 461–1934
Home Affairs
Minister: DPA Schutte; Deputy: LH Fick
Tel: (012) 326–8081 / (021) 461–5818
Justice
Minister: JH Coetsee; Deputy: Sheila Camerer
Tel: (012) 315–1021/2 / (021) 461–0150
Law and Order
Minister: HJ Kriel; Deputy: GB Myburgh
Tel: (012) 323–8880 / (021) 45–2645 / 45–7400
Local Government
Minister: Dr JT Delport; Deputy: YM Makda
Tel: (012) 44–1879 / 343–8805 / (021) 45–7295

Manpower
Minister: L Wessels
Tel: (012) 322–6523 / (021) 461–6030
Mineral and Energy Affairs
Minister: GS Bartlett
Tel: (012) 322–8695 / (021) 462–2310
National Education and Education Co-ordination
Minister: PG Marais
Tel: (012) 324–4098 / (021) 45–5412
National Health and Welfare
Minister: Dr EH Venter; Deputy, Welfare: GME Carelse; Deputy, Health: Dr BL Geldenhuys
Tel: (012) 328–4773 / 323–5466 / (021) 45–7407
National Housing and Public Works
Minister: HL Shill
Tel: (012) 324–1510
Population Development
Minister: JA Rabie
Tel: (012) 20–0036 / (021) 461–4215
Public Enterprises
Minister: Dr J de Villiers
Tel: (012) 326–1110
Regional and Land Affairs
Minister: A Fourie
Tel: (012) 323–5212 / (021) 45–7690
Sport
Minister A Williams
Tel: (012) 21–1781 / (021) 461–4243
State Expenditure
Minister: AA Venter
Tel: (012) 21–9587/8 / (021) 45–4850

Tourism
Minister: Dr B Ranchod
Tel: (012) 322–7677
Trade and Industry
Minister: DL Keys; Deputy: D de V Graaff
Tel: (012) 323–8911 / (021) 45–3456
Transport and Posts and Telecommunications
Minister: Dr PJ Welgemoed
Tel: (012) 328–3084/5/6 / (021) 45–7260/1
Deputy Minister in the Office of the State President: CL Fismer
Tel: (021) 45–7300 / (012) 21222 / (021) 319–1500
Office of the Auditor-General
Tel: (012) 324–2874

Independent Electoral Commission (IEC)
Head office Tel: (011) 397–5000

South African members: Judge JC Kriegler (chairperson), Adv Dikgang Moseneke (vice-chairperson), Rev Frank Chikane, Dr Oscar Dhlomo, Johann H Heyns, Rosil Jager, Dawn Mokhobo, Charles Nupen, Helen Suzman, B van der Ross, Adv Z Yacoob.
International members: RKC de Silva (Sri Lanka), Donald Gould (Canada), Prof Walter Kamba (Zimbabwe), Gay McDougal (United States), Dr Amare Teckle (Eritrea).

Inkatha Freedom Party (IFP)
Head office Tel: (031) 307–4962
President: Mangosuthu G Buthelezi
National chairperson: Dr Frank T Mdlalose

Deputy secretary-general: Inkosi Simon H Gumede
Women's Brigade national chairperson: Faith X Gasa (acting)
Youth Brigade national chairperson: Musa K Zondi
National spokesman: Ziba Jiyane

Executive Committee portfolios

Community Development
MV Ngema Tel: (0358) 79–1039
Education and African Affairs
LPHM Mtshali Tel: (0358) 20–2492
Environment
Maurice M Mackenzie Tel: (031) 307–4962
External Relations
Dr Mangosuthu G Buthelezi Tel: (0358) 20–2016
Financial Affairs
S Johnny Mhlungu Tel: (0358) 70–0385 and
MZ Khumalo Tel: (0358) 79–1039
Internal Relations
Dr Frank T Mdlalose Tel: (0358) 20–2432/8
Liaison with AmaKhosi
Inkosi Simon H Gumede Tel: (0358) 20–2425
Media Liaison
Suzanne Vos Tel: (011) 444–1862
Party Organisation and Development
Walter S Felgate Tel: (0351) 53–3123
Public Relations
Inka Mars Tel: (031) 29–3614
Research and Documentation
Prof SJ Maphalala Tel: (0351) 93911
Security
Rev CJ Mtetwa Tel: (0358) 20–2447

Sport
Dr Ben S Ngubane Tel: (0358) 20–2471
Training
Dr Dennis RB Madide Tel: (0358) 20–2481
Women's Affairs
Faith X Gasa (acting chairperson) Tel: (035872) ask for 5
Youth Affairs
Musa K Zondi Tel: (0358) 79–1226

Regional offices
Southern Natal: Maurice M Mackenzie (chief) Tel: (031) 307–4962 or MT Sabela Tel: (031) 368–1897
Information Centre: Peter Smith Tel: (031) 309–6803
Inkatha Institute: Dr Gavin Woods Tel: (031) 304–9305
Ixopo: Philip Halliday Tel: (0336) 34–1705
Northern Natal
Empangeni: MR Mkhize Tel: (0351) 92–3756
Ulundi: NE Sithole Tel: (0358) 79–1031
Natal Midlands
Pietermaritzburg: Themba BM Ndulini Tel: (0358) 20–7374
Transvaal
PWV areas: Themba Khoza Tel: (011) 339–3647
Suzanne Vos Tel: (011) 444–1862
Vaal Triangle: Mandla Sibisi Tel: (016) 21–4724
Cape Province
Western Cape: Nicolas Myburgh Tel: (0291) 42828

National Party (NP)
Head office Tel: (012) 342–2050
Leader: FW de Klerk

Federal Information Service Chief Director: Marthinus van Schalkwyk

Regional offices
Cape Province
Leader: DJ de Villiers Tel: (021) 23–4156
Natal
Leader: GS Bartlett Tel: (031) 301–2737
Orange Free State
Leader: HJ Coetsee (minister of Justice) Tel: (051) 47–3365
Transvaal
Leader: Pik Botha (minister of Foreign Affairs) Tel: (012) 21–8848

Pan Africanist Congress (PAC)
Headquarters Tel: (011) 836–0457 or (011) 836–0491/2
President: Mlamli Makwetu
Deputy president: Johnson Mlambo
Secretary-general: Benny Alexander
Deputy secretary-general: Thobile Gola
National organiser: Maxwell Nemadzivhanani

Departments and secretaries
Economic Affairs
Mosebjane Malatsi Tel: (011) 836–0457
Education and Human Resources
Mogale Mphahlele Tel: (012) 375–6558
Finance
Thomson Gazo Tel: (0401) 95–2237
Foreign Affairs
Gora Ebrahim Tel: (011) 836–0457 or 836–0491/2

Health
  Selva Saman Tel: (031) 43–6658
Labour
  Lesaoana Makhanda Tel: (011) 836–0457
Land and Environment
  Solly Skosana Tel: (011) 424–2407/3407
Legal and Constitutional Affairs
  Willie Seriti Tel: (012) 28–7347
Local Government and Civics
  Molefi Litheko Tel: (05265) 2250/1
Political Affairs
  Jaki Seroke Tel: (011) 339–1871/3
Projects and Development
  Elizabeth Sibeko Tel: (011) 836–0457
Publicity and Information
  Barney Desai Tel: (021) 448–1642/55
Relief and Aid
  Patricia De Lille Tel: (021) 448–1642
Religious Affairs
  Mike Matsobane Tel: (011) 410–1279
Sports and Culture
  Fitzroy Ngcukana Tel: (031) 43–6658
Transport
  Mark Shinners Tel: (011) 836–0457
Women's Affairs
  Ellen Mothopeng Tel: (011) 936–2509 or 492–1380
Azanyo chairperson
  Mosotho Petlane Tel: (011) 836–0457

South African Communist Party (SACP)
Head office Tel: (011) 339–3621/2
National chairperson: Joe Slovo

Deputy chairperson: Ray Mhlaba
General secretary: Charles Nqakula
Treasurer: Kay Moonsamy

Regions
PWV Tel: (011) 834–4657
Western Transvaal Tel: (018) 462–1395
Eastern Transvaal Tel: (0132) 20611
Western Cape Tel: (021) 448–7908
Eastern Cape Tel: (041) 41–5106
Border Tel: (0433) 22673
Southern Natal Tel: (031) 305–6186/7
Natal Midlands Tel: (0331) 94–4651
Orange Free State Tel: (051) 48–2486
Transkei Tel: (0471) 31–1745

Transitional Executive Council (TEC)
Head office Tel: (012) 328- 5490
Liaison officer: Dries van Heerden (012) 328–5490

Subcouncils
Defence: Prof DMD Mahlangu, Brig L Bengu, Brig MG Ramushwana, Adv SJ Maake, Gen AJ Liebenberg, J Modise, WN Breytenbach, R Kasrils
Finance: J Douw, Dr JN Reddy, Dr TG Alant, T Mboweni, TJ Ndaba, SOM Moji
Foreign Affairs: GKN Hetisani, Princess SN Sigcau, O Ganie, Prof CJA Barratt, A Pahad, L Wessels
Intelligence: LT Landers, Col WM Nszwayiba, Lt Gen RHD Rogers, Brig MW Mokoena, GH Rothmann, A Nzo, SJ Schoeman, R Shaik
Law and Order: Maj Gen J Nembambula, PHP Gas-

trow, Lt Col PN Bohlolo, Lt Gen L Malan, S Mufamadi, GB Myburgh, K Naidoo, MS Gininda
Regional/Local Government: DM Malatsi, Chief GSK Nota, V Makda, W Cobbett, AT Meyer, JSS Phatang
Status of Women: MVK Bassier, MT Moroke, NS Mtsweni, M Mamzini, Dr T King, E Gandhi
An eighth subcouncil, to deal with the post-election transition, had not been constituted at the time of going to press.

TEC members and alternates
African National Congress: C Ramaphosa (member), M Maharaj (alternate)
Cape Traditional Leaders: M Nonkonyana (member), K Gwasiso (alternate)
Democratic Party: C Eglin (member), M Andrew (alternate)
Dikwankwetla Party: TJ Mohapi (member), SOM Moji (alternate)
Intando Yesizwe Party: MJ Mahlangu (member), Q Vilankulu (alternate)
Inyandza National Movement: SS Ripinga (member), FS Baloi (alternate)
Labour Party: HJH Hendrickse (member), I Richards (alternate)
Natal/Transvaal Indian Congress: PJ Gordhan (member), C Salojee (alternate)
National Party: D de Villiers (member), L Wessels (alternate)
National People's Party: A Rajbansi (member), O Ganie (alternate)
Orange Free State Traditional Leaders: RH Mopell (member), MB Mota (alternate)

Solidarity Party: DS Rajah (member), JN Reddy (alternate)
South African Communist Party: J Slovo (member), T Mtintso (alternate)
South African government: RP Meyer (member), SS van der Merwe (alternate)
Transkei government: Z Titus (member), N Jajula (alternate)
Transvaal Traditional Leaders: LM Mokoena (member), MA Netshimbupte (alternate)
United People's Front: NM Ramodike (member), MJ Mahlangu (alternate)
Venda government: SE Moeti (member), S Makhuvha (alternate)
Ximoko Progressive Party: EE Ngobeni (member), PT Shilubana (alternate)
Management Committee: RP Meyer, MC Ramaphosa, J Slovo, Z Titus, P Gordhan, C Eglin, EE Ngobeni
Executive secretaries: M Maharaj, SS van der Merwe
Chairpersons: DJ de Villiers, P Gordhan, C Eglin, Z Titus
Representatives to the National Peacekeeping Force
Kwandebele Police Force: Maj MC Phatlane. Alternate: Capt SL Mashiyane
Transkei Police Force: Col DZ Sigotyana. Alternate: Capt ND Ntoyi
Gazankulu Police Force: Col MW Makhubela. Alternate: Maj MA Rikhumba
SA Defence Force: Lt Gen JH Pretorius (Army). Alternate: Maj Gen CJ Serfontein, Brig JJ Kasselman
Lebowa Police Force: Brig MA Dolamo. Alternate: Col DM Makwala

Venda Defence Force: Col W Swanepoel. Alternate: Lt Col NK Ludick
Qwa-Qwa Police Force: Brig MJ Koahela. Alternate: Col LM Kgwathela
KaNgwane Police Force: Maj NA Mabusa. Alternate: Lt MA Mahlongo
Umkhonto weSizwe: Lombert Moloi (Chief of Operations). Alternate: Manella Dwara
South African Police: Maj Gen WA van der Merwe. Alternate: Brig JR Beyl

Representatives to the JMCC
Transkei Defence Force: Gen Matanzima.
SA Defence Force: Gen GL Meiring. Alternates: Maj Gen WG Kritzinger, Brig M Oelschig
Umkhonto weSizwe: Siphiwe Nyanda (Gwebuza). Alternate: A Ishmael (Rashid Patel)
Venda Defence Force: Col W Swanepoel. Alternate: Lt Col NK Ludick

Tripartite Parliament
Office bearers
Speaker: E van der M Louw
Chief Whip: A van Breda

House of Assembly
Leader: AJ Vlok
Chairman: Dr HM Janse van Rensburg
Chairman of Committees: PL Mare
Deputy Chairman of Committees: KD Swanepoel
Leader of the Official Opposition: Dr the Hon F Hartzenberg

Chief Whip of the Majority Party: JJ Niemann
Chief Whip of the Official Opposition: FJ le Roux

House of Representatives
Leader: PJ Kleinsmidt
Chairman: NM Isaacs
Chairman of Committees: CA Wyngaard
Deputy Chairman of Committees: PRE da Gama
Leader of the Official Opposition: Rev HJ Hendrickse
Chief Whip of the Majority Party: WJ Dietrich
Chief Whip of the Official Opposition: JC Oosthuizen

House of Delegates
Leader: PI Devan
Chairman of the House: S Abram
Chairman of Committees: AS Kahn
Deputy Chairman of Committees: YI Seedat
Leader of the Official Opposition: K Moodley
Chief Whip of the Majority Party: MY Baig
Chief Whip of the Official Opposition: K Chetty

8
Acronyms

An A-Z of the alphabet soup of South African politics

AAC	Alexandra Action Committee
AAC	Anglo American Corporation
ANC	African National Congress
ANCYL	African National Congress Youth League
Apla	Azanian People's Liberation Army
ARAG	Abortion Reform Action Group
AVK	Afrikaner Volksfront
AWB	Afrikaner Weerstandsbeweging
Azanla	Azanian National Liberation Army
Azapo	Azanian People's Organisation
BCMA	Black Consciousness Movement of Azania
BVB	Boerevryheidsbeweging
BWB	Boereweerstandsbeweging
Codesa	Convention for a Democratic South Africa
Contralesa	Congress of Traditional Leaders of South Africa
Cosatu	Council of South African Trade Unions
Cosaw	Congress of South African Writers
CP	Conservative Party
CSIR	Council for Scientific and Industrial Research
CTPA	Cape Teachers' Professional Association
Comsa	Commonwealth Observer Mission to South Africa

DAC	(ANC) Department of Arts and Culture
DBSA	Development Bank of Southern Africa
DP	Democratic Party
DPSC	Detainees Parents' Support Committee
Ecomsa	European Community in South Africa
Edupol	(Urban Foundation) Education Policy Unit
ETB	Eastern Transvaal Boerekommando
ETG	(Cosatu) Economic Trends Group
FA	Freedom Alliance
Glow	Gay and Lesbian Organisation of the Witwatersrand
HNP	Herstigte Nasionale Party
HoD	House of Delegates
HoR	House of Representatives
HRC	Human Rights Commission
IBC	Independent Broadcasting Authority
Idasa	Institute for a Democratic Alternative for South Africa
IDT	Independent Development Trust
IEC	Independent Electoral Commission
Ifee	Independent Forum for Electoral Education
IFP	Inkatha Freedom Party
IMC	Independent Media Commission
IMPD	Institute for Multi-Party Democracy
Inocsa	Interim National Olympic Committee of South Africa
ISU	(SA Police) Internal Stability Unit
JSC	Judicial Services Commission
LHR	Lawyers for Human Rights
LRC	Legal Resources Centre
MDT	Media Defence Trust

MI	Military Intelligence
MK	Umkhonto weSizwe
Naawu	National Automobile and Allied Workers' Union
NAC	National Arts Coalition
Nactu	National Council of Trade Unions
Nadel	National Association for Democratic Lawyers
NAI	National Arts Initiative
NEC	(ANC) National Executive Committee
NEF	National Economic Forum
Nehawu	National Education, Health and Allied Workers' Union
NELF	National Electrification Forum
NETF	National Education and Training Forum
NEUM	Non-European Unity Movement
NGK	Nederduits Gereformeerde Kerk
NHF	National Housing Forum
NIS	National Intelligence Service
Nocsa	National Olympic Committee of South Africa
NP	National Party
NPKF	National Peacekeeping Force
NSC	National Sports Congress
NUM	National Union of Mineworkers
Numsa	National Union of Metalworkers of South Africa
Nusas	National Union of South African Students
Olga	Organisation of Gay and Lesbian Activists
PAC	Pan Africanist Congress of Azania
Pact	Performing Arts Council of the Transvaal
PAM	Pan Africanist Movement

PBKG	Pretoria Boerekommandogroep
Popcru	Police and Prisons Civil Rights Union
PWV	Pretoria-Witwatersrand-Vereeniging (region)
SABC	South African Broadcasting Corporation
SACBC	Southern African Catholic Bishops' Conference
SACC	South African Council of Churches
Sacob	South African Chamber of Business
Sacos	South African Council of Sport
SACP	South African Communist Party
Sactwu	South African Clothing and Textile Workers' Union
SADF	South African Defence Force
Sadtu	South African Democratic Teachers' Union
Sanco	South African National Civic Organisation
Sanroc	South African Non-Racial Olympic Committee
SAP	South African Police
Sarfu	South African Rugby Football Union
Saru	South African Rugby Union
Saso	South African Students' Organisation
Sayco	South African Youth Congress
SRC	Students' Representative Council
Swapo	South West African People's Organisation
TAU	Transvaal Agricultural Union
TBVC	(states) Transkei, Bophuthatswana, Venda, Ciskei (the four nominally independent homelands)
TEC	Transitional Executive Council
TMA	Transvaal Municipal Association

UCT	University of Cape Town
UDF	United Democratic Front
UF	Urban Foundation
Unibop	University of Bophuthatswana
Unisa	University of South Africa
Unitra	University of the Transkei
UWC	University of the Western Cape
Wecco	Western Cape Community Organisation
Wecusa	Western Cape United Squatter Association
WK	Wenkommando

List of Contributors

Julia Beffon is the sports editor of the *Weekly Mail & Guardian*.

Farouk Chothia is the Durban bureau chief of the *Weekly Mail & Guardian*, covering politics in Natal.

Carole Cooper is the research director of the South African Institute of Race Relations.

Lesley Cowling is the chief training officer of the South African Newspaper Education Trust.

Gaye Davis is the Cape Town bureau chief of the *Weekly Mail & Guardian*.

Shaun de Waal is the literary editor of the *Weekly Mail & Guardian*. Several of his short stories have been published in anthologies and journals.

Claire Gordon-Brown is a researcher for the South African Institute of Race Relations.

Jacqui Golding, formerly a journalist on the *Weekly Mail & Guardian*, is a reporter on *Business Day*.

Anton Harber is a founder and co-editor of the *Weekly Mail & Guardian*.

Ferial Haffajee is a labour reporter for the *Weekly Mail & Guardian*.

Stephen Heyns is resource developer for the Community Development Resource Association in Cape Town.

Claire Keeton is a journalist for the East London News Agency (Elnews).

Bafana Khumalo is a journalist and columnist for the *Weekly Mail & Guardian*.

Stephen Laufer has worked as a journalist in South Africa and Europe and is senior reporter for the *Weekly Mail & Guardian*.

Chris Louw, formerly co-editor of the political magazine *Die Suid-Afrikaan* in Cape Town, is now senior political reporter for the *Weekly Mail & Guardian*.

Barbara Ludman is assistant editor of the *Weekly Mail & Guardian*.

Mondli waka Makhanya is a business and political writer for the *Weekly Mail & Guardian*.

Irwin Manoim is a founder and co-editor of the *Weekly Mail & Guardian*.

Eric Naki is a journalist for the East London News Agency (Elnews).

Phila Ngqumba is a journalist for Veritas, based in King William's Town.

Cathy Powers is assistant to the news editor of the *Weekly Mail & Guardian*.

Carmel Rickard, a Nieman fellow and former Durban bureau chief of the *Weekly Mail*, writes on legal affairs for the *Sunday Times*.

Reg Rumney is a published poet and business editor of the *Weekly Mail & Guardian* with a special interest in social investment issues.

Pat Sidley is a prize-winning journalist working for the *Weekly Mail* and the Dutch news agency ANP.

Paul Stober is a news reporter for the *Weekly Mail & Guardian* covering politics and security issues.

Jan Taljaard is a consultant and *Weekly Mail & Guardian* specialist writer on the right wing.

Andrew Trench is a journalist for the East London News Agency (Elnews).